Two-Dimensional Sonata Form

Two-Dimensional Sonata Form

Form and Cycle in Single-Movement
Instrumental Works by Liszt, Strauss,
Schoenberg, and Zemlinsky

Steven Vande Moortele

LEUVEN UNIVERSITY PRESS

First edition: 2009
Second edition (unchanged): 2024

© 2024 by Leuven University Press / Universitaire Pers Leuven /
  Presses Universitaires de Louvain. Minderbroedersstraat 4, B-3000 Leuven (Belgium).

All rights reserved. Except in those cases expressly determined by law, no part of this publication may be multiplied, saved in an automated datafile or made public in any way whatsoever without the express prior written consent of the publishers.

ISBN 978 90 5867 751 8 (harcover, 2009)
ISBN 978 94 6270 438 1 (paperpack, 2024)
D/2024/1869/40
NUR: 663

Typesetting: Friedemann Vervoort
Cover: Jurgen Leemans

Contents

Acknowledgements		VII
Introduction		1
Chapter 1	Two-Dimensional Sonata Form:	
	A terminological and conceptual framework	11
	Levels of form	11
	Analogies between levels	15
	Projection of hierarchies	20
	Identification, interpolation, and exocyclic units	24
	Integration, process, and tension	26
	Further terminological considerations	28
	Notes	31
Chapter 2	Liszt's B-minor Sonata	35
	The *locus romanticus* of two-dimensional sonata form	35
	The exposition of the overarching sonata form	39
	Identification: first movement and exposition	44
	Interpolation: the slow movement	48
	Identification: scherzo–finale and recapitulation–coda	50
	Notes	57
Chapter 3	Liszt: *Tasso* and *Die Ideale*	59
	Two-dimensional sonata form in the second half of the nineteenth century	59
	Form in Liszt's symphonic poems	60
	Tasso: Lamento e trionfo (1847–54)	63
	Die Ideale (1856–57)	71
	Notes	78
Chapter 4	Strauss: *Don Juan* and *Ein Heldenleben*	81
	Strauss and Liszt	81
	Don Juan Op. 20 (1888–89)	82
	Ein Heldenleben Op. 40 (1897–98)	93
	Notes	99

CHAPTER 5	SCHOENBERG'S *PELLEAS UND MELISANDE*	101
	Before *Pelleas*	101
	Pelleas und Melisande Op. 5 (1902–03)	102
	Notes	123
CHAPTER 6	SCHOENBERG'S FIRST STRING QUARTET	127
	From program to absolute music	127
	Issues of form in the overarching sonata form	131
	Identification	138
	Interpolation and integration	142
	Overall form and tonal plan	149
	Notes	156
CHAPTER 7	SCHOENBERG'S FIRST CHAMBER SYMPHONY	159
	Overview	159
	Identification	162
	Interpolation	167
	Recapitulation, coda, and finale	173
	Notes	177
CHAPTER 8	ZEMLINSKY'S SECOND STRING QUARTET	179
	First approach	179
	Identification	183
	Interpolation	185
	Notes	193
CONCLUSION:	THE SIGNIFICANCE OF TWO-DIMENSIONAL SONATA FORM	195
APPENDIX:	MEASURE-NUMBER TABLES	203
BIBLIOGRAPHY		207
INDEX OF NAMES AND WORKS		217

Acknowledgements

The origins of this book lie in a dissertation entitled *Two-Dimensional Sonata Form in Germany and Austria between 1850 and 1950: Theoretical, Analytical, and Critical Perspectives* that I completed in 2006 under the supervision of Mark Delaere at the University of Leuven. Differences between the book and the dissertation are considerable: I cut large portions of the original text and changed my mind about much of the rest ("So it is a new book!" a generous colleague once exclaimed).

The initial research for this project as well as work on the dissertation that resulted from it was enabled by a series of PhD studentships from the University of Leuven and the Research Foundation – Flanders (FWO – Vlaanderen). The latter also generously funded my work as a postdoctoral fellow at the University of Leuven and McGill University, during which I was able to undertake additional research and reworked the dissertation into a book. A subvention from the Research Council of the Faculty of Arts at the University of Leuven helped prepare the book for publication.

Of the many colleagues and friends who have helped shape this project over the past eight years at the University of Leuven, McGill University, and elsewhere, I want to thank six in particular. Mark Delaere, my mentor during my years as a graduate student in Leuven, accompanied my first steps on the academic path. His critical attitude, intellectual rigor, and insistence that knowledge of the technical fabric of a musical composition is a *sine qua non* for anyone writing about music at a serious level, are lasting influences on my own work. I also benefited enormously from working closely together with Pieter Bergé, whom I have come to value not only as a favorite colleague, but also as a dear friend; over the last few years, it has been a pleasure and honor to help him put Leuven on the map of international music theory. To William Caplin, my host during my stay at McGill University in 2007 and 2008, I am grateful for the generosity with which he shared his knowledge, ideas, and experience, as well as for making me feel at home in Montreal long before I could even start to imagine what that city would mean to me. My editors Marike Schipper and Beatrice Van Eeghem, along with their dynamic team at Leuven University Press, impressed me with their accuracy, efficiency, and flexibility throughout the publication process. Finally, I am more than grateful to Sarah Gutsche-Miller for her unusually careful and critical editorial assistance. Without her, this book—as so much else—wouldn't have been what it is.

INTRODUCTION

This book is about two-dimensional sonata form. Although the term may not be familiar, the phenomenon it denotes is. "Two-dimensional sonata form" refers to a principle of formal organization that is used in several large-scale instrumental compositions of the second half of the nineteenth and early twentieth centuries. In these compositions, the different movements of a sonata cycle are combined within one single-movement sonata form. Forms such as these have previously been known as "double-function forms," but, as I will argue, this term is problematic and needs to be replaced. Although the repertoire of two-dimensional sonata forms is modest in quantity, many of them are among the most significant compositions of their time. In the hands of composers such as Franz Liszt, Richard Strauss, and Arnold Schoenberg, two-dimensional sonata form becomes a highly innovative formal type that can hold claim to a central place in the history of large-scale instrumental music.

The composition usually considered to be the prototype of "double-function" or two-dimensional sonata form is Liszt's Piano Sonata in B minor of 1853. In an influential discussion of this composition, William Newman complained about a lack of musicological and analytical interest in it [Newman 1969, p. 359]:

> In spite of their importance, Liszt's sonatas have yet to be treated to a full study that will pull together the scattered bits of information about their background, genesis, and further circumstances, and one that will provide more detailed style-critical analyses than the numerous summary statements now to be found on the thematic elements and peculiar structure of the Sonata in b.

Although Newman's complaint was justified in 1969 and could then easily have been extrapolated to other compositions, it is no longer valid forty years later. Since the early 1970s, musicologists and theorists alike have published numerous and often outstanding analyses of compositions that I refer to as two-dimensional sonata forms. Practically all of them have acknowledged that the crucial characteristic of these works is the combination of multi-movement elements in a single-movement form. This is true for Liszt's B-minor Sonata in particular, but also of Schoenberg's First String Quartet Op. 7 and, to a somewhat lesser extent, his First Chamber Symphony Op. 9. Nonetheless, Newman's assertion retains some of its truth even today. Analysts who have discussed two-dimensional sonata forms over the past four decades have all had to operate without a theoretical framework, unless they designed one *ad hoc*. In a sense, this is hardly surprising. Too narrow a focus on the music of Haydn, Mozart, and Beethoven has always been characteristic of *Formenlehre* in both its original continental and its modern American variants, and textbooks on musical form only exceptionally discuss music written after 1825.

The single comprehensive contribution to the study of large-scale musical form from the late nineteenth and early twentieth centuries is the so-called "theory of structural deformation" that James Hepokoski and others have been developing since the early 1990s.[1] Although the concept of deformation may be applied to any standard pattern of formal organization, most of the relevant literature has focused on deformations of sonata-form patterns, hence the more common term "sonata deformation." For Hepokoski, large-scale post-1850 (or even post-1800) instrumental compositions are "in dialogue" with normative models of musical form. These models derive either from mid-nineteenth-century music theory or directly from the late-eighteenth- and early-nineteenth-century repertoire on which this theory is based. In one of his first publications on the matter, Hepokoski states [Hepokoski 1992, p. 143]:

> The term "deformation" is most appropriate when one encounters a strikingly nonnormative individual structure, one that contravenes some of the most central defining traditions, or default gestures, of a genre while explicitly retaining others.

Elsewhere he explains [2001, p. 447]:

> What is presented on the musical surface of a [sonata deformation] ... may not be a sonata in any "textbook" sense, and yet the work may still encourage, even demand, the application of one's knowledge of traditional sonata procedures as a rule for analysis and interpretation.

A pattern of expectation for the formal course of the composition, in other words, is created only to be subsequently frustrated, and a specific composition derives its meaning from the interaction with the generic background against which it operates. The concept of sonata deformation—many aspects of which are prefigured in the writings of Carl Dahlhaus[2]—appears especially promising for those analyzing large-scale instrumental forms from the second half of the nineteenth and early twentieth centuries. Here is an approach to musical form that enables one to acknowledge the obvious innovatory aspects in instrumental music from 1850 onwards while still allowing for the use of traditional sonata-form terminology.

Hepokoski has drawn up a useful catalogue of deformations of normative sonata-form patterns and arranged them in a number of recurring "families." The most common strategies are the "breakthrough deformation," the "introduction–coda frame," "episodes within the developmental space," "strophic/sonata hybrids," and "multi-movement forms in a single movement" [1993, pp. 6–7]. Apart from these five central categories, Hepokoski has identified a large number of other deformation families, some of which partly overlap with the above categories. These include "content-based form," "rotational form," "teleological genesis," "*Klang* meditation," and the "interrelation and fusion of movements" [1993, pp. 21–30], the "off-tonic sonata" [1997, p. 328], the "nonresolving recapitulation" [2001a, pp. 128–135], the "two-block exposition," the "loosely knit, discursive exposition," the "distorted recapitulation," and "progressive tonality" [2001b, pp. 448–453].

Some have argued that deformation theory is not without difficulties when it comes to defining what, exactly, a normative sonata form is. Julian Horton has pointed out that it is particularly precarious to equate normative sonata form with "the *Formenlehre* model of sonata form established by A.B. Marx and others" [Horton 2005, p. 7]. This conflation is most evident in Hepokoski's writings from the early 1990s. The problem disappears in his more recent contributions, where the emphasis shifts from a theoretical norm derived from mid-nineteenth-century composition manuals to a generic one derived from the repertoire of sonata forms from the late eighteenth and early nineteenth centuries. In the recent *Elements of Sonata Theory*, mid-nineteenth-century theory plays no role whatsoever in the definition of what Hepokoski and his co-author Warren Darcy consider normative sonata form to be [Hepokoski & Darcy 2006].

For Horton—writing before the publication of the *Elements of Sonata Theory*—the generic norm is no less insecure than the theoretical one. "[I]t is not at all clear," he argues, "that a common conception of sonata form as an architectural pattern ... existed in classical practice either" [Horton 2005, p. 10]. Here I have to disagree with Horton, who seems to be operating with Mark Evan Bonds's distinction between generative and conformational approaches to eighteenth-century musical form at the back of his mind. Whereas generative approaches stress "the unique shape of a specific work," conformational approaches emphasize "those various structural elements that a large number of works share in common" [Bonds 1991, pp. 13–14]. Given the absence of a contemporaneous theoretical model of sonata form in the late eighteenth century,[3] it may indeed seem as if the best way to approach this repertoire is from a generative point of view. Yet even a purely generative approach to eighteenth-century musical form—a position that, as Bonds has argued, is problematic to the point of being absurd[4]—cannot change the fact that a group of sonata forms from the past was available to composers working in the second half of the nineteenth century. Surely this situation allowed for—or even invited—generalizations about the formal procedures present in those works. Therefore, it does seem legitimate to assume, with Hepokoski and Darcy, the existence of a normative pattern of form derived from a large body of compositions *a posteriori*, even if those compositions themselves were written in the absence of such a normative pattern, and even if none of them exactly coincides with the *a posteriori* norm.

According to Hepokoski and Darcy, however, the situation is more complex than this. In their view, there is no such thing as "the" normative sonata form, no ideal type that is subsequently subject to deformation. In their most recent writings, both authors emphasize that they see normative sonata form not as a static object, but as a "constellation of flexible norms and options" that changes over time [Hepokoski 2006, p. 30 n. 70], thus *de facto* reconsidering Hepokoski's own previous mention of a "set of reified defaults" [1992, p. 143]. The relationship between works and norms is now described as "dialogic." This notion occupies a position somewhere between generative and conformational: what happens in a specific composition interacts with what occurs in other compositions and thus helps to shape what comes to be perceived as normative. This is the case not only for sonata forms in the late eighteenth and early nineteenth centuries; the same mechanisms remain at work throughout the nineteenth century and into the twentieth. Moreover, the dialogic moment is not restricted to the interaction between a composer (or a composition) and a norm (or other compositions). Also the listener (or the analyst) enters into and can even influence the dialogue with the constellation of norms and works [2009, pp. 71–72].

Although it is beyond doubt that the dialogic approach makes for a highly valuable contribution to music analysis, the idea that the definition of normative sonata form can change over time warrants further reflection. Given that norms are anything but inflexible, it should not come as a surprise that what initially is a deformation of a normative sonata-form pattern can over time itself become normative. Hepokoski and Darcy acknowledge this possibility [Hepokoski 2006, p. 30 n. 69, Hepokoski & Darcy 2006, passim], but although it is fully in keeping with their dynamic view of form, it remains somewhat underdeveloped in their writings. When it comes to actual analytical practice, the classical norm turns out to be remarkably stubborn: rather than a chronologically (and geographically) more specific set of conventions, the classical norm often continues to be the measure against which Hepokoski and Darcy assess the deformational character of a specific form from the nineteenth or early twentieth centuries.

This is unfortunate, because the flexible nature of what counts as normative can have profound consequences. It opens up the possibility that there will be cases in which deformations are so numerous and drastic that it becomes impracticable to interpret them against the background of a set of norms that can be described as sonata form. It seems to me that within the flexible set of norms and options that characterize sonata form—and exactly because of that flexibility—more or less self-contained subsets can come into being that make reference to the larger set superfluous or even inadequate. Another way of saying this is that in certain cases it seems advantageous to study post-1850 musical form, even when apparently related to sonata form, against the background of a more specific set of conventions that establish a context of their own.

The need for a more specific set of formal conventions becomes particularly pressing when one is dealing with single-movement compositions. To measure a single-movement composition against a norm derived from a movement of a multi-movement composition ignores the singularity of single-movement patterns of formal organization.[5] The compositions that I call two-dimensional sonata forms are one group of single-movement compositions that are better not regarded as deformations. In this study, I will discuss nine of them: Liszt's Piano Sonata in B minor and his symphonic poems *Tasso* and *Die Ideale*, Strauss's tone poems *Don Juan* and *Ein Heldenleben*, Schoenberg's symphonic poem *Pelleas und Melisande*, his First String Quartet, and his First Chamber Symphony, and the Second String Quartet by Alexander Zemlinsky. Although all of these compositions fall under Hepokoski's deformation family of "multi-movement forms in a single movement," it does not seem particularly useful to relate them back to a normative sonata form derived from late-eighteenth- and early-nineteenth-century repertoires. In the present study, I consequently treat two-dimensional sonata form as an autonomous type of formal organization.

In doing so, I have a threefold goal. First, I develop a typology that defines what a two-dimensional sonata form is and establishes how it works, especially with regard to the relationship between the multi-movement sonata cycle and the single-movement sonata form. Second, I offer a thorough analytical investigation of the nine two-dimensional sonata forms listed above in the specific context of this particular type of formal organization. Finally, I position two-dimensional sonata form in the history of large-scale musical form, looking at the context in which it emerges and the questions it answers, as well as at the path that leads from Liszt's

B-minor Sonata (1853) to Zemlinsky's Second String Quartet (1913–15), the first and last two-dimensional sonata forms I discuss in this study. My hypothesis is that on the one hand, two-dimensional sonata form is an attempt to solve a number of problems typical of the post-Beethovenian sonata form and cycle, but that on the other, the combination of a multi-movement with a single-movement design creates its own complications. Different compositions tackle these complications in different ways, but it remains to be seen whether a two-dimensional sonata form exists in which all of them are solved—and, indeed, whether such a completely satisfactory solution is possible in the first place.

A comparison of the different ways in which two-dimensional sonata forms deal with the same problems also reveals a remarkable continuity that spans more than half a century and connects the works of Liszt and Strauss to those of Schoenberg and Zemlinsky. This continuity has far-reaching implications, for Liszt, Strauss, Schoenberg, and Zemlinsky may strike one as an odd quartet. I will show that all of them mutually benefit from each other's company. This is the case for Schoenberg in particular. Although for many Schoenberg scholars Strauss still is the devil incarnate, no adequate interpretation of Schoenberg's early instrumental music is possible without a thorough knowledge of the Liszt–Strauss tradition. To be sure, Schoenberg's early instrumental works have been granted pride of place in Schoenberg scholarship, figuring prominently in such important books as Walter Frisch's magisterial study of 1993 or the recent monographs by Ethan Haimo and Michael Cherlin of 2006 and 2007. Yet none of these authors fully addresses the enormous debt that Schoenberg's formal language from 1899 to 1906 owes to Liszt and, especially, Strauss. In this study, I claim that understanding the form of Schoenberg's early instrumental music as a product of the Beethoven-Brahms tradition is one-sided and underestimates the significance of instrumental music in the "New German" tradition. The discussion of Zemlinsky's Second String Quartet enriches and nuances this new perspective on Schoenberg. It shows that even within Schoenberg's circle, two-dimensional sonata forms were written that exist relatively independently of Schoenberg's contribution to this work group.

Conversely, Liszt and Strauss also benefit from Schoenberg's company. Serious analysis (formal and otherwise) of Liszt's and Strauss's large-scale instrumental music is still a relative rarity, in stark contrast to the overwhelming attention Schoenberg's music has received over the last five decades. It is hoped that bringing Liszt's and Strauss's two-dimensional sonata forms together with Schoenberg's in one study will help change the scholarly attitude towards the formers' works, some of which rank among the most important of the second half of the nineteenth century.

My emphasis in this book is on the development of a powerful tool for the analysis of two-dimensional sonata forms and its demonstration by means of the discussion of a limited number of representative compositions. I have not attempted to compile a comprehensive inventory of two-dimensional sonata forms. It is therefore possible, and even likely, that other compositions exist that are constructed according to the same pattern of formal organization. There is, moreover, no denying that the present selection of two-dimensional sonata forms is extremely one-sided, displaying an exclusive focus on the works of Austro-German composers. A broader geographical perspective would, however, have gone beyond the scope of this study. If one were to pursue future research on this topic, one would need to inquire into the dissemination of two-dimensional sonata form and related patterns of formal organization in other important centers of instrumental music in the second half of the nineteenth and early twentieth centuries. It is likely that a considerable number of other large-scale single-movement compositions of this period—particularly those in the symphonic repertoire—belong to the category of two-dimensional sonata form. Liszt's influence on composers such as César Franck and Camille Saint-Saëns in France, Bedřich Smetana and Antonín Dvořák in Bohemia, and Pyotr Ilyitch Tchaikovsky and Alexander Skrjabin in Russia is not to be underestimated, and it might very well be that this influence affects not only their style, composition technique, or aesthetics, but also their treatment of large-scale musical form.

Equally absent is a substantial discussion of what might be called the prehistory of two-dimensional sonata form: the many large-scale single-movement compositions of the first half of the nineteenth century that allude to multi-movement patterns. This very heterogeneous group of compositions ranges from epochal works such as the finale of Beethoven's Ninth Symphony, Schubert's *Wanderer* Fantasy, or Schumann's Fourth Symphony, to more obscure compositions such as Franz Berwald's String Quartet in E♭ major or the piano concertos of Ignaz Moscheles. Although some of these works are briefly touched upon in Chapter 2, a more detailed inquiry was impossible within the framework of this study. This repertoire too would provide a fertile ground for further investigation.

Even though the focus of this study is on the technical and formal aspects of two-dimensional sonata form, its methodology is characterized by a deliberate eclecticism. My main objective is to study musical works, not to present a theory or method that degrades the compositions to which it is applied to mere illustrations. Nonetheless, this book relies strongly on two methodological pillars. First and foremost is the *Formenlehre* tradition, in both its continental European variant—the "authentic" Schoenberg–Ratz tradition—and its American revival by William Caplin. Throughout this study I not only adopt most of Caplin's terminology, but also rely heavily on his notion of "formal function." The question of what role formal units play, from the lowest to the highest hierarchical level in a form, is present (implicitly or explicitly) on every page of this study. As I noted before, *Formenlehre* traditionally has a relatively limited historical focus. Consequently, an adaptation of some of its concepts and strategies was necessary for it to be applicable to music from the second half of the nineteenth and the early twentieth centuries. Most importantly, Caplin's bottom-up approach to musical form (from a two-measure basic idea to a complete movement) is not always practical for the repertoire I study in this book. Not only are large-scale forms after 1850—and especially two-dimensional ones—frequently much more complex than classical forms, they also less often allow the immediate deduction of a unit's function from its internal organization. Therefore, I systematically complement Caplin's bottom-up approach with a top-down strategy that at times even supersedes it. This double approach takes for granted the presence of a specific succession of formal units at the mid-level range and allows the analysis of the lower-level units to be colored by the expectations generated by the higher levels.

At the same time, my method is indebted to Hepokoski and Darcy's approach to musical form. Rather than study self-contained "works" and emphasize each individual composition's originality, I adopt their dialogic stance. Although I deliberately refrain from formulating anything that comes close to a "normative" two-dimensional sonata form and use a vague notion of normative (one-dimensional) sonata form only as a heuristic tool, the compositions mentioned in this book form a context for each individual composition that I analyze in detail. They come together in an "ecology" [Klein 2005, p. 46] of texts that mutually shed light on each other. Each of these musical texts brings with it a number—in some cases an impressive number—of existing interpretations. In that respect too, my approach is an emphatically dialogic one, building upon, refining, or criticizing existing analyses of the works I discuss.

I have organized my book into eight chapters and an epilogue. Chapter 1 develops a terminological and conceptual apparatus that will be applied in the analyses that follow. Chapters 2 through 8 analyze the nine two-dimensional sonata forms by Liszt, Strauss, Schoenberg, and Zemlinsky.[6] Each analysis can be read separately but, taken together, they constitute an informal "problem history" of two-dimensional sonata form that at the same time refines the analytical apparatus presented in Chapter 1. I conclude the book with a historical perspective that has modestly Adornian overtones.

Many of the two-dimensional sonata forms I discuss exist in multiple editions, not all of which indicate measure numbers. In an appendix, I provide tables that convert the orientation system used in the most widespread editions to the measure–number system that I apply throughout this book.

Notes

[1] The following paragraphs are adapted from Vande Moortele 2008. In addition to Hepokoski's essays on the matter of sonata deformation, Warren Darcy has contributed an important study of deformation strategies in the symphonies of Anton Bruckner [Darcy 1997]. Timothy Jackson has studied the deformational procedure of what he calls "tragic reversed sonata form" in works by a very diverse range of composers [Jackson 1997] and draws heavily on the concept of deformation in his monograph on Pyotr Ilyitch Tchaikovsky's Sixth Symphony, where he proposes the alternative but in fact very similar concept of "diachronic transformation" [Jackson 1999]. In many respects, Kenneth Hamilton's work on Liszt's large-scale instrumental forms [Hamilton 1996 & 1997] also resonates with the theory of sonata deformation.

[2] The idea that the interpretation of a composition should be guided by the generic context to which it belongs—a core idea in deformation theory—is particularly prominent in Dahlhaus's mode of thought. In an article on Liszt's *Faust* Symphony, for example, he insists that "[g]eneric traditions are a part of history that is present in the matter itself, as a partial moment of both the conception and the musical hearing that takes as a starting point certain expectations of form" ("Gattungstraditionen sind ein Stück Geschichte, das in der Sache selbst—als Teilmoment sowohl der Konzeption als auch des musikalischen Hörens, das von bestimmten Formerwartungen ausgeht—gegenwärtig ist") [Dahlhaus 1979, p. 131]; translations are my own unless otherwise indicated. Already in the much earlier *Analyse und Werturteil*, Dahlhaus had stated: "[O]ne may establish in analysis the rule that a movement is to be interpreted, within sensible limits, as a variant of the form characteristic of the genre, and not as exemplifying another schema unusual for the genre" ("Es darf … als Regel der Analyse gelten, daß ein Satz, solange es irgend sinnvoll erscheint, als Variante der für die Gattung charakteristischen Form und nicht als Ausprägung eines anderen, in der Gattung ungewöhnlichen Schemas aufgefaßt wird") [1970, p. 93; English translation 1983, pp. 82–83]. It is no coincidence, of course, that Hepokoski quotes the same passage [1992, p. 144].

[3] There is, of course, Heinrich Christoph Koch's description of "[d]as erste Allegro der Sinfonie" in the third volume of his *Versuch einer Anleitung zur Composition* [Koch 1793, pp. 304–307]. It seems unlikely, however, that anyone would have been able to write a sonata form based solely on the information Koch provides.

[4] One would, for instance, have to "explain the remarkable phenomenon of composers 'discovering' sonata form over and over again with each new work" [Bonds 1991, pp. 28–29].

⁵ This is not to say that the concept of sonata deformation cannot be fruitfully applied to certain single-movement compositions. For a case study see Vande Moortele 2006b.

CHAPTER 1
Two-Dimensional Sonata Form:
A terminological and conceptual framework

Levels of form

Musical form is hierarchically organized. It consists of several large and small functional components that all play a specific role. A functional component at any given level of this hierarchy consists of several subcomponents that operate at the level below. Together with other components at the same level, that first component forms a unit that functions at the level above. A hypothetical "textbook" sonata form, for instance, can be divided into components and subcomponents as shown in figure 1. These subcomponents can be further divided, and the subdivision can go on down to the lowest level, that of the individual notes. Figure 2 continues the subdivision for one of the units shown at the lowest level in figure 1: the main theme (which, in this hypothetical example, is a sentence). At each of the levels shown in figures 1 and 2, form is articulated by the sophisticated interplay of syntactic structure, cadential organization, thematic-motivic content, and rhetorical gestures.

Somewhat surprisingly, traditional *Formenlehre* textbooks rarely provide adequate labels for the different levels and functional components that constitute a musical form. Quite rightly, William Caplin has criticized them for "using ill-defined concepts and ambiguous terminology derived from theories that have long fallen into disrepute" [Caplin 1998, p. 3]. Caplin mentions no names, but there is no denying that even a basic text such as Arnold Schoenberg's *Fundamentals of Musical Composition* contains many an unpleasant surprise in this respect. In his preface to Schoenberg's book, the editor Gerald Strang explicitly states that Schoenberg reorganized his formal terminology when teaching in the United States [Strang 1967, p. xiii]:

> He rejected much of the traditional terminology in both languages [German and English], choosing, instead, to borrow or invent new terms. For example, a whole hierarchy of terms was developed to differentiate the subdivisions of a piece. *Part* is used non-restrictively as a general term. Other terms, in approximate order of size or complexity, include: *motive, unit, element, phrase, fore-sentence, after-sentence, segment, section* and *division*. These

CHAPTER 1

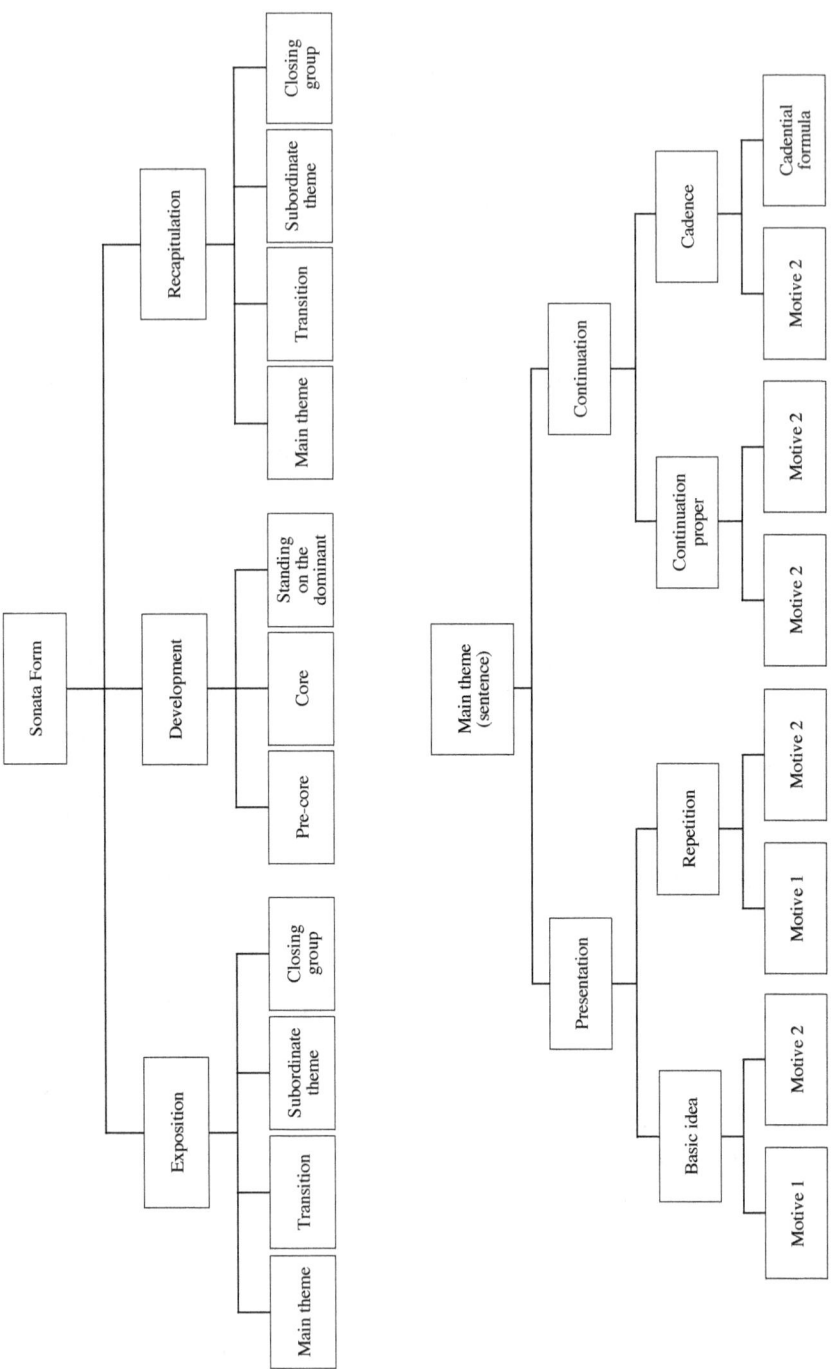

Figure 1: hierarchical organization of a hypothetical sonata form

Figure 2: hierarchical organization of a hypothetical sonata-form main theme (sentence)

terms are used consistently and their meanings are self-evident. Other special terms are explained in the text.

Unfortunately, Strang's assertion is incorrect in almost every respect. In *Fundamentals*, neither does Schoenberg use the terms Strang mentions in a consistent way, nor is their meaning always self-evident. Moreover, by confusing three different categories of terms that cannot possibly be part of one single hierarchical arrangement, Strang's list is itself not entirely logical. Some of the terms Strang lists refer to a specific functional component, others apply to all components at one specific hierarchical level, and yet others refer to any component at any hierarchical level (or at a number of hierarchical levels). In Schoenberg's system, "unit," "element," "segment," and "section" belong to the last category. "Unit," a term that Schoenberg rarely uses anyway, is synonymous with "part" and can designate any portion of a composition, regardless of its place in the hierarchy of a form. "Element," "segment," and "section" are somewhat more restricted in their meaning. "Element" can refer to any formal unit at the lower hierarchical levels, whereas "segment" and "section" refer to a formal unit at any of the middle or higher levels; as a rule, "segment" seems to apply to lower formal levels than "section." "Motive," "phrase," and "division," by contrast, are terms that can refer to different components at only one specific hierarchical level. "Division," for example, always refers to the level of exposition, development, and recapitulation. Finally, terms like "fore-sentence" and "after-sentence" refer to specific functional components (concrete realizations of a unit at a specific level), thus belonging to the same category as "small ternary," "main theme group," and "exposition."[1]

One of the merits of Caplin's 1998 treatise *Classical Form* is that it manages to straighten out existing terminology. His solution is as simple as it is effective. On the one hand, he only uses terms that either refer to any more or less self-contained portion of music at any hierarchical level, or that refer exclusively to a specific functional component at one specific level. The synonyms "group," "unit," "part," and "section" belong to the first category, while the second contains terms such as "contrasting middle," "small ternary," "subordinate theme," and "exposition." On the other hand—and this is even more crucial to his undertaking—Caplin defines almost every formal unit that can occur in classical instrumental music by ascribing to it one or more specific formal functions and by describing the ways in which these functions can be articulated.

Needless to say, the "ill-defined concepts and ambiguous terminology" used in earlier textbooks did not prevent analysts from successfully analyzing musical form. As far as their hierarchical organization is concerned, most forms from the late eighteenth and early nineteenth centuries—the core repertoire of *Formenlehre*—

are straightforward enough to allow for a certain degree of inconsistency and even obscurity in their description. As a result, the terminological problem could in most cases remain a latent and therefore unsolved one. The same hierarchical straightforwardness is, however, also a precondition for Caplin's terminological clarification by means of two distinct sets of terms. Both the ambiguous traditional terminology and the unequivocal alternative Caplin provides, then, ironically depend on the same characteristic of classical form.

A consequence of this shared dependence on hierarchical simplicity is that using either Schoenberg's or Caplin's terminological systems for the analysis of hierarchically more complex forms reveals new and unforeseen problems. The compositions referred to as "two-dimensional sonata forms" in the present book are one type of these hierarchically more complex forms. One of their most striking characteristics is the high frequency of complex interactions between different levels of the formal hierarchy. More specifically, elements of a single-movement sonata form and elements of a multi-movement sonata cycle, which normally operate at different hierarchical levels, reside at one and the same hierarchical level in a two-dimensional sonata form. When analyzing two-dimensional sonata forms and theorizing about them, it is not enough to be able to distinguish between specific functional components such as "main theme" or "exposition." It is also necessary to differentiate clearly between the hierarchical levels to which these components belong, and to be able to refer to those levels as a whole, irrespective of any specific realization in the shape of a concrete formal unit.

Neither Schoenberg's nor Caplin's terminological system allows for this. Schoenberg uses a number of terms that have the potential to refer to any component at a specific hierarchical level and consequently to that level as a whole, but he fails to apply them in a consistent way. Only some of his terms are used in connection with just one specific level ("motive," "phrase," "division"), while others ("element," "segment," "section") can apply to a number of different levels. Caplin, on the other hand, abandons the use of abstract terms related to a restricted number of hierarchical levels altogether: apart from general terms that can refer to any unit at any level, he only uses terms that refer to specific formal units. In the next paragraphs, I propose an alternative terminological system based on elements from both Schoenberg's and Caplin's theories. This should allow one to refer both to every specific functional component and to every hierarchical level of a musical form in its entirety. When confronted with traditional sonata forms, this system may seem pedantic; for the description of two-dimensional sonata forms, however, it will turn out to be of great use.

As a general term that can refer to any functional component at any hierarchical level, I borrow Caplin's term "(formal) unit." I also adopt most of Caplin's terms for specific formal units.[2] In addition to this, I introduce a number of terms that can be used to refer to any formal unit at one specific hierarchical level, and, as a result, to that level as a whole. None of these terms is new; what is new is their arrangement in a fixed hierarchical order. The top level in the hierarchy will be referred to as the level of the *cycle* and the second level as that of the *forms*. The third level is that of the *sections*, the fourth that of the *segments*. In a classical sonata, the level of the *cycle* is that of the multi-movement work as a whole, while the term *form* refers to each of its individual movements (e.g., a sonata-form first movement). Within this movement, the exposition, development, and recapitulation, as well as the introduction and coda, are at the level of the *sections*. Each of these sections comprises several *segments*. An exposition, for instance, comprises a main theme (group), a transition, a subordinate theme (group), and a closing group. If a theme group consists of multiple themes, each of these can be referred to as a *subsegment*.

Although these four or five levels—from the cycle down to the (sub)segment—are the ones that play the most significant role in the interaction between sonata form and sonata cycle in a two-dimensional sonata form, the labeling of hierarchical levels can be extended to what Caplin calls "intrathematic" or "phrase functions." One could, for instance, apply terms such as part, phrase, idea, and motive in a fixed order. For example, if a sonata-form main theme is a sentence, this sentence as a whole is at the level of the *segments*, its presentation and continuation at the level of the *phrases*, and the basic idea and its repetition at the level of the *ideas*. Ideas consist of *motives*; motives in turn consist of *notes*. To give another example, if a sentence is part of a theme that takes the form of a small ternary, the small ternary is at the level of the segments, and the sentence at the level of the parts; the subdivision then goes on in the same manner as in the sentence described above. Labeling the lower hierarchical levels can become a complicated and cumbersome affair: the number of levels that are actually present below the level of the segments can vary to a considerable extent, even within a composition. This is not the case for the level of the segments and above: they are present in every form. It is the interaction between these upper levels that will be the main focus of this study.

Analogies between levels

In spite of the relative frequency of two-dimensional sonata forms in instrumental music from the second half of the nineteenth and early twentieth centuries, traditional theories of form seldom treat musical forms like these, nor do they offer tools that can readily be used to analyze them. Analysts have, of course, successfully adapted the analytical and theoretical apparatus of *Formenlehre* for the analysis of instrumental music from the Austro-German tradition dating from the later nineteenth and early twentieth centuries. Traditional theory's lack of tools for the description of two-dimensional sonata forms, then, is not due solely to its limited historical scope, but at least as much to its exclusive focus on musical form. Indeed, the highest hierarchical level typically treated is that of the "form": *Formenlehre* hardly ever goes beyond the boundaries of the individual movement. Yet the most readily apparent characteristic of a two-dimensional sonata form is that it combines sections of a sonata form and movements of a sonata cycle within one single movement. Consequently, it cannot adequately be approached with a theory of musical form alone. The higher hierarchical level, that of the cycle, needs to be taken into account as well.

Only one aspect of the sonata cycle has received ample attention from twentieth-century theorists: that of thematic interconnections between movements. Continental European analysts in particular have proven keenly interested in the way the separate movements of a composition are integrated into a cycle by means of thematic or motivic interconnections.[3] To find a theory of the sonata cycle that is not about such interconnections, however, one has to hark back to the writings of Adolf Bernhard Marx and Hugo Riemann.

Both Marx and Riemann ask how it is that a piece containing a certain number of movements in a certain order is perceived as a meaningful musical whole. In the third volume of his *Lehre von der musikalischen Komposition* (1845, third edition 1857), Marx argues that only three movements are essential to a sonata cycle [Marx 1857, pp. 319–333].[4] For Marx, the presence of a fourth movement (i.e. a second interior movement), does not influence the way in which the other movements relate to each other; it merely realizes the function of the other interior movement in a different way. Marx then advises his readers to write sonatas with movements that contrast in tempo, key, meter, form, and content. Although these aspects primarily serve to differentiate between successive movements, two of them simultaneously fulfill a crucial function in the constitution of the cycle. Because both the tonic key and the fast tempo of the first movement are absent from the interior movement(s) but return in the finale, Marx claims, an overarching unity between the different movements is achieved. Strikingly, motivic interrelations between movements are of no importance in Marx's theory of the musical cycle. He writes:

> Occasionally, returning phrases—reminiscences from the earlier parts of the sonata that are taken up in the later ones (for instance in the finale)—are already an external indication of this unity; ... such retrospections are neither necessary nor always applicable—that is grounded in the idea of the whole.[5]

In his 1889 *Katechismus der Kompositionslehre*, renamed *Grundriß der Kompositionslehre* as of the third edition (1905), Riemann introduces a similar theory of the sonata cycle. His argumentation for the most part relies on the same elements as Marx's. It is, however, formulated more explicitly in relation to single-movement form, from which Riemann derives the three-movement pattern of a sonata. Riemann's starting point is the observation that in a large ternary form, the contrasting middle section often tends towards emancipation:

> It is a mere expansion of proportions when many concert pieces insert a lofty middle section between the presentation and the return of the main section (Allegro), and connect this to the return, and sometimes also to the exposition, of the main section. In the end, it is only an enrichment of the same form when the contrasting middle section is not followed by the return of the first section, but by a new section that is related to the first in character and gesture. That is how we obtain the form of the three-movement sonata ... With the thematic emancipation of the last section from the first, the simple unitary form becomes cyclic: the scheme A-B-A is replaced by the new A-B-C. [In this scheme,] only the key organization guarantees the unity by leading back to the starting point, even though the characters of the opening and closing movements are also usually related.[6]

Taking the theories of Marx and Riemann as a starting point, the following paragraphs will investigate the possible relationships between a sonata form and a sonata cycle, as well as the ways in which those relationships allow for the combination of elements of both in two-dimensional sonata forms. For the time being, this investigation will be conducted in a purely abstract manner, i.e. without reference to any existing composition. Marx and Riemann clearly show that the overall formal organization of a three-movement sonata cycle is analogous to that of a sonata form: both consist of a succession of three essential large formal units (first movement – interior movement – finale and exposition – development – recapitulation respectively).[7] In addition, they suggest a functional analogy between units that occupy equivalent positions in the different successions. The relationship between the finale and the first movement in a sonata cycle can, for instance, be seen as being roughly equivalent to that between the recapitulation and the exposition in a sonata form: because it reaffirms the tempo, the home key, and sometimes also the basic "character" of the first movement, the finale has a recapitulatory effect. The interior movements in the cycle, by consequence, more or less correspond to the development in the sonata form, not only because they occupy the same position in the three-unit succession, but also because they fulfill a contrasting function and express or extend a non-tonic key area.[8]

Needless to say, analogies between formal units in a sonata form and a sonata cycle are limited. Both the specific internal organization and content of a first movement, one or two interior movements, and a finale obviously differ from those of an exposition, a development, and a recapitulation. Moreover, although these units share a number of functions with their equivalents at the other hierarchical level, they also fulfill some functions that are different from or even opposite to those of their counterparts. One of the functions of a development in a sonata form is, for example, to elaborate the material presented in the exposition. There is usually no corresponding function in the interior movements of a sonata cycle. Nonetheless, it seems reasonable to discern a functional and positional analogy between the movements of a sonata cycle and the sections of a sonata form. Figure 3 represents this graphically.

sonata cycle

first movement	interior movement(s)	finale
exposition	development	recapitulation–coda

sonata form

Figure 3: positional and functional analogy between sonata cycle and sonata form

The analogy between the movements of a sonata cycle and the sections of a sonata form is only the most obvious implication of Marx's and Riemann's theories of the sonata cycle. Marx describes the overall tonal organization of the multi-movement sonata as an emanation of the pattern "rest–motion–rest" ("Ruhe–Bewegung–Ruhe"), while the succession of different tempi realizes its opposite, the pattern "motion–rest–motion."[9] To Marx, the pattern "rest–motion–rest" is the fundamental principle of any musical construction. In the conclusion of his discussion of what he calls the "first rondo form," he writes:

Here again we encounter the primal antithesis of all musical design, rest–motion–rest, which we first found in the opposition of tonic and scale, then of tonic and dominant harmony, and later in the ternary song (as well as, though less developed, in the binary [song] and any period). This once more confirms the continuing validity of our first insights. We will be able to observe them through all forms, even though we will not always have the time to point them out.[10]

By stating that the pattern "rest–motion–rest" acts as a fundamental principle at any level of a form, Marx implies that it is possible to extrapolate the analogy between sections and movements to other hierarchical levels. One has to proceed cautiously here. Postulating the presence of analogies between numerous different levels of form comes dangerously close to the sort of over-reductionism Leonard B. Meyer has called "the fallacy of hierarchic uniformity": the erroneous assumption that "the principles or 'laws' governing the organization of one hierarchic level are necessarily the same as those of some other level" [Meyer 1967, p. 258]. Nonetheless, it seems safe enough to pursue the analogy between hierarchical levels yet one step further. If the cycle's outer movements are in sonata form, it can be enlightening to extend the analogy to the level of the sections of these movements on the one hand, and the segments of their outer sections on the other (figure 4).

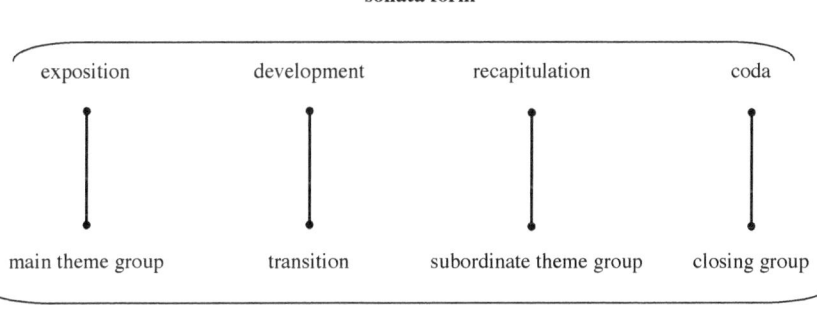

Figure 4: analogies between sonata form and exposition/recapitulation

The positional analogy between the sections of a sonata form and the segments of an exposition or recapitulation is self-evident: the main theme group corresponds to the exposition, the transition to the development, the subordinate theme group to the recapitulation, and the closing group to the coda. For some of these formal units, the functional analogies are equally obvious. The function of the coda in a sonata form is, for instance, very much akin to that of the closing group in an exposition or recapitulation.[11] The functions of the transition in an exposition or recapitulation—destabilization of the tonic,[12] increase of dynamic impetus, transition to and preparation of the subordinate theme group—likewise partially resemble those of the development section in a sonata form.

For other units at these levels, the idea of a functional analogy is more problematic. What could, for instance, be the functional analogy between an exposition and a recapitulation on the one hand, and a main and subordinate theme group on the other? Obviously, a subordinate theme group does not relate to a main theme group in the same way that a recapitulation relates to an exposition. The function of a subordinate theme group as the bearer of thematic contrast and, in an exposition, as an articulator of the subordinate key area is even diametrically opposed to that of a recapitulation. In most cases, the analogy between an exposition and a main theme group and between a recapitulation and a subordinate theme group seems to be restricted to their relative stability in comparison to the essentially loose and unstable transition and development.

Analogies grow increasingly vague when one descends down the hierarchy. The analogy between the segments of an exposition or recapitulation and the parts of a main or subordinate theme, for example, is restricted to their position within the larger formal unit. There seems to be hardly any functional analogy at all. Moreover, even the positional analogy is there only under very specific circumstances, namely in those cases in which the main or subordinate theme group displays a ternary organization. Nevertheless, composers writing two-dimensional sonata forms have not only eagerly exploited the functional and positional analogies between the movements of a sonata cycle and the sections of a sonata form, or those between the sections of a sonata form and the segments of an exposition or a recapitulation. They have also made specific compositional decisions that allowed them to make use of the potential and merely positional analogy between the segments of an exposition or a recapitulation and the parts of a main or subordinate theme or theme group.

Projection of hierarchies

Analogies between different hierarchical levels have significant implications for the relationship between sections of a sonata form and movements of a sonata cycle that are combined at the same hierarchical level in a two-dimensional sonata form. Traditionally, this relationship has been conceptualized in terms first proposed by William Newman in his influential discussion of Liszt's B-minor Sonata. Newman argued that Liszt's Sonata "is not a simple 'sonata form' but a double-function form, because its several components also serve as the (unseparated) movements of the complete cycle" [Newman 1969, p. 134]. According to Newman's definition, all formal units in such a form simultaneously function as sections of the sonata form and as movements of the sonata cycle. The multi-movement sonata cycle and the single-movement sonata form coincide completely: the overarching sonata form's exposition is at the same time the sonata cycle's first movement, the cycle's interior movements establish the overarching sonata form's development, and one and the same formal unit functions as both the recapitulation (with coda) and the finale. In Newman's view, none of the sections of the sonata form can contain formal units that are not simultaneously part of one of the movements of the sonata cycle, nor can these movements contain units that do not belong to the overarching sonata form.

Newman's concept of "double-function form" is not without problems, which I will address presently. Nonetheless, it forms an ideal starting point for the development of a theoretical model of two-dimensional sonata form. Behind Newman's model lies the assumption that a sonata form and a multi-movement sonata cycle are projected onto each other. The hierarchical organization of the sonata form is analogous to that of the sonata cycle, except that the former is incomplete, lacking the cycle as an upper hierarchical level. The result is an oblique relationship between both hierarchies. The levels of the form's hierarchy do not correspond to those of the cycle's: every formal unit in a two-dimensional sonata form simultaneously functions at two *different* levels, one in the complete and one in the incomplete hierarchy. In the incomplete hierarchy, units function at the level immediately below the level at which they function in the complete hierarchy. A cycle in the complete hierarchy is a form in the incomplete hierarchy, while a form in the complete hierarchy is a section in the incomplete one; a section in the complete hierarchy is a segment in the other, and a segment in the complete hierarchy is a part in the incomplete one. More specifically, the same formal unit that is a sonata cycle in the complete hierarchy functions as a sonata form in the incomplete hierarchy, the sonata form in the complete hierarchy is an exposition in the incomplete one, the exposition in the complete one is a main theme group in the incomplete hierarchy, and the main theme group in the complete hierarchy is a part of the main theme group in the incomplete hierarchy. Throughout this book, I will refer to these two hierarchies—the incomplete hierarchy of the sonata form and the complete hierarchy of the sonata cycle—as "dimensions": the dimension of the cycle on the one hand and the dimension of the form on the other. Figure 5 shows the oblique projection of the hierarchy of the cycle onto that of the form.

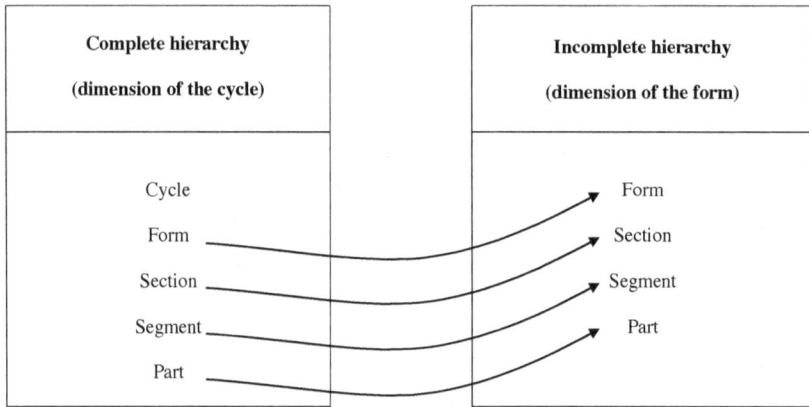

Figure 5: oblique relationship between complete and incomplete hierarchies

In Newman's conceptualization of double-function form, this projection results in a one-to-one relationship between the sections of the form and the movements of the cycle. Movements and sections neatly coincide, and every unit in the piece fulfills a double function: one in the form and one in the cycle (hence, of course, the term "double-function form"). This one-to-one relationship between sections of the sonata form and movements of the sonata cycle is, however, fictitious. In none of the two-dimensional sonata forms discussed in this study (nor, for that matter, in any other two-dimensional sonata form of which I am aware) do the sections of the overarching sonata form coincide with the movements of the sonata cycle as seamlessly as Newman's definition suggests.

To be sure, the situation in which a movement and a section perfectly coincide does occur. Yet it is equally common for a movement to coincide with only part of a section or to overlap with portions of several consecutive sections. Often—and this is the major difference between my two-dimensional sonata form and Newman's double-function form—entire movements stand between two different sections of the sonata form, thus fulfilling a function in only one of the two dimensions. The projection of a sonata form and cycle onto each other in a two-dimensional sonata form is, in other words, a loose projection: sections and forms can coincide, but they do not have to. Every two-dimensional sonata form contains a number of movements that exclusively belong to the dimension of the cycle and therefore lack a function in the dimension of the form. Conversely, every two-dimensional sonata form contains units that have a function in the dimension of the form but play no role in the dimension of the cycle. Only a limited number of fragments fulfill a function in both the overarching sonata form and the sonata cycle. A two-dimensional sonata form, then, can be defined as the combination of the movements of a sonata cycle and the sections of a sonata form at the same hierarchical level of a single-movement composition. It includes all essential sections of the sonata form and all movements of the sonata cycle, but these can interact in a variety of ways.

Figure 6 illustrates this by means of a rudimentary overview of form and cycle in Liszt's B-minor Sonata—the two-dimensional sonata form that will be analyzed in greater detail in Chapter 2. This figure also introduces the format that I will use throughout this study to present formal overviews of complete two-dimensional sonata forms: the uppermost row describes the sections of the single-movement sonata form (the dimension of the form) and the bottom row the movements of the sonata cycle (the dimension of the cycle). The middle row provides measure numbers for both dimensions, and dotted diagonal lines indicate that one dimension is temporarily inactive.

INTRODUCTION	EXPOSITION b – D – (F♯)	DEVELOPMENT	
1–7	8–204	205–330	331–452
SONATA-FORM FIRST MOVEMENT B			SLOW MOVEMENT F♯

INTRODUCTION RETURN	RECAPITULATION b♭ – b – B		CODA B
453–459	460–532	533–672	673–760
	SCHERZO b♭	⇒ FINALE b – B	

Figure 6: Liszt, B-minor Sonata: form and cycle

As becomes immediately evident from figure 6, Liszt's B-minor Sonata, like any two-dimensional sonata form, contains not one, but two distinct sonata forms: one spanning the entire composition, the other constituting the first movement of the sonata cycle. I will refer to these sonata forms as the "overarching sonata form" and the "local sonata form" respectively. The figure also clearly shows that the relationship between both dimensions changes in the course of the composition: some formal units fulfill a function in both dimensions, while others function only in one while the other is temporarily inactivated. In Liszt's B-minor Sonata, the first movement of the sonata cycle (the local sonata form) coincides with the introduction and the exposition of the overarching sonata form. The recapitulation and the coda of the overarching sonata form coincide with the scherzo and the finale in the dimension of the cycle.[13] The development and the return of the introduction before the onset of the recapitulation, by contrast, have a function only in the overarching sonata form—they play no role in the dimension of the cycle. The opposite is true for the slow movement, which belongs exclusively to the dimension of the cycle and has no function in the overarching sonata form.

In principle, the direction of the projection is irrelevant. It makes no difference whether it is conceptualized as the projection of a sonata form onto a sonata cycle or of a sonata cycle onto a sonata form. However it is the sonata form, rather than the sonata cycle, that ultimately appears to be the principal mode of formal organization. The movements of the sonata cycle seem to be added onto a conceptually preexistent sonata form and not the other way round. This is why I speak of two-dimensional sonata form rather than of two-dimensional sonata cycle.

Identification, interpolation, and exocyclic units

Inspiration for an alternative to Newman's all too rigid definition of double-function form can be found in Anton Webern's early discussion of Schoenberg's First String Quartet:

> Essentially, the form of this quartet is that of a single large-scale sonata movement. The scherzo and the large-scale development have been inserted between the first development and the recapitulation, and the recapitulation is extended by the adagio that stands between the main and subordinate themes. In this case, the rondo-finale can be understood as an extended coda.[14]

Even though the actual content of Webern's description is anything but unproblematic,[15] for our immediate purposes what he says is less important than the way he says it. Webern leaves no doubt that the relationship between both dimensions changes over the course of a two-dimensional sonata form. On the one hand, he writes that the finale simultaneously functions as the overarching sonata form's coda. The relationship between this movement and this section is, in other words, the one defined by Newman. But Webern also indicates another possibility. The scherzo—along with the formal unit he refers to as the "large development"— is "inserted between" the sonata form's "first development" and its recapitulation, and the slow movement "stands between" the main and subordinate theme groups in the recapitulation. In these instances, movements of the sonata cycle do not coincide with sections of the sonata form, but operate exclusively in the hierarchy of the cycle.

In an article on Liszt's Piano Sonata and Schoenberg's First String Quartet, Carl Dahlhaus expands upon Webern's argument. After quoting the passage from Webern's essay included above, he takes issue with Newman's definition of "double-function form." Regarding Liszt's Piano Sonata, he writes:

> [I]f one takes as a starting point the notion that the essence of the "double-function-form" is to equate the parts of the sonata form and the movements of the sonata cycle, then [there is only one thing] one can do with a slow movement that stands between an exposition as a first movement and a recapitulation as a finale: [one has] to force it into the definition of a development. However, the formal idea that lies at the basis of the B-minor Sonata becomes understandable only when one realizes that categories belonging to different classes can be both juxtaposed and melded together.[16]

In the same article, Dahlhaus introduces—*en passant*—two simple concepts that are very useful for the description of the relationship between sonata cycle and sonata form in a two-dimensional sonata form: "identification" and "interpolation" [Dahlhaus 1988, pp. 207–208]. The present study adopts both concepts and complements them with the notion of "exocyclic" units.

The two dimensions of a two-dimensional sonata form coincide only when the relationship between the form and the cycle is one of identification, that is at those points in the form at which the same formal unit simultaneously functions as a movement in the sonata cycle and as one or several units in the sonata form. When a movement of the sonata cycle is identified with a unit of the sonata form, either function leaves its mark on the formal unit in question, imposing upon it a number of its own defining characteristics and inactivating some of those of the other dimension. As a result, that formal unit can no longer be regarded purely as a movement, nor simply as a unit in the sonata form. The only satisfactory interpretation is as a combination of both: as a unit to which the tension between the non-identical requirements of both dimensions has become essential.

When a movement of the cycle is interpolated into the overarching sonata form, the two dimensions do not coincide but stand next to each other. For the duration of the interpolation, the overarching sonata form is suspended, to resume only when the interpolation is over. The opposite of an interpolated movement is an exocyclic unit: a unit that belongs exclusively to the overarching sonata form and plays no role in the sonata cycle.[17] For the duration of such units, the dimension of the cycle remains temporarily inactive. The presence of such exocyclic units is, as we will see in Chapter 2, a defining characteristic of two-dimensional sonata form, distinguishing it from similar, but not identical types of form.

Integration, process, and tension

Interpolated movements are not necessarily entirely unrelated to the overarching sonata form. There are several methods of integration that relate the overarching sonata form and the sonata cycle to each other, even in those formal units in which they do not coincide. Most often, such integration is achieved through thematic connections between the interpolated movement and units that belong to the overarching sonata form.

A variety of subcategories can be distinguished here. First, interthematic relationships can exist between different movements of the cycle. When they are restricted to interpolated movements, these thematic correspondences do not, of course, affect the relationship between the different dimensions, since all movements in question then belong exclusively to only one dimension. Thematic integration within the dimension of the cycle is, however, not necessarily restricted to interpolated movements. It may also involve movements that are identified with units of the overarching sonata form. If, then, the presence of shared thematic material relates an interpolated movement to a movement that is identified with a unit of the overarching sonata form, this automatically contributes to the integration of the interpolated movement in the dimension of the form. I will refer to this first method of integration as *indirect integration*, because it operates via the detour of thematic integration in the dimension of the cycle.

A second method is *direct integration*. As the term suggests, this differs from indirect integration in that it does not establish a thematic link between an interpolated movement and another movement of the cycle, but between an interpolated movement and a formal unit that belongs exclusively to the dimension of the form. A further distinction can be made between three different types of direct integration:
(1) Thematic material essential to one or more of the interpolated movements is prefigured in one or several of the exocyclic units of the overarching sonata form that precede the interpolated movement(s) in question.
(2) Thematic material essential to and first introduced in one or several of the

interpolated movements is referred to, quoted, or worked out in one or several of the exocyclic units of the overarching sonata form that follow the interpolated movement(s) in question.

(3) Thematic material essential to one or several of the exocyclic units of the overarching sonata form that precede the interpolated movements returns in one or several of those interpolated movements.

The direct integration of the first type has a prospective character, announcing something that has yet to come. Types 2 and 3 are retrospective, recalling material that has been prominent in preceding formal units.

It will have become clear by now that the relationship between the dimensions in a two-dimensional sonata form is not static, but dynamic. This is not only because every two-dimensional sonata form displays an alternation of identification, interpolation, and exocyclic units; there is also a perceptual aspect involved. Every two-dimensional sonata form discussed in this book begins as if it were a one-dimensional sonata form. Initially, the presence of two dimensions (i.e., of formal units fulfilling a function in two dimensions) remains imperceptible, because each unit fulfils exactly the same function in both dimensions. In Liszt's B-minor Sonata, for example, we will see that mm. 1–8 and 9–31 function as an introduction and main theme group in both the overarching and the local sonata form. Only when the functions that one unit has to fulfill in the two dimensions start to differ—in Liszt's B-minor Sonata, this point is at m. 32—does the two-dimensionality become noticeable. I will refer to this point in the form as the "dimensional disconnection." Along with revealing the presence of two dimensions, this dimensional disconnection urges a retrospective reinterpretation of the preceding formal units: listeners are invited to retrace their steps and reconsider what has happened prior to the dimensional disconnection in light of what happens afterwards: what initially seemed to be only the beginning of a one-dimensional sonata form "becomes" the beginning of a two-dimensional sonata form.[18]

One important consequence of this dynamic concept of form is that formal overviews, such as the one of Liszt's B-minor Sonata given in figure 6, are only one-sided representations of what actually happens in the musical form at hand. Commenting on similar overviews in Walter Frisch's book on Schoenberg's early music [Frisch 1993], Michael Cherlin has suggested an analogy with architecture [Cherlin 1994, p. 180]:

> [A] formal "overview" is much like a floor plan. To construct a floor plan, we must place ourselves outside of the space being considered. It is not that this outside-in view is unimportant, but that it needs to be complemented by perspectives that are inside-out. To this end, the architect's imagination

must be placed inside the space, a space we can move through, perceiving shifting perspectives with every step, as space, light, and matter interact. The floor plan is static and singular. The "in-side" walk-through is dynamic and manifold.

Although Cherlin's point cannot be dismissed, the limits of a formal overview are a problem only if one expects more from such an overview than it can offer. If, to elaborate on Cherlin's comparison, one accepts that it is only a "floorplan"— merely a tool towards the adequate understanding of a complex and dynamic musical form—then there is not really a problem, provided, of course, that one is aware of the floorplan's limitations and willing to transcend them either mentally or, as I will try to do in the following chapters, through verbal description.

A final point that merits consideration is that the specific relationship between dimensions in actual two-dimensional sonata form should not be regarded as less perfect alternatives to an imaginary ideal two-dimensional sonata form in which both dimensions entirely coincide. There is no denying that two-dimensional sonata forms tend as much as possible to integrate the sonata form and the sonata cycle. Yet where identification and interpolation are concerned, a composer writing a two-dimensional sonata form and trying to integrate both dimensions is confronted with numerous and partly insurmountable problems. In spite of the often ingenious manipulation of potential analogies between a sonata form and a sonata cycle, in spite of crafty attempts to find a balance between both dimensions in units in which they are identified, and in spite of the sometimes very intense integration of interpolated movements in the overarching sonata form, an unresolved tension between both dimensions of a two-dimensional sonata form never disappears.

Further terminological considerations

Apart from the term double-function form, which should be abolished given its close association with Newman's unsatisfactory definition, a number of other terms have been used to refer to the kind of form I call two-dimensional sonata form. The most current term in the Germanic world is "Mehrsätzigkeit in der Einsätzigkeit" (along with its somewhat less common inversion "Einsätzigkeit in der Mehrsätzigkeit"). The term has been used most notably by Dahlhaus in a number of influential writings on Liszt and Schoenberg [Dahlhaus 1980, 1981, and 1988]. Variants of the term have also been coined by Sigfried Schibli, who argued for the term "integrale Einsätzigkeit" [Schibli 1984, p. 276], and by Mathias Hansen, who proposed the term "gegliederte Einsätzigkeit" [Hansen 1993, p. 73].

The main drawback to all of these terms—apart from their being rather difficult to translate—is their lack of specificity: they fail to make clear that the compositions under consideration should be interpreted within the referential framework of sonata form.

A more promising German term has been proposed by Heinrich Helge Hattesen. He refers to the formal organization of Schoenberg's First String Quartet as "mehrschichtige Form" or "multi-layered form" [Hattesen 1990, p. 191]. What makes Hattesen's term particularly attractive is that it can be used in conjunction with the term "Formschichten" ("formal layers"). This allows Hattesen to refer to the hierarchies of the sonata cycle and the sonata form as separate entities. Yet although it is more attractive than other German terms, the term "mehrschichtige Form" fails to specify the number of layers involved and does not indicate that the form in question is a sonata form. Moreover, the concept "layer" is very close to the concept "level"; its use in the context of this book might cause terminological confusion between the hierarchies as a whole (the "dimensions" or "layers"), and the levels of which those hierarchies consist.

In a study of Tchaikovsky's Sixth Symphony, Timothy Jackson introduced the term "super-sonata form" [Jackson 1999, pp. 26–27]. He uses it to refer both to forms I call two-dimensional sonata forms and to sonata cycles that in some way suggest an overarching form spanning the entire composition, but in which the different movements are nonetheless clearly separated (such as Schumann's Fourth, Brahms's Third, Bruckner's Eighth, and, obviously, Tchaikovsky's Sixth Symphony). Although both phenomena are indeed related, I prefer to preserve a clear terminological distinction between single-movement compositions that incorporate a complete sonata cycle and multi-movement cycles that suggest the presence of an overarching form. Therefore, I choose to reserve the term "super-sonata form" for the latter phenomenon.

My term two-dimensional sonata form was initially inspired by Dahlhaus's use of the term "Mehrdimensionalität" (multi-dimensionality) in his aforementioned discussion of Liszt's B-minor Sonata and Schoenberg's First String Quartet [Dahlhaus 1988, p. 212]. Dahlhaus understands "Mehrdimensionalität" in a particularly idiosyncratic sense. In a musical form, he writes, an "Unterschied der 'Ordnungen'" (a "difference of classes") can be distinguished from an "Unterschied der 'Dimensionen'" (a "difference of dimensions"). By the former, Dahlhaus means the difference between formal section, movement, and cycle ("Satzteil, Satz und Satzzyklus"), by the latter, that between super- and subordinated forms or formal sections ("über- und untergeordnete Formen oder Formteilen"). "Classes" are the levels of a formal hierarchy as such, while "dimensions" refers to their actual hierarchization. While classes and dimensions usually coincide, they no longer do so in Liszt's Sonata and Schoenberg's String Quartet. The formal unit we call a movement, for instance, is no longer always hierarchically superior to a section. Both can operate at the same level, and the movement may even be hierarchically inferior to a section. According to the meaning Dahlhaus himself gives to the term "Dimension," however, any musical form that is hierarchically organized consists of several "Dimensionen," and is, by consequence, "mehrdimensional." The difference between traditional forms in which "Dimensionen" and "Ordnungen" coincide and more complex forms in which both are organized independently is of no influence on a composition's being "dimensional."

With this definition of "dimension," there is no point in restricting the application of the term "multi-dimensional form" to Liszt's B-minor Sonata, Schoenberg's First Quartet, or other compositions of similar formal organization. Rather than adopt Dahlhaus's concept of "dimension" as a whole, I therefore propose to keep the term, but to modify its meaning. In the present book, "dimension" is understood not as a hierarchical level that is hierarchically ordered, but as a hierarchy in its entirety. A composition in which a sonata form and a complete sonata cycle are projected onto each other thus comprises two dimensions: the complete hierarchy of the sonata cycle and the incomplete hierarchy of the overarching sonata form.

One might object that the term "dimension" has already been used in relation to music in completely different contexts. It has, for instance, been employed to refer to the size of a piece, or as a synonym for parameter (a tone is sometimes said to have a number of dimensions), and Schoenberg himself has famously written about the vertical and horizontal dimensions of musical space. Confusion with the dimensions of a composition, the dimensions of a tone, and the dimensions of musical space is, however, easily avoided by specifying the kind of dimension at stake here as the "dimensions of musical form." Apart from that, the term "two-dimensional sonata form" seems to have nothing but practical advantages. It is easily translatable, it allows for reference to the sonata cycle and the overarching sonata form as distinct entities, it explicitly associates the compositions that belong to this category with the tradition of sonata form, and it specifies the number of dimensions involved. As such, it can easily be distinguished from "ordinary" sonata forms, which can be referred to as one-dimensional.[19]

By way of concluding this chapter, Newman's "double-function form" must be revisited one more time. Although his term can no longer be used for the description of a two-dimensional sonata form, this does not necessarily mean that the concept of double-functionality as such—the idea that one single formal unit simultaneously fulfills two different functions—can no longer be useful. Double-functionality does occur in compositional practice, and a distinction can be made between vertical and horizontal double-functionality. Vertical double-functionality is typical of two-dimensional sonata forms. This is the kind of double-functionality Newman had in mind, and it involves identification of a formal unit of the sonata form with one of the sonata cycle. Horizontal double-functionality is a broader phenomenon that is not exclusively related to two-dimensional sonata form. It means that one single formal unit combines the functions that are usually fulfilled by a number of different formal units. Concerning the instrumental music of Haydn, Mozart, and Beethoven, for instance, Caplin has written about "fusion": two different functions that are normally realized by two consecutive but separate formal units (e.g. a main theme and a transition) combined in one single formal unit [Caplin 1998, pp. 165–167 & 203]. James Webster has even used the actual term "double functioning" to describe the similar phenomenon of the combination of introductory and expository functions in the late music of Beethoven [Webster 1992, p. 38]. Another form of horizontal double-functionality occurs in the extremely condensed music of Schoenberg's atonal period. In the first of his Five Orchestral Pieces Op. 16, for example, the subordinate theme group is omitted, and its contrasting function is adopted by the development section, so that the latter becomes in fact double-functional [see Vande Moortele 2006a, pp. 59–62].

Notes

[1] Neither "fore-sentence" nor "after-sentence" appears in Schoenberg's printed text; both terms are systematically replaced by their respective synonyms "antecedent" and "consequent."
[2] Some of this terminology is used in figures 1 and 2; other terms will be introduced in the course of this study. Although James Hepokoski and Warren Darcy have recently proposed an alternative terminological system [Hepokoski & Darcy 2006], I prefer to continue using Caplin's terms, except in those cases in which Hepokoski and Darcy propose terms for phenomena that Caplin does not discuss (e.g., the "medial caesura").
[3] This is the case in the work of Rudolph Réti in particular. See Réti 1951.
[4] Marx does not use the term cycle, which was introduced in 1857, but became current only in subsequent years [see Finscher 1998, col. 2528].
[5] "Bisweilen bezeichnen zurückkehrende Sätze, Anklänge aus den erstern Partien der Sonate, die man in die spätern, z. B. in das Finale hinübernimmt, diese Einheit schon äusserlich erkennbar; ... dergleichen Rückblicke sind weder nothwendig, noch stets anwendbar, das heisst: in der Idee des Ganzen begründet" [Marx 1857, p. 328].
[6] "Es ist nur eine Vergrößerung der Dimensionen, wenn manche Konzertstücke zwischen Aufstellung und Wiederkehr des Hauptsatzes (Allegro) einen getragenen Mittelsatz einschieben, der mit der Wiederkehr, manchmal auch mit der ersten Aufstellung des Hauptsatzes verbunden ist; schließlich ist es doch aber nur eine wohlverständliche

Bereicherung derselben Form, wenn statt der Wiederkehr des ersten Satzes nach dem kontrastierenden Mittelsatze ein neuer aber in Charakter und Bewegungsart dem ersten nahe stehender folgt; damit haben wir aber die Form der dreisätzigen Sonate ... Mit der thematischen Emanzipation des letzten Satzes gegenüber dem ersten wird aber aus der einfachen einheitlichen Form die zyklische, d.h. wir erhalten statt des Schemas A-B-A das neue A-B-C, bei welchem nur die Tonartenordnung die Einheit wahrt, d.h. zum Ausgang zurückleitet, aber, wie gesagt, gewöhnlich auch die Charaktere des Anfangs- und Schlußsatzes Verwandtschaft zeigen" [Riemann 1905, vol. 1, p. 231].

[7] The introduction of a sonata form seems to stand apart from this analogy. The coda can often be grouped with the recapitulation as a pendant to the finale.

[8] Obviously, this is true only when the sonata cycle contains just one interior movement, or when both interior movements are in a non-tonic key. When one of the interior movements is in the tonic, it extends the tonic of the first movement or prefigures that of the finale. In either case, the tonal function of one of the interior movements is detached from its other functions.

[9] Wilhelm Seidel has shown how the tempo succession fast–slow–fast can, paradoxically, be understood as an emanation of the rest–motion–rest principle as well [Seidel 1986, pp. 208–209].

[10] "[Hier] tritt uns ... wieder der Urgegensatz und die Grundform aller musikalischen Gestaltung, *Ruhe, – Bewegung, – Ruhe*, entgegen, den wir zuerst ... im Gegensatze von Tonika und Tonleiter, dann von tonischer und dominantischer Harmonie, später im dreitheiligen Liede (so wie, unentwickelter, im zweitheiligen und jeder Periode) gefunden hatten. Es bestätigt sich wieder einmal das Fortwirken unsrer ersten Erkenntnisse, wir werden es durch alle Formen hindurch verfolgen können, wenn sich auch nicht immer Zeit findet, es aufzuweisen" [Marx 1857, p. 103].

[11] "A coda is ... analogous to a closing section—made up of codettas—that follows a perfect authentic cadence ending a theme" [Caplin 1998, p. 179].

[12] In an exposition, this destabilization obviously serves as a preparation for the entry of the contrasting tonal region at the beginning of the subordinate theme. In recapitulations too, however, transitions often set out to explore different tonal regions in order to compensate for the otherwise tonally "monotonous" course of the recapitulation.

[13] I will discuss the complex relationship between the scherzo and the finale in Chapter 2.

[14] "Im Grunde ist die Form dieses Quartetts die eines einzigen großen Sonatensatzes. Zwischen der ersten Durchführung und der Reprise sind das Scherzo und die große Durchführung eingeschoben, und die Reprise ist durch das zwischen Hauptthema und Seitensatz stehende Adagio ausgedehnt. Das Rondo-Finale könnte man in diesem Falle als eine weitausgebaute Coda auffassen" [Webern 1912, p. 16].

[15] As will become clear in Chapter 6, Webern fails to see that the formal unit he calls "große Durchführung" is part of the overarching sonata form rather than of the sonata cycle, that the finale is better described as an exclusive part of the sonata cycle, and that the coda of the sonata form starts only when the finale is over.

[16] "[G]eht man von der Vorstellung aus, daß es der Sinn der "double-function-form" sei, die Teile des Sonatensatzes und die Sätze des Sonatenzyklus einander gleichzusetzen, so bleibt nichts anderes übrig, als einen langsamen Satz, der zwischen einer Exposition als erstem Satz und einer Reprise als Finale steht, in den Begriff der Durchführung zu pressen. Die Formidee, die der h-moll-Sonate zugrunde liegt, wird aber erst verständlich, wenn man

sich bewußt macht, daß Kategorien, die verschiedenen formalen Ordnungen angehören, sowohl nebeneinander gestellt als auch miteinander verschmolzen werden können" [Dahlhaus 1988, p. 206].

[17] The term "exocyclic" comes from chemistry, where it means "situated outside the ring."

[18] Both the notion of retrospective reinterpretation and the concept of becoming are Janet Schmalfeldt's [see Schmalfeldt 1995]. I adopt her symbol "⇒" to indicate this "becoming."

[19] Interestingly, the term "unidimensional" occurs in a very similar sense in an essay by James Webster. In his discussion of the form of the finale of Beethoven's Ninth Symphony, Webster uses it to refer to interpretations of this movement that discern only one strain of formal organization in it [Webster 1992, p. 36].

CHAPTER 2

LISZT'S B-MINOR SONATA

The *locus romanticus* of two-dimensional sonata form

In this chapter, the terminology and concepts developed in Chapter 1 will be put to the test by means of an analysis of an entire two-dimensional sonata form. No composition seems more appropriate to this task than Franz Liszt's Piano Sonata in B minor of 1853, a work one might call—as a play on a pun by Walter Frisch—the *locus romanticus* of two-dimensional sonata form.[1] As early as 1904, the German musicologist Eugen Schmitz recognized that Liszt's B-minor Sonata, although a single-movement composition, comprised "three organically interwoven movements" ("drei allerdings organisch ineinandergeflochtene Sätze") [Schmitz 1904, p. 451].[2] Ever since, and particularly since Newman's prototypical description of the sonata as a "double-function form," it has arguably remained the most widely analyzed of all two-dimensional sonata forms.

Composed shortly after the middle of the nineteenth century, Liszt's Sonata and its much-discussed formal organization did not appear out of the blue. Liszt had, since the early 1840s, been experimenting with similar patterns of formal organization in some of his symphonic poems (see Chapter 3) and in a number of keyboard compositions such as the "fantasia quasi sonata" *Après une lecture de Dante* (1837–49), the *Großes Konzertsolo* (1849–50), the Fantasy and Fugue on *Ad nos, ad salutarem undam* for organ (1850), and the A-major Piano Concerto (1839–61).[3] In a broader historical perspective, two-dimensional sonata form is firmly rooted in the nineteenth-century tendency towards cyclic integration of the different movements in multi-movement instrumental compositions. Compositions by others that predate Liszt's Sonata and display a similar combination of movements from the sonata cycle with sections from the sonata form are, however, few in number. Moreover, in none of them is that combination as clear-cut as in Liszt's B-minor Sonata.

One composition from the first half of the nineteenth century that nonetheless comes very close to being a two-dimensional sonata form is Robert Schumann's Fourth Symphony (1841/51). Consisting of four movements that are played without interruptions and related by numerous thematic interconnections, Schumann's Fourth is especially notable for the formal relationship between its outer movements. More specifically, the first movement is not formally closed and thus creates an openness to which the finale responds. Although the first movement clearly contains an exposition (mm. 29–86) and a development (mm. 87–312), it lacks an actual recapitulation. Instead, the development is immediately followed by a coda (mm. 313–358).[4] The finale responds to the absence of a recapitulation in the first movement and in so doing brings about an overarching formal relationship.

Crucial in this respect is the finale's main theme, which is a transformation of a theme that was first introduced in the development of the first movement. As example 1 shows, this new theme in the development (1b) retains a close association with the first movement's main theme because it uses the latter's head motive (1a) as a counterpoint. Example 1c shows the transformation of this new theme at the beginning of the finale. In combination with the lack of a recapitulation in the first movement, its return at the beginning of the finale has the marked effect of a large-scale recapitulation. Its absence from the recapitulation of the finale, which is restricted to the subordinate theme group and the closing group, confirms this interpretation. The main theme's function in the finale is that of a recapitulation rather than of an exposition, and after its first appearance, its part is played.

Example 1: Schumann, Fourth Symphony: (a) first movement, main theme, beginning (mm. 29–30); (b) first movement, new theme in the development, beginning (mm. °121–124); (c) finale, main theme, beginning (mm. 17–18)

The similarities with two-dimensional sonata form are obvious: Schumann's Fourth Symphony too can be conceptualized as the projection of a sonata form and a complete sonata cycle onto each other. In the first movement and the finale in particular, this entails a number of significant changes to the anticipated formal course, allowing those movements to suggest a simultaneous function of exposition and recapitulation in an overarching form.

The most often cited influence on the formal organization of Liszt's Sonata is Franz Schubert's 1822 *Wanderer* Fantasy (D760). Liszt was certainly well acquainted with Schubert's Fantasy, having arranged it for piano and orchestra in 1851, two years before he composed his Sonata.[5] In the *Wanderer* Fantasy, the four movements of a sonata cycle are thematically interrelated and played without interruption. The first movement (mm. 1–188, C major) lacks a recapitulation: it breaks off after the development section and yields to a slow movement (mm. 189–244, C♯ minor). In the scherzo (mm. 245–597) that follows the slow movement, most of the thematic material from the exposition returns in a transformed shape. Yet the scherzo can be construed as a recapitulation only from a thematic point of view, because the entire movement appears off-tonic (A♭ major). Only in the finale (mm. 598–720) does the home key return. But although thematic material in this unit is also obviously derived from the main theme, it no longer has the effect of a recapitulation, especially given the complete absence of subordinate-theme-group material. Like Schumann's Fourth Symphony, Schubert's *Wanderer* Fantasy comes very close to what I call a two-dimensional sonata form. As will become clear towards the end of this chapter, however, both works also differ in crucial ways from the pattern of formal organization exemplified by Liszt's B-minor Sonata.[6]

In the analytical literature on Liszt's B-minor Sonata there is a broad consensus that it is a two-dimensional sonata form. Opinions differ, however, on the number of movements involved, as well as on the exact nature of the relationship between the sonata cycle and the overarching sonata form.[7] The interpretation that I will defend in the further course of this chapter—and which draws heavily on Carl Dahlhaus's reading of the piece—was already shown in figure 6 in Chapter 1. In this reading, the first movement of the sonata cycle is identified with the exposition of the overarching sonata form, and its scherzo and finale with the recapitulation and the coda. The slow interior movement, by contrast, is interpolated between the development and the recapitulation of the overarching sonata form. The development section and the return of the slow introduction between the slow movement and the scherzo are exocyclic units that belong exclusively to the overarching sonata form.

In the following paragraphs, I will investigate exactly how the interaction between both dimensions in Liszt's Sonata is realized. After an analysis of the

Example 2: Liszt, B-minor Sonata, transition (beginning), mm. 32–44

overarching sonata form's exposition, I will focus on the identification of the first movement of the sonata cycle with the exposition of the overarching sonata form, the interpolation of the slow movement, and the complex relationship between the sonata cycle's scherzo and finale and the overarching sonata form.

The exposition of the overarching sonata form

The opening measures of Liszt's Sonata present a fundamental ambiguity.[8] Mm. 1–7 are almost always interpreted as a slow introduction. But what about the measures that follow? The fragmented and harmonically unstable surface of mm. 8–31 strongly contrasts with the striking stability of mm. 32–44, shown in example 2. Not only do the latter clearly articulate the tonic B minor, they also have a sentential layout, with a double basic idea in mm. 32–35, its sequential repetition in mm. 36–39, and a continuation beginning in m. 40. From this perspective, mm. 32ff have a distinct thematic quality, whereas mm. 8–31 still seem to belong to the introduction.

At the same time, the perfect authentic cadence (PAC) in the tonic in m. 32 is an unmistakable "main theme cadence," signaling the main theme's conclusion rather than its beginning.[9] The ensuing passage, in spite of its initial stability, eventually starts to modulate, reaching its goal only at the quasi half-cadential arrival on the dominant of the mediant D major in m. 81. Mm. 8–31 may initially appear to function as an introduction, but when mm. 32ff turn out to be a transition rather than a main theme, they are retrospectively reinterpreted as the main theme—without, however, losing their introductory quality.[10]

The ambiguity of the opening is reinforced at the beginning of the recapitulation of the overarching sonata form. Mm. 453–459 are a transposition (down a minor second) of mm. 1–7, and mm. 460–522 develop a transformation of the material from mm. 8–17 (likewise transposed down a minor second). Only from m. 523, which corresponds to m. 25, does the recapitulation parallel the exposition. As a result, there is a very strong sense that the actual recapitulation begins only with the rhetorically reinforced return of mm. 32ff in m. 533, the preceding units (mm. 453–532) assuming a more preparatory function, perhaps in the manner of a modified return of the introduction. As we will see, this ambiguity plays a central role in the articulation of the finale as a movement, and thus of the sonata cycle as a whole.

An argument in favor of an interpretation of mm. 8–31 as a main theme is that their internal formal organization comes quite close to a small ternary. Mm. 8–17 constitute a first part (A) with two contrasting thematic ideas (the first in

Example 3: Liszt, B-minor Sonata: (a) main theme, first two thematic ideas (mm. 8–17); (b) subordinate theme group, beginning of the second thematic idea (mm.°125–130); (c) subordinate theme group, beginning of the third thematic idea (mm. 153–160)

mm. °9–11,[11] the second in mm. 14–15), the more repetitive and thematically less profiled mm. 19–24 suggests the function of a contrasting middle (B), and mm. 25–31 form an abridged recapitulation of the first part (A'). Although this recapitulation is condensed, the first thematic idea from part A returns at pitch (but now harmonized), and the second thematic idea resurfaces as the cadence approaches.

There is no question that the new beginning in D major in m. 105 marks the onset of the subordinate theme group. The unit that follows comprises three different thematic ideas: mm. 105–120, mm. °125–140, and mm. 153ff respectively. Only the first of these thematic ideas is really new; as example 3 illustrates, the second and third are transformations of the two contrasting thematic ideas from the main theme group. Each transformation is immediately preceded by a very explicit reminiscence of the original shape of the idea it transforms.

Thematic transformations like these are a hallmark of Liszt's style. A useful definition of the technique has been offered by Frisch, who posits that "a transformed theme retains its original melodic outline, but may change its mode, harmony, tempo, rhythm, and meter" [Frisch 1984, p. 36]. This definition should not be interpreted rigidly. Not only entire themes, but also theme fragments or motives can be transformed. It often happens, moreover, that something begins as a thematic transformation but soon takes another direction. Finally, a transformation retains the melodic outline of its model, but not necessarily its interval structure. Minor changes in pitch are always possible, and in some cases it seems appropriate to use terms such as "free transformation" or "distorted transformation" to indicate the extent to which the pitch content has been altered. Nevertheless, non-pitch modifications always predominate over pitch-related ones.

Thematic transformation is, however, more than just a characteristic of Liszt's personal style; as will become clear throughout this book, it is also closely allied with the phenomenon of two-dimensional sonata form itself. It is not difficult to see why this is the case: thematic transformation is an ideal tool for the mediation of single-movement and multi-movement patterns. Allowing for the presentation of the same thematic material in shapes that markedly differ in tempo and character, it meets the requirements both of unity within a single movement and of contrast between separate movements.

A particularly striking feature of the internal organization of Liszt's subordinate theme group is that it initially eschews tonal stability for almost fifty measures. The opening thematic idea begins with a strong sentential impulse (two-measure basic idea, two-measure repetition, continuation from m. 109 onwards), but disintegrates from m. 114 onwards and fails to achieve cadential closure. Instead, it lingers on b: VII$^{°7}$ (a dominant in the movement's tonic key!) and even restates the first thematic idea of the main theme at pitch (mm. 119–124). Through an enharmonic reinterpretation of the a♯ (b: $\overset{\wedge}{7}$) as b♭, the music moves to F major for the beginning of the second thematic idea. This too takes a sentential shape, but is even more loosely organized than the beginning of the subordinate theme group. The presentation of an eight-measure model (mm. 125–132) is followed by a sequential repetition in D minor and, from m. 141 on, a continuation that eventually leads to an imperfect authentic cadence (IAC) in D major at the onset of the third thematic idea. The effect is that in spite of the obvious initial thematic rhetoric of mm. 105ff (and, to a lesser extent, of mm. 125), the impression that they are actual subordinate themes is retrospectively undermined later on. Only the third thematic idea develops into a fully-fledged subordinate theme. It takes the form of a compound period with a sentential antecedent leading to a half cadence (HC) in m. 170 and a dissolving consequent starting in m. 171.

From m. 183, after a varied repetition of part of the third subordinate theme, the texture once again becomes tonally unstable. The increased developmental activity in mm. 183–204 has led Dahlhaus to label this passage as a miniature development that functions as a transition to the actual development beginning in m. 205 [Dahlhaus 1988, p. 205]. A more accurate label might be that of a *Spielepisode*: the optional and often somewhat development-like segment that is sometimes inserted between the subordinate theme group and the closing group.[12] In any case, mm. 183–204 are an integral part of the exposition's tonal trajectory. They lead to what appears to be a cadential $^6_4$ chord in F♯ major in m. 197. Instead of resolving over a dominant to its tonic and thus potentially marking the beginning of a closing group, however, the cadential motion is interrupted and followed by a new and very similar gesture, now suggesting E♭ minor (mm. 201–204).

This second cadence-like gesture is abruptly juxtaposed with a new formal unit based on the head of the main theme from m. 205 onwards. In mm. 205–212, an eight-measure model (2+2+4) is presented over a C-major $^6_4$ chord and immediately repeated over a B-major $^6_4$ chord in mm. 213–220. A new two-measure model follows in mm. 221–222 (dominant in B♭ minor), which is—just like the first measures of the preceding model—based on the first idea from the main theme group. The repetition of this model in mm. 223–224—now over a B♭-minor $^6_4$ chord—is followed by an incomplete repetition on the dominant of F♯ minor, which initiates a fragmentation process that results in a liquidation in the second half of m. 232. The model-sequence-fragmentation technique and the concomitant tonal instability in which sonorities from different keys are juxtaposed, never confirmed, and never enter into a functional relationship with each other, clearly mark this unit as part of a developmental core.

The exposition is, in other words, limited to mm. 1–204 and constitutes a virtual three-key exposition, modulating from B minor in the main theme group to D major at the beginning of the subordinate theme group and then to F♯ major just before m. 200. F♯ major is, however, not fully realized, and there is no closing group. Figure 7 summarizes the course of the exposition.

1–7	8–31		32–104	
INTRODUCTION	MAIN THEME (ternary)		TRANSITION (sentential)	
	(b)	b: PAC	b →	D: HC⇒PAC

105–124	125–152	153–204		
SUBORDINATE THEME GROUP				
Thematic idea 1	Thematic idea 2	Thematic idea 3 (period)		⇒ *Spielepisode*
(sentential)	(sentential)	antecedent	dissolving consequent	
D	F D: IAC	D	D: HC →	~~F♯: PAC~~ ~~e♯: PAC~~

Figure 7: Liszt, B-minor Sonata: formal overview of the exposition

A sonata-form exposition that lacks a closing group and is not even rounded off by a cadence may seem remarkable, but it was not a complete novelty in 1853. One obvious source of Liszt's strategy is the variant of sonata form typically used in overtures, a genre Liszt was certainly interested in around the time he composed the Sonata (see Chapter 3). Liszt's Sonata resembles the typical form of an overture not only in its use of an unrepeated exposition, but also in the merger of the expositional closing group with the beginning of the development, a standard option for overtures of the second quarter of the nineteenth century. In most cases, the onset of the closing group itself is marked by an unambiguous PAC in the goal key of the exposition, which is followed by a more or less brief postcadential unit that then leads smoothly into the development. Random examples include Hector Berlioz's *King Lear* (1831, V: PAC in m. 223),[13] Richard Wagner's *Rienzi* (1835,

V: PAC in m. 195), and Schumann's *Manfred* (1848–49, ♭iii: PAC, enharmonically spelt as ♯ii, in m. 82). In a number of overtures, however, the exposition is not concluded by a PAC (nor, consequently, by a closing group). This practice seems to have been initiated by Berlioz, notably in his overture to *Benvenuto Cellini* (1836–38), an opera Liszt conducted in Weimar in 1852. In this overture, the subordinate theme begins in D major (G: V) and reaches a first PAC in m. 159. This cadence is elided with a varied repetition of the entire theme that omits the concluding cadence: in m. 197–198, the anticipated V–I in D major is abruptly replaced by a V–I in B minor, which is then elided with a first developmental core. Several years later, Berlioz would adopt a similar strategy in *Le Corsaire* (1844), as would Schumann in his overture to the *Szenen aus Goethes Faust* (1853).[14]

Identification: first movement and exposition

In his analysis of Liszt's Sonata, Newman locates the beginning of the development at m. 331. For him, mm. 205–330 play no significant role in the overarching sonata form. They fulfill a function in the dimension of the cycle only, constituting the recapitulation of a first movement cast in an "incomplete sonatina form" [Newman 1969, p. 375]. Newman's reading implies that the first movement of the cycle is partly identified with the exposition of the overarching sonata form and partly interpolated between the latter's sections.

Strictly speaking, the presence of a section that exclusively belongs to one of both dimensions is at odds with Newman's own concept of double-function form. There are ways to accommodate mm. 205–330 to Newman's definition, however. They could, for instance, be regarded as a recapitulation in the dimension of the cycle that functions as a repeat of the exposition in the dimension of the form. One may, of course, object that there are numerous arguments against an interpretation of mm. 205–330 as a varied exposition repeat, but the very same objections can be raised against their interpretation as a recapitulation. If Newman felt comfortable calling mm. 205–330 a recapitulation, in other words, he would probably also have agreed with an interpretation of this formal unit as a varied expositional repeat.

Authors after Newman have found it difficult to see how mm. 205–330 could function as a recapitulation (or, for that matter, as a varied exposition repeat). The passage contains only transformed or developed versions of themes from the exposition, the succession of formal units does not correspond at all to that in the exposition, and the key relationships are—to say the very least—at odds with those of a recapitulation. A more plausible option is to identify the introduction and the entire exposition of the overarching sonata form with the first movement of the sonata cycle. In this reading, both units end in m. 205 before the onset of the development, which stretches until m. 330 and belongs exclusively to the dimension of the form.

The identification of the local sonata form with the introduction and the exposition of the overarching sonata form is realized in a most ingenious way. The introduction, main theme group, transition, and subordinate theme group of the exposition of the overarching sonata form function as the same formal units in the exposition of the local sonata form. They are, in other words, vertically double-functional. At the same time, the transition and the subordinate theme group are horizontally double-functional in the dimension of the cycle. They may be heard simultaneously as a development and a recapitulation respectively, i.e. as the two sections of the sonata form that follow the exposition. As Dahlhaus notes:

> The transition (mm. 32–104) is a development not only technically, but also because of the size that it attains. One therefore expects a recapitulation.[15]

The interpretation of the transition and the subordinate theme group as a development and recapitulation may initially seem far-fetched, but it is supported by impressive evidence. First, and as noted before, both contrasting thematic ideas from the main theme group return in the subordinate theme group, not only as transformations (mm. °125–140 and 153–182), but also in their original shape (mm. 120–124 and 141–152). The first of them even returns in the original key. Second, the transition is unusually long—especially in comparison to the main theme—and exhibits an unusual amount of developmental activity. The threefold sequenced return of the first thematic idea from the main theme group (on B♭ major, G minor, and F major respectively) and the subsequent fragmentation in mm. 55–81 in particular suggest something beyond a mere transitional function. The standing on the dominant (mm. 81–104) preceding the subordinate theme group is, moreover, too long and too strong to be the preparation of a mere subordinate theme group. The sense of arrival—at least at the surface level—generated by the entry of the subordinate theme group itself (marked *Grandioso* and *fortissimo*) seems equally to breach the boundaries of a mere exposition. The standing on the dominant behaves as if it were the end of a development section rather than the end of a transition. This impression is further strengthened by the reappearance of the descending scale figure from the introduction, which takes on a strong form-articulating function throughout the composition.

A final argument in favor of an interpretation of mm. 32–104 as both a transition and a development, and of mm. 105–204 as a recapitulation as well as a subordinate theme group, is that none of the extraordinary features just described return in the recapitulation. There, the transition (mm. 523–599) and the subordinate theme group

CHAPTER 2

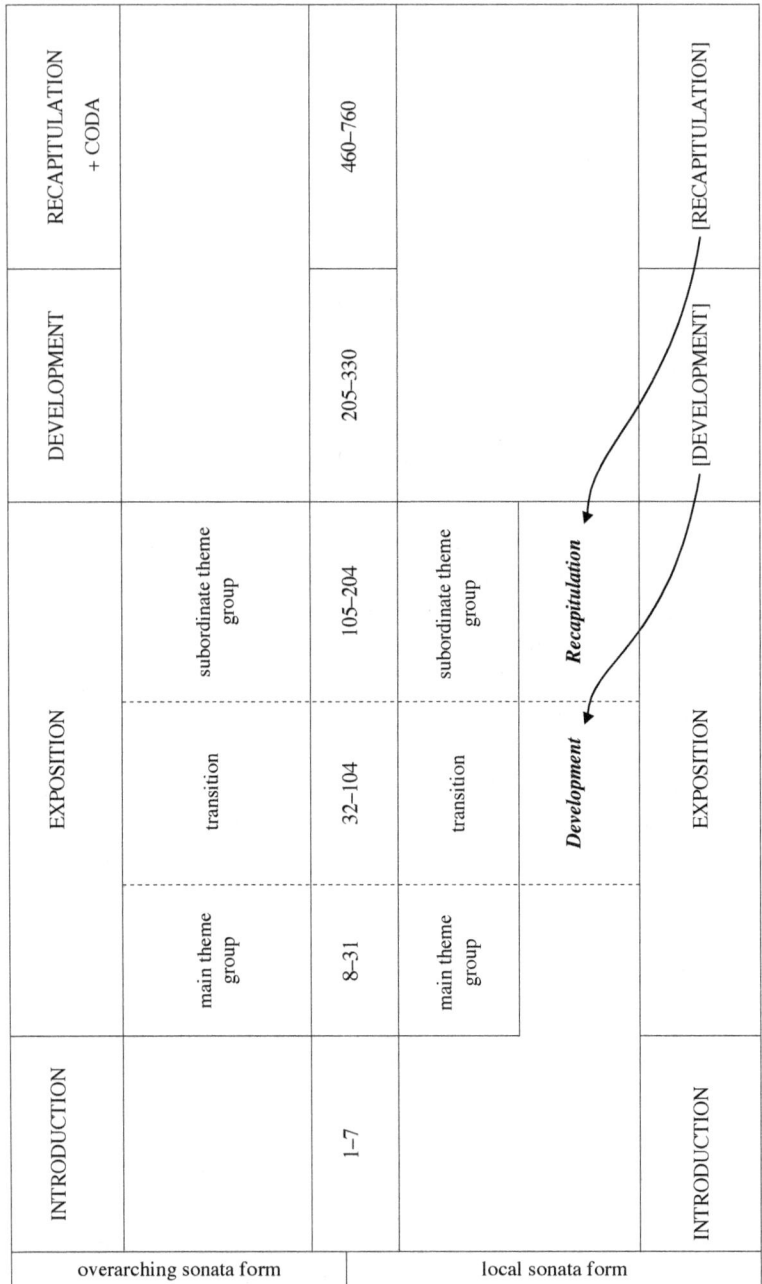

Figure 8: Liszt, B-minor Sonata: identification of the local sonata form with the introduction and exposition of the overarching sonata form

(mm. 600–672) obviously do not fulfill the simultaneous function of a development and recapitulation. Accordingly, the subordinate theme group enters in a modest *mezzoforte*, lacks the marking *grandioso*, and contains far fewer references to main-theme material. Neither thematic idea from the main theme reappears in its original shape, and the first is even omitted completely. Although the transition in the recapitulation is hardly any shorter or less developmental in character than the one in the exposition, it is striking that its forward dynamics decline in m. 595, immediately before the entry of the subordinate theme group. As a result, the latter begins in a far less emphatic way than in the exposition. And although the descending scale figure is prominent in mm. 555–581, its absence from the final part of the transition (mm. 582–599) weakens its form-articulating effect.

If one takes mm. 104 and 600 to be what James Hepokoski and Warren Darcy have termed the medial caesura—the "rhetorically reinforced break or gap that serves to divide an exposition [or recapitulation] in two parts" [Hepokoski & Darcy 2006, p. 24]—then the medial caesura in the recapitulation seems to be much more orthodox than the one in the exposition. In the exposition, the expected caesura is overridden: there is a very strong sense in which the standing on the dominant at the end of the transition, which initially may seem to be an arrival, is reactivated to lead to the tonic arrival at the onset of the first subordinate theme. The effect is similar to what Hepokoski and Darcy call "caesura-fill of the 'juggernaut' type" [2006, p. 44]. In the recapitulation too, there is a considerable amount of "caesura-fill," but it never jeopardizes the effect of a dominant arrival in m. 582.

The relationship between the overarching and the local sonata forms in mm. 1–204 can be summarized as follows (a schematic overview is given in figure 8). Mm. 1–7 and 8–31 function as an introduction and a main theme group in both the local and the overarching sonata forms. Both dimensions completely coincide, so that the double-functionality remains as yet latent: in contrast to real double-functionality, in which the same formal unit has two different functions in two different dimensions, a latently double-functional unit has the same function in two different dimensions. The situation changes in m. 32. This is the point of dimensional disconnection: both dimensions, which entirely coincided in the previous units, no longer do so now. In the dimension of the form, mm. 32–104 and 105–204 constitute the transition and the subordinate theme group. In the dimension of the cycle, these units combine the function of a transition with that of a development, and that of a subordinate theme group with that of a recapitulation. They are, in other words, horizontally double-functional within the dimension of the cycle, combining formal functions that would normally be separated in time. Because of this horizontal double-functionality within the dimension of the cycle, mm. 32–204 become openly—as opposed to latently—double-functional. In these formal units, a tension arises between what they are expected to do in the dimension of the cycle and how they are expected to behave in the dimension of the form.

Even though the change in the relationship between form and cycle in m. 32 is the most crucial turning point in Liszt's B-minor Sonata, the listener comes to realize this only gradually. It is unlikely that a listener would start to realize that he or she is not just dealing with a one-dimensional sonata form as early as the transition. Rather, it is the subordinate theme group, with its *grandioso* beginning and several literal references to the main theme group, that urges the listener to reinterpret the preceding portions of the composition against the background of two-dimensional sonata form. Yet even then, an interpretation as a two-dimensional sonata form initially appears as only one of several possibilities. Because of the horizontal double-functionality of mm. 32–204 in the dimension of the cycle, there is still a possibility that they merely consist of an unusual transition and subordinate theme group in a one-dimensional sonata form. The validity of an interpretation as a two-dimensional sonata form is definitively confirmed only in m. 331, with the arrival of the interpolated slow movement. Only this movement, which cannot be accounted for in the dimension of the form, makes it perfectly clear that more has been going on than just a sonata form.

Interpolation: the slow movement

Interpolated movements in two-dimensional sonata forms generally display two apparently contradictory tendencies: a tendency towards individuation on the one hand, one towards integration on the other. The former no doubt is the most obvious. It is expressed by contrast and potential autonomy. Practically every interpolated movement in a two-dimensional sonata form contrasts with the overarching sonata form in which it is interpolated. Several factors can articulate this contrast. First and foremost, it can be articulated thematically. An interpolated movement tends, at least where its principal or initial themes are concerned, to make use of thematic material that is, or appears to be, new and proper to that particular movement only. There are two possibilities here: either the main thematic material of the interpolated movement is radically new, or it stems from the overarching sonata form but is altered to such an extent that it obtains a distinctive new thematic quality, often by means of thematic transformation. Second, practically every interpolated movement differs from the immediately preceding formal unit of the overarching sonata form in tempo, meter, and key.

In m. 331 of Liszt's B-minor Sonata, the development of the overarching sonata form is interrupted by an interpolated slow movement. The theme that opens this movement is entirely new and cannot be traced back to any of the themes from the exposition. It even is the first new theme to appear since the beginning of the subordinate theme group. The slow movement's tempo (*Andante sostenuto* and, later, *Quasi Adagio*) obviously contrast with the overarching sonata form's *Allegro energico*. Metrically as well, the beginning of the interpolated movement is clearly distinct from the unit directly preceding it ($\frac{3}{4}$ in the slow movement, ¢ in the overarching sonata form). The F♯-major tonic of the slow movement is, of course, simply fifth-related to the tonic of the overarching sonata form; in the large-scale tonal plan of the Sonata, it realizes the F♯ major that was merely implied at the end of the exposition (as shown in example 4 later in this chapter). The actual approach to the new key at the beginning of the slow movement, however, is remarkable. The final chord before the *Andante sostenuto* being a dominant ninth chord in E major, the move to F♯ major (via a briefly tonicized G♯ major) marks a sudden change in direction that very effectively helps to distinguish the interpolated movement from the preceding measures.

The other individuating factor in an interpolated movement is its potential formal autonomy: the movement has to be able to stand on its own—that is to say, as an independent movement within a hypothetical one-dimensional sonata cycle. It is this potential formal autonomy that distinguishes an interpolated movement from the mere interpolated episode that sometimes appears in the development of nineteenth-century sonata forms. A first requirement for potential autonomy is simply that the movement's temporal expanse be in keeping with the proportions of the other movements in the cycle. A second and analytically more interesting prerequisite is that the movement display a potentially closed formal and tonal organization. This means that only relatively minor changes, additions, or omissions would have to be made to the interpolated movement in order to enable it to function as a separate movement in a one-dimensional sonata cycle and generate an impression of well-roundedness similar to that of an "ordinary" movement. Often, but not always, potential formal autonomy is related to the presence of a traditional pattern of formal organization.

Mm. 331–452 of the B-minor Sonata clearly constitute a self-contained movement. Yet even though this movement is both formally and tonally closed, the extent to which it corresponds to a traditional pattern of formal organization is open to discussion. Wolfgang Dömling, for instance, has located the beginning of the slow movement in m. 347 instead of m. 331. In doing so, he reveals a striking large-scale parallelism between the sequences of formal units on either side of the slow movement (mm. 8–330 and mm. 460–728 respectively). The formal units that precede the slow movement return in the same order and in very much the same proportions after the slow movement, where they constitute the recapitulation [Dömling 1985, pp. 124–125].[16] The price Dömling has to pay is that he cannot conceive of the slow movement as a fully-fledged musical form, but only as "fantasy-like free" ("fantasieartig frei"). Without mm. 331–345, the slow movement becomes almost nonsensical as a musical form. It starts in C♯ major—modulating to A major after as few as two measures—but ends in F♯ major, and the theme that returns at its climax in mm. 395ff is not the theme with which it begins, but the one that immediately precedes it. With mm. 331–346 included, by contrast, the slow movement can be analyzed as a ternary form, in which mm. 331–334 are an introduction, mm. 335–362 a first section, mm. 363–397 a middle section, and mm. 398–452 a modified recapitulation of the first section. Instead of the expected final chord of the slow movement in m. 453, the slow introduction returns (transposed down a minor second), signaling the resumption of the overarching sonata form.

After establishing itself as an interpolated movement, the slow movement is gradually integrated into the overarching sonata form. More specifically, it is infiltrated by thematic material that originates in the exposition of the overarching sonata form. This process begins in the second half of the first section. In mm. 349–362, the transformed second thematic idea from the main theme group returns. The integration goes on in the middle section, which is entirely constructed out of material from the exposition. Mm. 363–367 and 376–379 vary the first subordinate theme and in mm. 385–386 and 389–390, the first thematic idea from the main theme group returns. In mm. 433–452, the movement's concluding measures, the transformed second thematic idea from the main theme group is subject to a process of liquidation. The integration that takes place in the course of the slow movement is retrospective: material that played a central role in earlier portions of the overarching sonata form reappears in the interpolated movement. Much later in the composition, there is another instance of retrospective integration: mm. °712–728 of the coda of the overarching sonata form refer back to the opening of the slow movement, now transposed to B major.

Identification: scherzo–finale and recapitulation–coda

The most persistent question in the literature on Liszt's B-minor Sonata is undoubtedly whether its sonata cycle consists of three or four movements. Is there, more specifically, a scherzo between the slow movement and the finale or not? In Newman's view there is. He describes the B♭-minor fugato on a transformation of part A of the main theme in mm. 460–522 as a "scherzando fugue" and grants it the status of a second interior movement [Newman 1969, p. 375]. According to Dahlhaus, by contrast, mm. 460–522 do not function as a scherzo, but as the beginning of the finale, so that the sonata cycle comprises only three movements [Dahlhaus 1988, pp. 206–207]. Rey Longyear, finally, defends an intriguing intermediate position. He interprets mm. 460–522 as the beginning of the finale, but at the same time includes them as a scherzo in his list of movements [Longyear 1973, pp. 198 & 207–208].

The question whether there is a scherzo in the dimension of the cycle affects the interpretation of mm. 460–522 in the dimension of the form. One way of looking at this unit is as a second interior movement that precedes the recapitulation. In this interpretation, it can be seen either as an identification with part of the development or as an interpolation between the slow movement and the recapitulation. If, by contrast, mm. 460–522 are interpreted as the beginning of the finale, the most natural conclusion seems to be to include them in the recapitulation. Only in Longyear's analysis are they at the same time a separate scherzo movement and part of the recapitulation, since he lets the scherzo coincide with the beginning of the finale.

Each of these interpretations has its defects. Longyear's view implies a complex combination of horizontal and vertical double-functionality. Not only do mm. 460–522 simultaneously function as a scherzo and as the beginning of a finale—and therefore as a horizontally double-functional unit in the dimension of the cycle—they are also vertically double-functional, combining their double function in the cycle with that of the beginning of the recapitulation in the dimension of the form. Interpreting mm. 460–522 as an interpolated scherzo movement is problematic too, not so much because it would have to account for a movement that is disproportionately short in comparison to the others, but mainly because the passage is neither tonally nor formally closed and thus constitutes no movement at all. It begins as a fugue (with a regular fugue exposition in mm. 460–488 that evolves into a first episode in m. 489), but increasingly opens up until the polyphonic texture disappears completely as of m. 502.

Given that a developmental texture becomes evident from m. 489, one might, along with Newman, be inclined to interpret mm. 460–522 as a scherzo that is identified with the final segment of the development. Yet in that case, it would be hard to see why this segment is preceded by the same material that precedes the exposition. As was noted before, this material assumes a strong form-articulating function throughout the Sonata, returning at all major formal junctures: in mm. 81–104 before the entry of the subordinate theme group (which also functions as the recapitulation of the local sonata form), in mm. 277–286 just before the transition to the slow movement, and in mm. 673–682 at the beginning of the coda. It would be highly remarkable that the same material reappears at the beginning of the scherzo, but not at the beginning of the recapitulation or the finale.

Finally, the interpretation of m. 460 as the beginning of the recapitulation is also open to debate. The main objection is not that such a reading would imply that the sonata cycle contains no scherzo: as shown in the discussion of Adolf Bernhard Marx's theory of the sonata cycle in Chapter 1, a sonata requires only one interior movement. The more serious problems are that the main theme returns in a transformed shape and in the wrong key (B♭ minor instead of B minor) and that its treatment suggests a developmental function. In the Sonata's large-scale tonal plan, moreover, mm. 460–532 are much more closely associated with the slow movement than with the rest of the recapitulation. Being enharmonically equivalent to A♯ minor, B♭ minor prolongs the slow movement's F♯ major.[17] B♭/A♯ minor functions as the mediant of the dominant, so that the latter extends from the beginning of the slow movement all the way to the dominant chord in B minor at the first exact correspondence to the exposition in mm. 531–532. Example 4 connects a number of important tonal centers in the large-scale tonal plan of the Sonata.

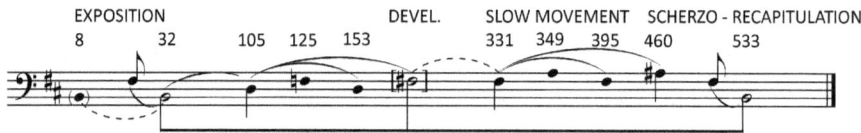

Example 4: large-scale tonal plan of Liszt's B-minor Sonata

The suggestion of a scherzo movement from m. 460 onwards is too strong to be ignored. Still, I maintain that the same moment acts as the beginning of the recapitulation, albeit not in any obvious way. The recapitulation begins stepwise, so to speak: the listener only gradually becomes aware of it. Here, Liszt reaps the harvest of the calculated ambiguity at the beginning of the exposition: the main theme's relatively vague profile in the exposition allows for a fundamental transformation when it returns. As a result, the return of introduction and main-theme material from m. 460 does not function as an emphatic recapitulation. Conversely, it is the very nature of the opening of the exposition's transition that enables it to bear the weight of the recapitulation when the main theme itself no longer does so. Because m. 533, the last possible moment when the attentive listener becomes aware that the recapitulation is underway, does refer back to the transition rather than to the beginning of the exposition, however, the introduction and the scherzando elaboration of the main theme in mm. 460–532 are retrospectively subsumed into the recapitulation, even though they are entirely off-tonic.

The radical and even structural modifications that mm. 460–532 have undergone in comparison to the exposition provide the finale with the amount of independence from the exposition/first movement that it requires in order to be perceived as a movement in its own right and not just as a recapitulation. The oblique move into the recapitulation in the dimension of the form is paralleled by the merger of two consecutive movements (scherzo⇒finale) in the dimension of the cycle. These are not the only changes to the recapitulation that help articulate the finale. Equally conspicuous is that in mm. 650–672, the original *Spielepisode* from the exposition has been replaced by the reprise of a passage from the development (mm. 255–276).

Although the recapitulation is identified with the finale, the relationship between both dimensions is different here from that in the exposition and the first movement. The vertical double-functionality of mm. 32–104 and 105–204 in the dimension of the cycle at least strongly suggests a form proper to the first movement. But although the recapitulation's simultaneous function as a finale does, of course, affect its outer shape too, these modifications do not result in a form proper to the finale. Because the finale lacks a form of its own, then—it borrows its form from the recapitulation—it is also difficult to determine unequivocally whether the coda of the overarching sonata form is part of it or not. Below I will suggest a reason why it probably is.

Identifying the finale of the sonata cycle with the recapitulation of the overarching sonata form is one of the major difficulties the composer of a two-dimensional sonata form has to confront. In principle, it is possible to realize this identification along the lines of the identification of a first movement with an exposition. Since the segments of a recapitulation are essentially those of an exposition, they are equally capable of functioning as the sections of a movement. But this is exactly where the problem lies. Because a recapitulation is by definition a more or less similarly organized return of the exposition, the movement with which it is identified will be very similar to the movement that was identified with the exposition earlier on. Yet an essential characteristic of the relationship between a first movement and a finale in a sonata cycle is, of course, that they differ from each other.

One might argue that to a progressive composer from the second half of the nineteenth century who had the ambition of modernizing sonata form—and there is no doubt that Liszt was such a composer—this difficulty must have appeared as a challenge. By modifying the recapitulation of the overarching sonata form to such an extent that it can serve as the finale of the sonata cycle, Liszt may have hoped to solve one of the central problems of sonata form after Beethoven. By the second quarter of the nineteenth century, the recapitulation had become what Theodor W. Adorno once called "the crux of sonata form" ("die Crux der Sonatenform") [Adorno 1960, p. 241]. Composers from the generation of Schumann, Mendelssohn, and Liszt became increasingly aware of a "recapitulation problem," finding it difficult to write full recapitulations of what had already been said in the exposition. Consequently, they experimented with modified recapitulations, avoiding the schematic and symmetrical model of classical sonata form while not altogether ignoring the idea of a recapitulation as one of the most essential aspects of the form.

It is against the very background of the recapitulation problem that the identification of the finale with the recapitulation and coda of the overarching sonata form may paradoxically appear as a flaw in the formal organization of Liszt's B-minor Sonata. There is no denying that the recapitulation of Liszt's Sonata reveals a number of important differences from the exposition. Because these differences fail to render the movement that is identified with this recapitulation a form of its own, however, one might argue that the recapitulation and the beginning of the coda do not function as a finale at all. The modifications made to mm. 460–672 in comparison to the exposition might be explained within the dimension of the form alone, in the sense that they could also have occurred in the recapitulation of a one-dimensional sonata form. A tendency to individuate the recapitulation from the exposition is typical of nineteenth-century sonata form in general and not necessarily related to two-dimensional sonata form.

But there is more to a musical form than meets the eye. As Hepokoski has argued [Hepokoski 2002, p. 135],

> the concept of "form" is not primarily a property of the printed page or sounding surface. Instead, "form" resides more properly in the composer- and listener-activated process of measuring what one hears against what one is invited to expect.

In the context of two-dimensional sonata form, this means that when the initial movements of a sonata cycle are present—be it in the form of an identification or an interpolation—these movements may be expected to be completed to form a full sonata cycle. This is particularly true of compositions called "sonata" or, for that matter, "symphony" or "string quartet." Here, a specific multi-movement pattern obviously is a very strong generic convention. If a recapitulation is preceded by other movements that normally belong to a sonata cycle, therefore, every modification of that recapitulation pointing in the direction of a finale is enough to effectively allow its interpretation as the finale of that cycle. The listener hears a finale not so much because of the modifications of the recapitulation, but rather because of what precedes the onset of the recapitulation in the dimension of the cycle. I call this the principle of cyclic completion, and it is of utmost importance in many two-dimensional sonata forms.

The notion of modifications that point in the direction of a finale can be defined more precisely. Michael Talbot has distinguished three main types of finales in Western art music: the relaxant finale, the summative finale, and the valedictory finale [Talbot 2001, pp. 50–51]. From the beginning of the nineteenth century onwards, the summative type clearly becomes the most important one. It is characterized by a double tendency to summarize the previous movements and to surpass everything that has been said in those previous movements in intensity and rhetorical power.

In two-dimensional sonata forms, finales are likewise generally summative in character. Finales that coincide with the recapitulation of the overarching sonata form are summative because of the very nature of identification. A finale that is identified with the recapitulation automatically contains thematic material from the first movement that was identified with the exposition of the overarching sonata form. In order to avoid too close a parallel to the exposition and the first movement, this thematic material often reappears in a modified or transformed version, and is joined by thematic material from the other movements. Because it coincides with the point of structural resolution in the overarching sonata form, moreover, a finale that is identified with the recapitulation automatically occupies the most crucial place in the composition.

Elements that point in the direction of a summative finale in Liszt's B-minor Sonata are numerous. The most obvious of these is that the scherzo is subsumed under the finale. It can hardly be coincidental, moreover, that in this scherzo the main theme group reappears transformed and in a fugal texture. This suggests intensification and outdoes the main theme's homophonous (in fact quasi monophonous) presentation in the exposition. The several increases in tempo in the second part of the transition (*Più mosso*, m. 555) and after the subordinate theme group (*Stretta quasi Presto* in mm. 650ff, *Presto* in mm. 673ff, and *Prestissimo* in mm. 682ff) equally contribute to the finale's summative character. The last sixty measures of the coda, finally, have an explicitly summative function, transposing the five thematic ideas of the entire composition to the tonic major and presenting them in close proximity: the first thematic idea from the subordinate theme group (mm. 700–710), the slow-movement theme (mm. 711–728), both ideas from the main theme group (in inverse order, mm. 729–736 and 737–747), and the slow introduction (mm. 750–760).

The two-dimensional sonata form in Liszt's B-minor Sonata makes ample use of the potential analogies between the sections of a sonata form and the movements of a sonata cycle explored in Chapter 1. The first movement of the sonata cycle coincides with the introduction and the exposition of the overarching sonata form; the slow movement occupies developmental space, standing between the actual development and the recapitulation; and the finale coincides with the recapitulation and the beginning of the coda. For the identification of the first movement and the exposition, Liszt also exploits the potential analogies between the sections of a sonata form and the segments of a sonata-form exposition. It is no coincidence that the development of the local sonata form coincides with the transition of the overarching sonata form, nor that the recapitulation of the local sonata form coincides with the overarching sonata form's subordinate theme group.

The identification of the first movement of the sonata cycle with the introduction and the exposition of the overarching sonata form is quite successful. The tension between both dimensions is not resolved, surfacing particularly in the subordinate theme group that simultaneously functions as a recapitulation, but it is held under control. The identification of the finale with the recapitulation and part of the coda of the overarching sonata form appears somewhat less convincing. In spite of the various gestures that articulate the presence of the finale, the last 230 measures of the Sonata regularly shift back to an emphasis on the recapitulatory aspect alone. It does not come as a surprise, then, that in later two-dimensional sonata forms, composers have focused on the finale problem, trying to find other ways of relating the finale of a sonata cycle with the overarching sonata form.

Now that we have a clear idea of how an actual two-dimensional sonata form works, we are better equipped to differentiate it from related patterns of formal organization such as those of Schumann's Fourth Symphony and Schubert's *Wanderer* Fantasy described near the beginning of this chapter. The crucial difference between a two-dimensional sonata form and Schumann's Fourth is that in the latter, the multi-movement pattern retains its priority, whereas in the former, the overarching sonata form is clearly the predominant dimension. As can be seen in Liszt's B-minor Sonata, this predominance manifests itself in three ways. First, the formal units preceding the first interior movement in a two-dimensional sonata form will not easily be mistaken for an autonomous first movement of a through-composed multi-movement cycle. This is different from Schumann's Fourth, in which the portion of the composition that precedes the first interior movement clearly and primarily functions as a first movement (albeit one with an unusual design). Second, almost every two-dimensional sonata form contains a development or development segment that is exocyclic. Needless to say, Schumann's Fourth is entirely lacking such a unit that functions exclusively in the overarching design and not in any of the movements of the sonata cycle. Finally, the overarching sonata form in a two-dimensional sonata form always contains a recapitulation. This recapitulation can be identified with the finale of the sonata cycle, but it can also belong exclusively to the dimension of the form. In either case its function as a recapitulation is unmistakable. Even when it is identified with the finale, there is no doubt that the recapitulatory aspect is, at least initially, its primary function. Again, this is not so in Schumann's Fourth. Although its recapitulatory aspects are undeniable, Schumann's finale functions primarily as a movement in a sonata cycle.

The situation is somewhat different in Schubert's *Wanderer* Fantasy. The initial sequence of large formal units, exposition/development/slow movement, strongly suggests that the exposition and the development belong to an overarching sonata form in which the slow movement is interpolated. Only in the scherzo and the finale does it become clear that the *Wanderer* Fantasy is not a two-dimensional sonata form. Although the recapitulatory aspects of these movements are as undeniable as those in the finale of Schumann's Fourth, they never really breach the dimension of the cycle. At no point do they perform the emphatic recapitulatory gesture that is typical of two-dimensional sonata forms. In both Schumann's Fourth Symphony and Schubert's *Wanderer* Fantasy, there is a super-sonata form, but not a two-dimensional sonata form.

Notes

[1] In his *Brahms and the Principle of Developing Variation*, Frisch refers to Liszt's B-minor Sonata as "a *locus romanticus* of the device of transformation" [Frisch 1984, p. 47].

[2] The question whether three or four movements can be distinguished in Liszt's Sonata will be addressed below.

[3] Various combinations of single-movement and multi-movement designs also occur in several of Liszt's operatic fantasies.

[4] Alternatively, one could interpret m. 321—the arrival on the tonic major—as the beginning of the coda. In that case, the development extends to m. 320.

[5] After 1851, Liszt arranged the *Wanderer* Fantasy a second time, now for two pianos.

[6] Other major early-nineteenth-century compositions that are sometimes mentioned as examples of the combination of elements from sonata form and sonata cycle at the same hierarchical level include Ludwig van Beethoven's *Große Fuge* and even the finale of his Ninth Symphony. A rather more exotic example is the String Quartet in E♭ major by Franz Berwald, a single-movement design with a slow movement, a scherzo, and a return of the slow movement between the development and the recapitulation. Berwald's Quartet was written in 1849, but published only in 1885.

7 Kenneth Hamilton frames his instructive introductory analysis of the B-minor Sonata as a confrontation of three such diverging viewpoints [Hamilton 1996, pp. 31–48].
8 I use the term ambiguity in the narrow sense of "open to two different interpretations," taking the Latin root "ambo" (both, two) literally.
9 By "main theme cadence" I mean the last half or authentic cadence in the main theme or main theme group. For a more detailed discussion of the concept see Vande Moortele 2009.
10 Beginning with an unstable main theme followed by a relatively stable transition, Liszt's B-minor Sonata is somewhat reminiscent of the first movement of Beethoven's Piano Sonata op. 31 no. 2 (the *Tempest*). On the opening of the *Tempest* Sonata see Schmalfeldt 1995 and Vande Moortele 2009.
11 Throughout this study, the symbol "°" signifies "with upbeat."
12 On the concept of *Spielepisode* (sometimes translated into English as "display episode") see Dahlhaus 1987, pp. 137–138.
13 Not an IAC, in spite of the $\hat{4}$-$\hat{3}$ in the first flute, which I consider to be merely covering the more structural $\hat{2}$-$\hat{1}$ in the first violins.
14 In sonata forms with a repeated exposition, the practice of blurring the boundaries between exposition and development is even rarer. One example is the first movement of Schumann's A-minor String Quartet op. 41 no. 1 (composed in 1842, but first published only in 1848). Here, the subordinate theme group ends on an IAC and is followed by a regular closing group (mm. 137–144) and a retransition to the exposition repeat (mm. 145–150). Both the closing group and the retransition, however, are notated in the *prima volta*. Consequently, both are omitted when the exposition is repeated. The *secunda volta* takes up at m. 129, abridges the extension of the subordinate theme, and inflects it to A♭ major, the key in which the development begins. Thus, the exposition repeat is not rounded off by a closing group or even a cadence; instead, its subordinate theme group unnoticeably leads over into the beginning of the development.
15 "Die Überleitung (T. 32–104) ist nicht nur technisch, sondern auch durch den Umfang, den sie erreicht – sie erstreckt sich über nicht weniger als 73 Takte – eine Durchführung. Man erwartet also eine Reprise" [Dahlhaus 1988, p. 205].
16 Dömling divides the exposition in a first theme (97 measures), a second theme (15 measures), an elaboration of the first theme (172 measures), a varied return of the second theme (14 measures), and an epilogue (16 measures). In the recapitulation, the first theme comprises 138 measures, the second theme 16 measures, the elaboration of the first theme 84 measures, the return of the second theme 11 measures, and the epilogue 18 measures. The abridgment of the elaboration of the first theme in the recapitulation, Dömling argues, is compensated for by the far more extensive treatment of the first theme itself. The presence of the elaboration units in the exposition and the recapitulation he explains as a compensation for the substitution of the central development by a slow movement.
17 The enharmonic substitution of b♭ for a♯ was prepared, at a foreground level, as early as mm. 119–124.

CHAPTER 3

LISZT: *TASSO* AND *DIE IDEALE*

Two-dimensional sonata form in the second half of the nineteenth century

There has never been any doubt that the concept of two-dimensional sonata form, as exemplified by Liszt's B-minor Sonata, was adopted by Arnold Schoenberg at the beginning of the twentieth century. One can only be amazed, however, to read Alan Walker's comment that the B-minor Sonata "was to have no successor until Schoenberg did something similar in his First Chamber Symphony more than 50 years later" [Walker, Eckhart & Charnin Mueller 2001, p. 774]. Not only was the First Chamber Symphony Op. 9 anything but Schoenberg's first two-dimensional sonata form, Schoenberg was also not the first to write a two-dimensional sonata form after Liszt's Sonata.

In the margin of his discussion of Liszt's Sonata, William Newman cites a number of works composed in its immediate wake, including the single-movement piano sonatas by Felix Draeseke, Rudolf Viole, and Julius Reubke [Newman 1969, p. 378]. It would be an exaggeration to claim that all of these are mere epigonal responses to Liszt's Sonata. Reubke's 1857 Piano Sonata in B♭ minor, for instance, is an interesting composition in its own right.[1] Nonetheless, none of these works can seriously be said to have influenced the course of music history in any way relevant to the present study.

Another group of works that is sometimes mentioned in this context are the symphonic or tone poems by Liszt and Richard Strauss.[2] These orchestral compositions have never been the subject of the kind of detailed analytical treatment that has been applied to Liszt's Sonata. In this and the next chapter, I aim to make clear how two-dimensional sonata form is employed in the genre of the symphonic poem, and how this genre has contributed to the transfer of that pattern of formal organization from the mid-nineteenth to the early twentieth century.

It is important to note that in this and in subsequent chapters I treat symphonic poems as if they were absolute music: their programmatic aspects are largely left aside. Strictly speaking, such an approach is quite unacceptable. It fails to do justice to the generic singularity of the symphonic poem, at the core of which stands the sophisticated interaction between a musical text and a programmatic paratext, both of which are an integral part of the symphonic poem as a work of art. In the present context, however, a one-sided emphasis on form might be forgiven, since my focus is not on symphonic poems as such, but on what they have in common with a number of compositions that unequivocally belong to absolute music.

Form in Liszt's symphonic poems

The genesis of the twelve symphonic poems Liszt wrote during his tenure as *Hofkapellmeister* in Weimar (from 1848 to 1861) is a complicated matter.[3] Most of them underwent numerous and sometimes extensive revisions prior to their first publication, and *Tasso*, *Les Préludes*, *Orpheus*, *Prometheus*, *Festklänge*, and *Hamlet* were initially conceived and used as overtures rather than as symphonic poems.[4] Only in February 1854, when eight of the symphonic poems had already been composed, did Liszt actually start to use the novel term "poème symphonique" [Altenburg 1998, col. 154].[5] Because of this complicated genesis, it is difficult to determine whether two-dimensional sonata form first emerged in the B-minor Sonata or in one of Liszt's symphonic poems. Although *Tasso*, one of the symphonic poems that I will discuss in detail, was begun well before the Sonata, it acquired its definitive shape only after the latter's completion.

The symphonic poem emerged as a genre in the early 1850s, at the beginning of what Carl Dahlhaus famously described as the "dry period of the symphony" ("die tote Zeit der Symphonie"). In the years between the completion of Schumann's Third (1850) and the premiere of Bruckner's First (1868), Dahlhaus argues, no new first-rate symphony saw the light in German-speaking Europe [Dahlhaus 1980, p. 65; English translation p. 78]. This thesis—and the concomitant thesis of a sudden revival of the symphony in the so-called "second era of the symphony" ("das zweite Zeitalter der Symphonie")—has been the subject of much discussion. Dahlhaus has been criticized mainly for judging the nineteenth-century situation from the standpoint of twentieth-century reception history. Siegfried Kross has argued that compositions which for Dahlhaus belong to the "second era of the symphony" are the same symphonies that are part of the regular concert repertoire in the second half of the twentieth century [Kross 1990]. Walter Frisch, by contrast, has rehabilitated the core of Dahlhaus's argument, pointing out that "a post-Schumann doldrum or decline in the symphony is not an invention of the twentieth century, but was acknowledged repeatedly by critics of the 1850–75 period" [Frisch 2003, p. 11]. Moreover, research by Frank Kirby into the quantitative aspect of symphonic production in the nineteenth century indicates that in the decade from 1850 to 1859 the number of new symphonies published was the lowest in the century, rising again from the next decade onwards [Kirby 1995, p. 197]. Even Richard Taruskin in his recent *Oxford History of Western Music* echoes Dahlhaus's argument, describing the years between 1850 and 1870 as "the dry decades" of the symphony and commenting that "not a single symphony composed in the 1850s and 1860 has survived in the repertoire" [Taruskin 2005, p. 675].

It surely is no coincidence that the genre of the symphonic poem came into being at a time when the genre of the symphony entered the deepest crisis of its history. And it is hardly coincidental that the new genre was created by one of the composers from the circle of those who signaled the crisis of the symphony most explicitly in their writings. To many, the symphonic poem must have appeared as a way out of the impasse in which the symphony then found itself. Although the appearance that it would actually replace the symphony was only temporary—lasting until the late 1860s or early 1870s at most—the symphonic poem did manage to win itself a place as one of the main public genres in the genre hierarchy of the late nineteenth century, and retained that place into the first decade of the twentieth century.

In 1862, shortly after the completion of the twelve Weimar symphonic poems, Liszt claimed to have "solved the greater part of the symphonic problem set to [him] in Germany."[6] This suggests that Liszt intended the symphonic poem—as the term itself indicates—to be a serious and worthy alternative to the symphony. Clear and tangible though the roots of the symphonic poem in the overture may be, the new generic designation nonetheless indicates a qualitative leap, an ennoblement of the previous genre.

This ennoblement entailed considerable formal implications. Although Liszt's symphonic poems clearly inherited the sonata-form framework (without exposition repeat) from the overture as a basic generic convention, at least a number of them tend towards a degree of formal complexity greater than that of the single-movement overture. Some of the symphonic poems displayed this formal complexity right from their inception, and may thus have prompted Liszt to change their generic designation from overture to symphonic poem. Others acquired a comparable degree of formal complexity only during the revision process, possibly because Liszt wanted them to correspond formally to the aesthetic level of the new genre. It is this tendency towards increased formal complexity that allowed the symphonic poem to play a part in the transfer of two-dimensional sonata form from the mid-nineteenth to the early twentieth century.

The formal organization of Liszt's symphonic poems has long been misrepresented. For over a century, their formal complexity has been interpreted as formlessness—or, less negatively, as a liberation from rigid formal patterns—because their form was supposedly determined by their program. In the sixth volume of the first edition of the *Oxford History of Music*, for instance, even as ardent a champion of the new music of the later nineteenth century as Edward Dannreuther described Liszt's symphonic poems as "mere sketches arranged in accordance with some poetical plan, extraneous, and more or less alien, to music" [Dannreuther 1905, pp. 149–150]. As late as 1980, Constantin Floros would cast a similar point in more positive terms:

> A further fundamental principle of Liszt's symphonic program music was the demand that the subject of a composition (the "poetic idea") must determine the form. Through the observance of this principle Liszt sought to free his music from the schematism of "classical" form and to open up for it unlimited possibilities of formal design.[7]

Although Floros is discussing the *Faust* Symphony, his comments apply equally well to Liszt's orchestral music in general and are representative of the Liszt image predominant for more than three quarters of the twentieth century. It is quite obvious that the "liberation from schematic form" Floros writes about is the formal aspect of the long-lived view of Liszt as the romantic composer par excellence, as one of the protagonists of the "music of the future" and, consequently, as a revolutionary iconoclast who severed all bonds with the past.

Only in more recent years have a number of authors tried to modify this traditional view. Detlef Altenburg, for instance, has insisted on Liszt's intimate alliance with the classical tradition, demonstrating that it was Liszt's ambition during his Weimar period to carry on the legacy of both the Viennese and the Weimar *Klassik*. As Altenburg correctly notes, the symphonic poems play a crucial role in this project [Altenburg 1994]. In an article appropriately subtitled "The Revolutionary Reconsidered," Richard Kaplan has demonstrated how the formal organization of a number of Liszt's symphonic poems depends heavily on the conventions of sonata form. Kaplan discusses *Tasso*, *Les préludes*, *Orpheus*, and *Prometheus* as sonata forms, while noting that *Die Ideale*, just like the B-minor Sonata, "combine[s] the sonata scheme with a continuous three- or four-movement design" [Kaplan 1984, p. 145].[8] Michael Saffle, in his overview of Liszt's orchestral music in *The Liszt Companion*, likewise emphasizes the importance of the sonata-form tradition for Liszt's symphonic poems [Saffle 2002, p. 242].

In nine of Liszt's twelve Weimar symphonic poems, sonata form is a fundamental layer of formal organization, though sometimes in combination with another form. Five of these symphonic poems (*Prometheus*, *Mazeppa*, *Festklänge*, *Hungaria*, and *Hamlet*) are one-dimensional sonata forms. Four others (*Ce qu'on entend sur la montagne*, *Tasso*, *Les préludes*, and *Die Ideale*) are two-dimensional forms, combining sonata form with an equally important concurrent pattern of formal organization. Whether *Ce qu'on entend sur la montagne* combines its relatively obvious overarching sonata form with an "allegro first movement, the slow movement, and the finale" ("Allegrosatz, langsame[r] Satz und Finale"), as Dahlhaus discerned, remains open to debate [Dahlhaus 1976, p. 99]. *Tasso*, *Les préludes*, and *Die Ideale*, however, are clear two-dimensional sonata forms, combining sections of a sonata form with movements of a sonata cycle at the same hierarchical level. In these works, the kinship of the symphonic poem to the symphony—and its distance from the overture—becomes most apparent in terms of formal organization. It is to the form of two of them, *Tasso* and *Die Ideale*, that we now turn.

Tasso: Lamento e trionfo (1847–54)[9]

Liszt's second symphonic poem *Tasso* originated as an overture. Accordingly, several aspects of its form resolutely point in the direction of a sonata form without exposition repeat. A slow introduction (mm. 1–26) is followed by what appears to be a sonata-form exposition complete with thematic contrast and a tonal trajectory leading in descending major thirds from C minor to A♭ major and E major. At least part of the thematic material from this exposition is recapitulated from m. 348 onwards, and themes that appeared off-tonic in the exposition return in the tonic major in the recapitulation.

At the same time, much of what happens in the form sits uneasily with even the most flexible conception of sonata form. First, the *Allegro strepitoso* unit that initially appears to function as a main theme (mm. 27–53) turns out not to behave as a main theme from a tonal-harmonic point of view and is followed by a return of introductory material in the original tempo (mm. 54–61). Second, the seeming group of contrasting themes (mm. 62–144) begins in the tonic and is in a different tempo from the main theme. Third, *Tasso* lacks a development section, its exposition being separated from the recapitulation by an extensive section marked *Quasi menuetto*. Fourth and finally, a considerable part of the thematic material presented in the exposition is omitted from the recapitulation, where it is often replaced by post-expositional material.

Several authors have tried to come to terms with this extraordinary formal plan. Kenneth Hamilton considers mm. 1–61 to be a multi-tempo introduction that partly returns at the beginning of the recapitulation. In his opinion, mm. 62–101 function as the main theme and are recapitulated in a transformed shape from m. 397 onwards. "Liszt's stroke of genius," he comments, "is to have a slow minor-key exposition subject (the *Lamento*) recapitulated in a fast major-key variation (the

Trionfo)" [Hamilton 1996, p. 24]. The so-called transformation of what Hamilton hears as the main theme is, however, no such thing at all. To be sure, there is a motivic connection between the theme in mm. 397ff and the one in mm. 62ff. Both themes contain the same basic motive, as the boxes in examples 5a and 5c indicate. In its entirety, however, the theme in mm. 397ff is a transformation of the theme that opens the *Quasi menuetto* section (compare examples 5b and 5c). The alleged main theme returns only considerably later, initially in a modulating context (mm. 475ff); only in mm. 534ff does it return in a firm tonic setting.

Example 5: Liszt, *Tasso*: (a) mm. 62–67; (b) mm. °166 –173; (c) mm. 397–400

While Hamilton's reading focuses only on the exposition and the recapitulation, James Hepokoski has suggested a way of coming to terms with the lack of a traditional development section. For Hepokoski, *Tasso* is a standard example of a sonata deformation with episodes in the developmental space.[10] More precisely, he distinguishes two episodes and, although he does not specify them, we may assume that he has the E-major passage in mm. 131–144 and the *Quasi menuetto* in mm. 165–347 in mind.

Whereas an interpretation of the *Quasi menuetto* as an episode is convincing, this is less so for the E-major passage in mm. 131–144. As one of the basic characteristics of episodes within a development is that they contrast with the context in which they occur, a slow episode in a sonata form that is itself already partly slow is unlikely. Admittedly, the basic tempo indication of the E-major passage (*Meno Adagio*) is slightly faster than that of the preceding units, but not sufficiently so to effect a genuine contrast. Another reason why mm. 131–144 make for an improbable episode is that they play an indispensable role in the exposition, where they complete the large-scale tonal progression from C minor to E major. This tonal progression is not unusual in Liszt's sonata-style music: in several of his works, the exposition ends in the key a major third above the tonic, "even," Kaplan remarks, "in the minor-mode pieces" [Kaplan 1984, p. 150].[11]

Hepokoski's idea is not entirely to be dismissed, but it does not go far enough. In my view, *Tasso* does not simply include two episodes in the developmental space, but rather comprises a complete multi-movement cycle that is spread out over the entire single-movement form. In the following paragraphs, I will analyze *Tasso* as a two-dimensional sonata form, first reinvestigating its overarching sonata form, then showing how many of the seeming eccentricities of that form can be explained by the simultaneous presence of a sonata cycle.

One wonders why previous analysts have been so fascinated by the question of where the introduction ends and where the exposition begins. It seems impossible not to consider the *Allegro strepitoso* in mm. 27ff as part of the exposition. Not only is a fast (and furious) unit following a slow opening a generically strong signal for the onset of a sonata-form exposition, it also is the only portion from the initial stages of the composition to return unaltered near the place where, given the form's overall proportions, the recapitulation may be expected to begin. Put the other way round, an interpretation of mm. 27–53 as part of a multi-tempo introduction fails to account for both their strong sense of "beginning" and their return in mm. 348–374. As for their lack of harmonic stability, this need not preclude a function as part of the exposition or even, as I will argue below, as part of its main theme group.[12]

Far more problematic is that the first tonic chord in the exposition enters only in m. 62, the very moment one might initially take to be the beginning of the subordinate theme group. The entire passage in mm. 62–90 is firmly rooted in the tonic, and even if one is willing to accept a more relaxed handling of key relationships in mid-nineteenth-century sonata-form expositions, it is unlikely that a theme will function as a subordinate theme when it is presented in the very key traditionally reserved for the main theme.[13] This, then, emerges as the first serious problem posed by the formal organization of *Tasso*: not that the *Allegro strepitoso* defies an interpretation as part of the main theme group, but rather that mm. 62–90 are difficult to understand as a subordinate theme.

In the context of Liszt's Weimar period, this situation is less exceptional then it initially seems. Main themes and main theme groups that begin off-tonic are not at all uncommon in this group of works. In the previous chapter, we saw how the main theme in the exposition of the B-minor Sonata fails to express the tonic key in an unambiguous way, the first tonic chord in root position entering only at the beginning of the transition. A similar situation—slow introduction, unstable off-tonic main theme, initially stable but eventually modulating transition—occurs in the symphonic poem *Hamlet*. In m. 74 of *Hamlet*, the initial slow tempo changes to an *Allegro appassionato ed agitato assai*, thus suggesting the beginning of an exposition. Yet only in m. 105 are both a tonic chord in B minor and a first thematic presentation of main-theme material attained. Harmonically, mm. 74–104 function as a long dominant preparation of m. 105, and from a thematic-motivic point of view too their character is preparatory rather than expository. Yet in spite of its stability, m. 105 marks the beginning of a modulating formal unit that will eventually turn out to function as a transition.[14]

Against this background, it becomes conceivable that *Tasso* condenses the contrast between an unstable main theme and an initially stable transition within one large and internally contrasting main theme group. In this reading, mm. 27–90 comprise not one, but two main themes. The first main theme (mm. 27–53) is fast, unstable, off-tonic, and has a sentential design (3+3+21; the consequent, obviously, is tremendously expanded). The second main theme (mm. 62–75) is slow, stable, and in the tonic and takes the form of a period. Its repetition in mm. 76–90 leads to a PAC that functions as a main theme cadence. Even though it does not yet explain the return of the slow introduction in the middle of the main theme group, this interpretation seems intuitively more plausible than one that considers mm. 1–61 as a multi-tempo introduction that is followed by a slow main theme. I will come back to the significance of the extraordinary layout of the main theme group below.[15]

The part of the exposition that comes after the main theme cadence is less problematic. Mm. °91–130 function as an internally modulating subordinate theme that resembles a period with dissolving consequent. Mm. °91–99 constitute an antecedent that duly leads to a (reinterpreted) HC. The consequent that seems to begin after a two-measure lead-in in m. °102 is, however, never rounded off. Instead, it modulates and leads to a VII°7 dominant in E major. The E-major passage in mm. 131–144, which is a thematic transformation of the first main theme, is not an episode that marks the beginning of developmental space, but a second subordinate theme that ends with a PAC in E major and thus concludes the exposition.[16] It returns in an analogous position at the end of the recapitulation (mm. 533–557), now in the tonic.

After the *Quasi menuetto* development substitute comes a patently obvious recapitulation in m. 348. This recapitulation is, however, restricted to the first main theme. In contrast to what happens in the exposition, the partial return of the slow introduction is followed here by an *Allegro con molto brio* section that is, as mentioned before, largely based on a transformation of the *Quasi menuetto* theme. Only at the beginning of the second subordinate theme (m. 533) is the parallel to the exposition re-established. Finally, the *Stretto* in m. 558 marks the beginning of the coda.

Many of the eccentricities of the overarching sonata form in *Tasso* are essential to make the two-dimensional sonata form work in the first place. Several units of the overarching sonata form have been modified to fulfill a simultaneous function as a movement of the sonata cycle. In the sonata cycle, mm. 62–144 function as a slow movement, mm. 165–348 as a minuet, and mm. 397–584 as a finale. Each of these movements is identified with units of the overarching sonata form.

The slow movement is identified with the second main theme and both subordinate themes. This partly explains the main theme group's layout: the slow subsegment of the main theme group in the overarching sonata form marks the beginning of the slow movement in the dimension of the cycle. As a consequence of its identification with part of the exposition of the overarching sonata form, the slow movement conforms to the latter's tonal plan and thus remains tonally open-ended (c – A♭ – E). It is nonetheless interesting to note that in terms of thematic units, the slow movement is organized as a ternary form, with the second main theme as an first section, the modulating first subordinate theme as a middle section, and the second subordinate theme (a transposed transformation of the second main theme) as a recapitulation.

In the minuet, the nature of the relationship between both dimensions is less self-evident. Given its size and the contrast with its environment in terms of key, meter, tempo and—because of the transformation—thematic content, the scherzo might appear to be a self-contained movement, an interpolation between the exposition and the recapitulation that occupies the entire developmental space without being more than a placeholder for the development. Although such an interpretation is not impossible, I prefer to conceive of the relationship between the minuet and development as an identification, because the former barely exhibits an autonomous formal organization. Its formal openness, in other words, may be interpreted as a requirement of the development with which it is identified.

The finale is identified with the later segments of the recapitulation and the coda. Like the scherzo, it has a very strong autonomous profile. It is clearly separated from the recapitulation of the first main theme and contrasts with it in tempo, meter, key, and character. Interpreting the finale as an interpolation is not an option, however, not only because it lacks a form of its own, but also because it occupies the place of the subordinate theme group and the coda of the overarching sonata form. Without the units that function as a finale in the dimension of the sonata cycle, the overarching sonata form would be incomplete.

Also the multiple returns of the slow introduction can be explained from the perspective of two-dimensional sonata form. In order to further emphasize their function as movements in a sonata cycle—and not merely as formal units in a sonata form that happen to look like movements of a sonata cycle—each of the

CHAPTER 3

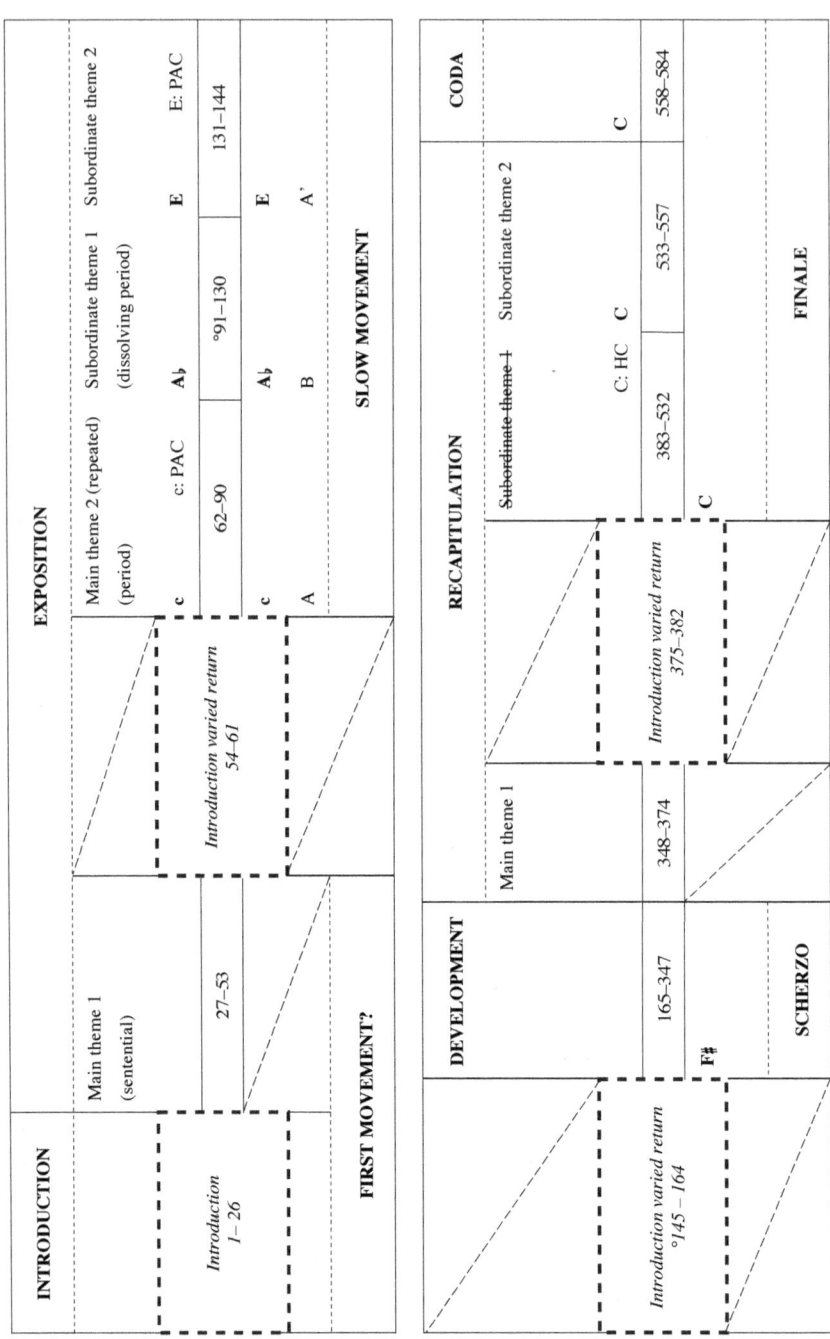

Figure 9: Liszt, *Tasso*: form and cycle

three movements is preceded by a varied return of material from the overarching sonata form's slow introduction: in mm. 54–61 before the slow movement (and, from the perspective of the overarching sonata form, in the middle of the main theme group), in mm. °145–164 before the scherzo, and in mm. 375–382 before the finale. To interpret mm. 54–61 as the first form-articulating return of the slow introduction seems more plausible than hearing it as the third part of a ternary multi-tempo introduction. Figure 9 gives an overview of the formal organization of *Tasso*.

As becomes clear from figure 9, I interpret the varied returns of the slow introduction as belonging neither to the form nor to the cycle, but as standing "between" both dimensions. The figure also shows that the projection of the dimensions onto each other is very different here than it was in the B-minor Sonata. The slow movement comes very early, being identified with the larger portion of the exposition, and the finale enters relatively late, well after the beginning of the recapitulation.

The most important difference between *Tasso* and the B-minor Sonata is that the former lacks a local sonata form. Nothing in the portion of the overarching sonata form that precedes the first interior movement indicates a simultaneous function as a first movement in the sonata cycle. This does not necessarily mean that the sonata cycle is incomplete. There are two ways of looking at the situation. One is to invoke an inversion of the principle of cyclic completion: the sequence of slow movement, minuet, and finale strongly suggest the presence of a complete sonata cycle, to such an extent that what precedes the first of these movements will be retrospectively reinterpreted as part of the cycle as well. Formulated in terms of the projection model from Chapter 1, the projection of the first movement of the sonata cycle onto the beginning of the overarching sonata form is so weak that it leaves no trace whatsoever of that movement. Alternatively, one could argue that in *Tasso*, the local sonata form coincides with the overarching sonata form, so that the entire overarching sonata form simultaneously functions as the first movement of the sonata cycle. This reading can be modeled not so much as the projection of a single-movement form and a multi-movement cycle onto each other, but rather as a first movement in the dimension of the cycle that has absorbed the three subsequent movements.

By not identifying the first movement of the sonata cycle with one or several units of the overarching sonata form, *Tasso* avoids one of the points in a two-dimensional sonata form at which the tension between both dimensions becomes most noticeable. At the same time, the avoidance of this tension implies that this solution is—at least from the analyst's point of view—a less interesting option than identification. Almost by way of compensation, the number of units in

Chapter 3

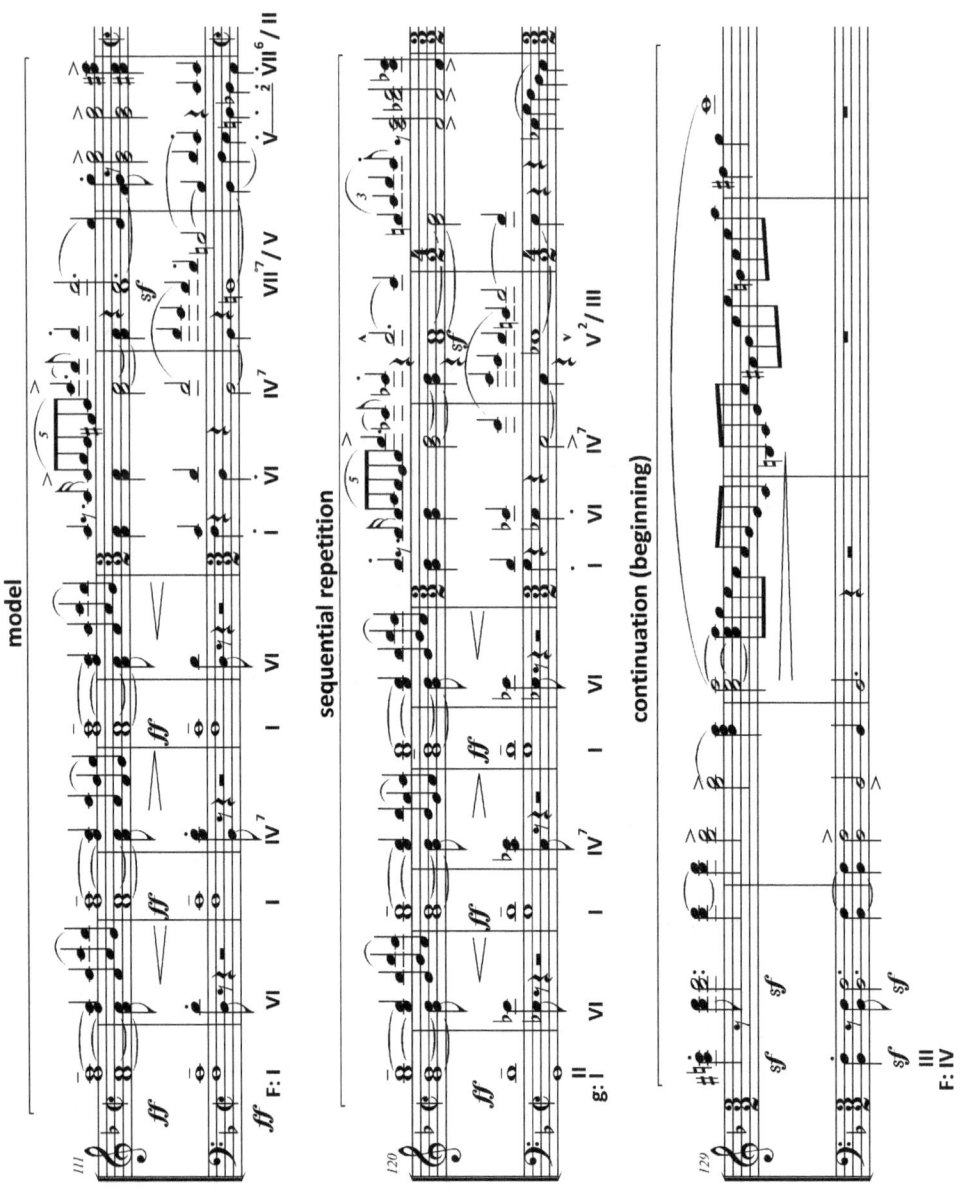

Example 6: Liszt, *Die Ideale*: main theme (presentation and beginning of continuation) (mm. 111–133)

the dimension of the form that do not coincide with a movement from the cycle is reduced to a minimum. The first interior movement begins remarkably early, with the tonic subsegment of the main theme group. A problem *Tasso* does not avoid is that of identifying the finale of the sonata cycle with the recapitulation and coda of the overarching sonata form. By identifying the finale only with the later units of the recapitulation and coda, the recapitulation and the finale are partly dissociated.

Die Ideale (1856–57)

Most analysts of *Die Ideale* agree that it incorporates a multi-movement design in a single-movement form. The latter can be described as a quite straightforward, albeit hugely proportioned sonata form up to m. 452.[17] The main theme group (mm. °26–156) is preceded by a slow introduction and begins with a long preparatory unit. The main theme proper enters only in m. 111 and stretches until the F-major main theme cadence in m. 158 that is elided with the beginning of the transition. Formally, the main theme is a sentence: as example 6 shows, the (enormous) model and its sequential repetition in mm. 111–119 and 120–128 respectively are followed by a continuation in mm. 129–157.

The transition (mm. 158–196) begins with a varied repetition of the main theme, which starts to modulate after its presentation phrase (from m. 178 onwards). It heads for D major, the key in which the subordinate theme group begins. The latter comprises two different themes. The first subordinate theme (thematic complex might be a more accurate term) is stated three times, thereby tonicizing three different regions: D major (mm. °197–221), B major (mm. °222–246), and E♭ major (mm. °247–263). Each statement comprises three parts: a four-measure phrase that is repeated twice down an octave (first presented in mm. °197–209), a sonic field on the tonic, under which the head of the main theme's basic idea is heard (mm. 210–216), and the return of thematic material from the slow introduction (mm. °217–221). The second statement is an exact and complete transposition of the first, while the third only lacks the theme's third part. The second subordinate theme (mm. 263–318) begins in E♭ major but immediately modulates to C major, the key in which the exposition ends.

Throughout the subordinate theme group, cadential confirmation of any of its key centers is conspicuously avoided. In the first subordinate theme group and both of its repetitions, there is not even a suggestion of a cadence, and a dominant pedal lies under the statements in D major and B major. Only the third statement, in E♭ major, appears over a tonic pedal. The second subordinate theme, by contrast, does seem to be heading for a cadence, but this is never achieved, so that the long dominant that enters in m. 313 never resolves.

Nonetheless, Christian Martin Schmidt has convincingly argued that m. 319 is clearly singled out as the beginning of the development [Schmidt 1990, p. 534]. It superimposes characteristics of the main theme's basic idea (the third f/a in the upper parts), its repetition (the g in the bass—carried over from the end of the exposition), and the first subordinate theme (the pedal point underlying the entire formal unit in mm. 319–340). This opening pre-core segment of the development is followed by two cores. The first of these (mm. 341–380) begins by establishing a model (mm. 341–345), which is repeated (mm. 345–353) and then subjected to fragmentation and recombination (mm. 353–365). The model itself has its origins in the upbeat to the main theme (compare m. °110) and the preparatory phase of the main theme group (compare m. °45).

The next core uses the opening of the main theme as a model (B major) that is immediately repeated sequentially in E♭ major (mm. 381–393 and 394–406). The unit that follows (mm. 407–452) begins as another sequential repetition of the model (now in E major), but evolves into an almost complete restatement of the main theme that begins to deviate from the exposition only in m. 447. This unit marks a major turning point in the form: in the overarching sonata form, it is a false recapitulation, but in the local sonata form, it functions as the actual recapitulation. M. 407 is, in other words, the point of dimensional disconnection. Mm. 1–406 were only latently double-functional: the introduction, the exposition, the pre-core, and the first two cores of the development in the overarching sonata form fulfill the same function in the local sonata form. In m. 407, however, the double-functionality becomes apparent, the subsequent measures fulfilling a different function in both dimensions (see figure 10).

mm.	overarching sonata form	local sonata form
1–25	slow introduction	
°26–318	exposition	
319–340	development: pre-core	
341–380	development: first core	
381–406	development: second core ⇓	development: second core
407–452	false recapitulation	**RECAPITULATION**

Figure 10: Liszt, *Die Ideale*: identification of the local sonata form with the initial units of the overarching sonata form

Once dimensions have been disconnected, each of them has to make concessions. In the dimension of the form, one has to accept the presence of a lengthy false recapitulation in the middle of the development. In the dimension of the cycle, a completely satisfactory recapitulation becomes impossible. Had the recapitulation in mm. 407–452 been in the tonic and included all or most of the material presented in the exposition, it would have deprived the overarching sonata form of every reason to continue. This explains why the recapitulation of the local sonata form is in E major instead of F major, and why it is restricted to the main theme proper, lacking the preparatory phase of the main theme group, the transition, and the entire subordinate theme group.

In m. 453, the recapitulation of the local sonata form is interrupted by an abridged return of the slow introduction. This signals the end of the first movement in the dimension of the cycle. In m. 474, an interpolated slow movement in C♯ minor begins. As figure 11 shows, it has a full-fledged and tonally closed ternary form: mm. 474–485 constitute an introduction, mm. 486–501 a first section (A), mm. 502–541 a more heterogeneous middle section (B), and mm. 542–557 a varied recapitulation of the first section (A') that is followed by a transition to the next formal unit.

Introduction (mm. 474–485)	
A (mm. 486–501)	c♯
B (mm. 502–541)	g♯ – E
A' (mm. 542–557)	c♯
Transition (mm. 558–567)	

Figure 11: Liszt, *Die Ideale*: formal plan of the interpolated slow movement

Like the interpolated slow movement in the B-minor Sonata, this movement is characterized by the interplay between contrast and integration. In conjunction with the return of the slow introduction, the change in tempo, meter ($^6_8$), and key clearly delineates it from the overarching sonata form, to which the movement is simultaneously related thematically. As example 7 illustrates, thematic material from the overarching sonata form reappears in each of the slow movement's sections. The introduction uses the first thematic idea from the subordinate theme group, which also returns in section B (examples 7a and c). Sections A and A' present a melody that begins as a transformation of the beginning of the main theme (example 7b).

Example 7: Liszt, *Die Ideale*: transformations of the main and subordinate-theme material in the slow movement: a) opening of the introduction (mm. 474–476); b) beginning of section A (mm. 486–489); c) last segment of section B (mm. 525–527)

Mm. 558–567 function as a transition to the next large formal unit (mm. 568–657), which unmistakably bears the rhythmic and gestural characteristics of a scherzo. Rather than, like the slow movement, being interpolated in the overarching sonata form, this movement is identified with part of the development, in which it occupies the position of a third core. The scherzo is neither formally nor tonally closed, but merely lends its character to one of the segments of the development. Its basic motive, moreover, originates in the exposition's main theme, as shown in example 8.

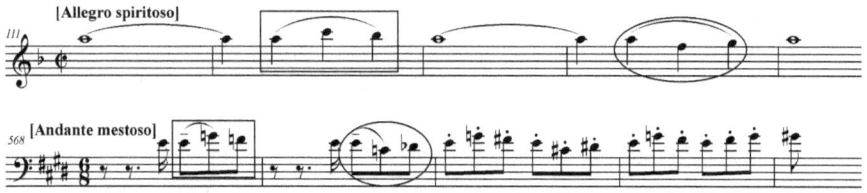

Example 8: Liszt, *Die Ideale*: mm. 111–115 and 568–574 (motivic connection main theme – scherzo)

In mm. 658–679, the last twenty-two measures from the preparatory unit of the main theme group return, followed in mm. 680–709 by the main theme itself in the original key and in a grandiose transformation. In contrast to the exposition, it seems more appropriate here not to include the preparatory unit in the main theme group, but to see it as the last segment (the standing on the dominant) of the development. Also in contrast to the exposition, the (altered) continuation of the main theme in the recapitulation simultaneously functions as the transition. It is immediately followed by a transformation of the first subordinate theme (mm. 710–739) and, after a short transition (mm. 740–748), a transformation of the second subordinate theme (mm. 749–808). All three statements of the first subordinate theme reappear untransposed, thus postponing eventual tonal resolution to the recapitulation of the second subordinate theme, which duly appears in the tonic. Mm. 809–872, a stretto on the head of the main theme that leads to a somewhat underarticulated cadence in m. 859, function as a coda.

The technique of thematic transformation is an essential tool for the realization of the two-dimensional sonata form in *Die Ideale*. Transformed versions of the overarching sonata form's main theme (and, at the same time, of the sonata cycle's first movement) reappear as the main thematic material in both the slow movement and the scherzo, mediating between the single-movement and multi-movement plans. The transformations of the main theme and each of the subordinate themes in the recapitulation have a different function: they serve to individuate the latter from the exposition. The individual character of the finale increases as the section proceeds. The recapitulation of the main theme differs from its exposition only in tempo and character. More specifically, it is a monumentalized version of the original main theme, not only because of the slower tempo, but also because of the omission of the turn figure from m. 117 in m. 686. Since there is no additional rhythmic modification, however, its dependence on the original theme is obvious. Both subordinate themes are recapitulated in more radically transformed shapes, as demonstrated by example 9. In either case, the transformation involves a much faster rhythm and an irregular rhythmic diminution. Nonetheless, each theme retains its original pitch constellation, the first subordinate theme even reappearing untransposed and with the original modulation pattern.

Given the presence of a first movement, a slow movement, and a scherzo before the beginning of the recapitulation, the modifications to the recapitulation can also be understood to articulate a finale in the dimension of the cycle. Even though the monumentalized transformation of the main theme might be taken as a first indication of the recapitulation's simultaneous function as a finale, the emphasis clearly lies on the recapitulatory function, as is hardly unexpected at the beginning of a recapitulation. The finale function comes more to the fore in the

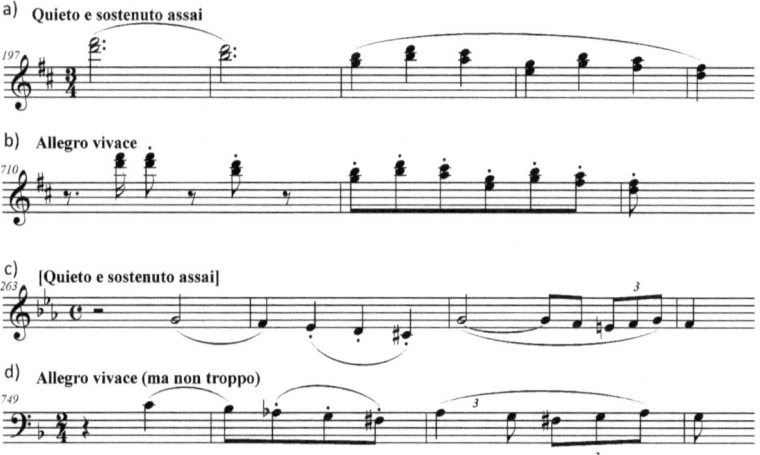

Example 9: Liszt, *Die Ideale*: thematic transformations in the recapitulation:
    (a) first subordinate theme in the exposition (beginning) (mm. 197–201);
    (b) transformed first subordinate theme in the recapitulation (beginning) (mm. 710–712);
    (c) second subordinate theme in the exposition (beginning) (mm. 263–266);
    (d) transformed second subordinate theme in the recapitulation (beginning) (mm. 749–752)

more radical transformations of both subordinate themes. Nonetheless, the finale remains relatively weakly profiled. The recapitulatory aspect always predominates, particularly because the identification with the finale does not influence the formal organization of the recapitulation. A formal overview of the entire composition is given in figure 12.

The two-dimensional sonata form of *Die Ideale* is very similar to that of the B-minor Sonata. In either case, the first movement is identified with the initial units of the overarching sonata form, the slow movement is interpolated in the development, and the finale is identified with the recapitulation and the coda. In both works, the finale is only moderately profiled: it fails to establish a potentially autonomous form of its own, thus drawing heavily on the principle of cyclic completion. There are also important differences between the formal organization of both works. Not only is the scherzo in *Die Ideale* identified with part of the development rather than with the beginning of the recapitulation, also the relationship between the first

FIRST MOVEMENT

INTRODUCTION	EXPOSITION				DEVELOPMENT (beginning)			
	Main theme group	Transition	Subordinate theme 1	Subordinate theme 2	Pre-core	Core 1	Core 2 ⇒	False recapitulation
	F: PAC		D – B – E♭	E♭ → C C: PAC				
1–25	26–157	158–196	197–262	263–318	319–340	341–380	381–406	407–452
F	F							E RECAPITULATION
INTRODUCTION	EXPOSITION				DEVELOPMENT			

FINALE

	DEVELOPMENT (continued)		RECAPITULATION				CODA
	Core 3	Retransition	Main theme – Transition (fusion)	Subordinate theme 1	Transition	Subordinate theme 2	
		F: V	F	D – B – E♭ (!)		F (no cadence)	F PAC
474–567	568–657	658–679	680–709	710–739	740–748	749–808	809–872
	(c♯?)		F				
SLOW MOVEMENT	SCHERZO		FINALE				

Return of introduction 453–473
c♯

Figure 12 : Liszt, *Die Ideale*: form and cycle

movement of the sonata cycle and the initial units of the overarching sonata form is very different in both compositions. In the B-minor Sonata, this identification fully exploits the potential analogies between sections of a sonata form and segments of a sonata-form exposition, identifying the development and the recapitulation of the local sonata form with the transition and the subordinate theme group of the overarching sonata form respectively. In *Die Ideale*, the first movement of the sonata cycle is identified not only with the exposition of the local sonata form, but also with the first segments of its development. This allows for a recapitulation in the local sonata form that is—at least thematically—far more explicit. This strategy seems to have been especially attractive to later composers. As we will see, similar strategies were deployed by both Strauss and Schoenberg.

Notes

[1] For a comparison of Liszt's and Reubke's sonatas see Keym 1998.
[2] In order to avoid repeating the cumbersome formulation "symphonic poems or tone poems" all the time, I will use "symphonic poem" as a general term, using "tone poem" only when referring specifically to Strauss.
[3] A thirteenth symphonic poem, *Von der Wiege bis zum Grabe,* was written in 1881, twenty years after Liszt's Weimar period. It is not in one, but in three movements, thus constituting an interesting generic hybrid.
[4] See, for instance, on the genesis of *Tasso*, Torkewitz 1995. A concise and up-to-date overview of Liszt's symphonic poems, their versions, and their chronology can be found in the work list of the *New Grove* article on Liszt [Walker, Eckhardt & Charnin Mueller 2001, pp. 832–835].
[5] As early as in 1849 Liszt had used the term to refer to Wagner's *Tannhäuser* overture [see Grey 1988, p. 4].
[6] Letter from Liszt to Franz Brendel, 8–11–1862 [La Mara 1894, p. 33].
[7] "Ein weiteres fundamentales Prinzip der symphonischen Programmusik Liszts war die Forderung, daß das Sujet einer Komposition (die 'poetische Idee') die Form bestimmen müsse. Durch die Befolgung dieses Grundsatzes suchte Liszt seine Musik von dem Schematismus der 'klassischen' Form zu befreien und ihr unbegrenzte Möglichkeiten formaler Gestaltung zu erschließen" [Floros 1980, p. 50, English translation Kaplan 1984, p. 143].
[8] Although Kaplan's general claim about the significance of sonata form in Liszt's symphonic poems is entirely justified, his actual analyses offer much cause for disagreement. The only symphonic poem he rightly qualifies as a (one-dimensional) sonata form is *Prometheus*. In my view, *Orpheus* is not a sonata form, but a symmetrical arch form, while both *Tasso* and *Les préludes* are two-dimensional rather than one-dimensional sonata forms.

9. Significant portions of this section rework (and, to some extent, reconsider) materials that were previously published in Vande Moortele 2008.
10. See, for instance, Hepokoski 1992a, p. 146.
11. Examples from the symphonic music include, for pieces starting in the major mode, *Les préludes* (C major to E major) and, for pieces starting in the minor mode, the first movement of the *Faust* Symphony (C minor to E major) as well as *Prometheus* (A minor to D♭ major). Likely precedents are, of course, the first movement of Beethoven's *Waldstein* Sonata Op. 53 and, in symphonic music, the third *Leonore* overture Op. 72b (both C major to E major).
12. Another reason not to include mm. 27–53 in the exposition is perhaps the superficial analogy between *Tasso* and the first movement of the *Faust* Symphony. Not only does the latter contain the same expositional tonal progression from C minor to E major, it also begins with a similar apparently multi-tempo introduction. An important difference, however, is that the fast unit in the introduction to the *Faust* movement (mm. 23–65)—which one might also consider to be what Caplin has called a "thematic introduction," belonging to the main theme group rather than to the actual slow introduction [Caplin 1998, p. 15]—is, after a short interruption (mm. 66–70), followed by another fast unit (mm. 71ff). Although not the firmest tonic confirmation imaginable either, this unit behaves as a main theme in every respect. In contrast to *Tasso*, moreover, the introductory fast unit in the *Faust* movement does not return before or at the beginning of the recapitulation. Admittedly, the slow segment of the introduction returns later in the *Faust* movement (mm. 359–381), but there it precedes an interpolated slow episode (mm. 382–420), the recapitulation following only in m. 421.
13. The existence of precedents for a sonata-form exposition with a tonic subordinate theme in early Chopin (e.g., the C-minor Piano Sonata Op. 4 and the G-minor Piano Trio Op. 8) hardly seems to make an interpretation along these lines less implausible.
14. For a more detailed discussion of *Hamlet*'s exposition see Vande Moortele 2006a.
15. There is no denying that the general pause after a dominant arrival in m. 61—in the middle of what I call the main theme group—is very much like a medial caesura. In my reading of the exposition, this is only an apparent medial caesura, separating the off-tonic and tonic subsegments of the main theme group. Ultimately, I could also agree with a reading that accepts m. 61 as a real medial caesura, provided that reading concedes that the ensuing tonic subordinate theme assumes some of the functions that are normally fulfilled by a main theme.
16. On a previous occasion, I have referred to this second subordinate theme as a "closing group" [Vande Moortele 2008, p. 53]. I changed my mind because I feel that a defining characteristic of a closing group is that it is in the same key as the subordinate theme that immediately precedes it. A unit that broaches new tonal territory can therefore never be a closing group, even when it expresses a clear rhetoric of closure.
17. The incomplete measure between mm. 25 and 26 is not counted in the measure numbers.

CHAPTER 4

STRAUSS: *DON JUAN* AND *EIN HELDENLEBEN*

Strauss and Liszt

From 1889 to 1894, Richard Strauss served as Kapellmeister in Weimar. In this capacity, he sought to emulate Liszt in many respects. Like his predecessor, Strauss modernized both the Weimar orchestra and its repertoire, and it is hardly coincidental that he attached great importance to the preparation of new productions of Wagner's *Tannhäuser* and *Lohengrin,* two operas Liszt had conducted—and, in the case of *Lohengrin*, even premiered—in Weimar. In addition, Strauss's concert programs throughout his conducting career included an unusually high number of Liszt's works. Between 1902 and 1904, when in Berlin, he even performed all twelve Weimar symphonic poems in numerical order spread over two concert seasons of the *Berliner Tonkünstler-Orchester* [see Birkin 2002, pp. 87–88].

Michael Walter surmises that these decisions were motivated not only by Liszt's success as a Kapellmeister, which was an example worth following, but also by Strauss's ambition to present himself as Liszt's legitimate heir, as an organizer, conductor, and composer [Walter 2000, p. 86]. When, after the completion of the four-movement symphonic phantasy *Aus Italien* in 1886, Strauss started to write single-movement orchestral compositions that he called "tone poems," he may indeed be said to have continued the tradition initiated by Liszt's symphonic poems.

It might come as a surprise, then, that in a letter to one of his uncles from 1888, Strauss apparently described his first tone poem *Macbeth* as some kind of symphonic poem, "but not after Liszt" ("aber nicht nach Liszt").[1] It is quite probable that this is merely an instance of youthful anxiety of influence, not least because Strauss himself explicitly reconsidered his view in a letter to Roland Tenschert from 1944. In this letter, Strauss thanks Tenschert for the copy of the latter's book *Dreimal sieben Variationen über das Thema Richard Strauss* he had recently received, but immediately points out an error: "Page 32 'but not after Liszt' must be a mistake. I don't remember that. If at all, it should read: 'but after Liszt'."[2] The terminological distinction between "symphonic poem" and "tone poem" in Strauss's oeuvre thus seems to be negligible, all the more so since Strauss alternately used both terms in letters, diary entries, and publications throughout his life [Werbeck 1996, p. 317].

Strauss's own ideas about the formal organization of Liszt's symphonic poems are very different from the interpretation developed in the previous chapter. In old age, he wrote:

> New ideas must find new forms—this basic principle of Liszt's symphonic works, in which the poetic idea was effectively also the form-building element, from then on became my guide for my own symphonic poems.[3]

This interpretation corresponds almost exactly to—and may even have influenced—the view of Liszt that has dominated most of the twentieth century as discussed in Chapter 3: that of a revolutionary iconoclast writing symphonic poems whose formal organization was entirely determined by their program. As a result, Strauss's tone poems have acquired a similar reputation, which is only confirmed by the discomfort with sonata form Strauss voiced in a letter to Hans von Bülow written at the time of his earliest tone poems *Macbeth* and *Don Juan*:

> From the F-minor Symphony onwards I have increasingly found myself in a contradiction between the musical-poetic content that I wanted to convey a[nd] the ternary sonata form that has come down to us from the classical composers.[4]

Nonetheless, elements of "ternary sonata form" are evident in most of Strauss's tone poems, just as they are in many of Liszt's symphonic poems. Moreover, in a number of these tone poems, Strauss, like Liszt, combines sonata form with aspects of a multi-movement sonata cycle. Two of these, *Don Juan* and *Ein Heldenleben*, will be analyzed in the next paragraphs. While the formal organization of *Don Juan* is still very close to that of *Tasso* and *Die Ideale*, more idiosyncratic strategies come to the fore in *Ein Heldenleben*.

Don Juan Op. 20 (1888–89)

In his influential essay on *Don Juan*, James Hepokoski offers a critical assessment of the analytical literature on Strauss's second tone poem [Hepokoski 1992a, pp. 142–152]. Most of the interpretations he cites belong to one of two categories: one group of authors understands the form fundamentally as a rondo, whereas others describe it as a sonata form. For his own interpretation, Hepokoski refuses to choose between both approaches, concluding that "the actual musical logic of *Don Juan* is best described as a process by which what initially appears to unfold as a rondo deformation is conceptually recast, toward the end, as a sonata deformation" [1992a, p. 150].

In Hepokoski's reading, the first 424 measures of *Don Juan* suggest a rondo (or rondo deformation) rather than a sonata form. Mm. 1–39, 169–196, and 313–350 function as recurrences of the rondo theme (or, in the case of the so-called *Heldenthema* in mm. 313–350, its substitute), while the B-major passage in mm. 90–160, the section in G minor and major in mm. 197–312, and the passage starting in D major in mm. 351–424 constitute three contrasting episodes; mm. 40–89 are ultimately interpreted as a transition from the rondo theme to the first episode.

According to Hepokoski, the rondo format gradually disintegrates over the course of the piece. While the off-tonic return of the rondo theme in m. 169 and other unusual characteristics that occur relatively early in the piece can still be explained as deformations, he considers the substitution of the rondo theme's third occurrence by the so-called *Heldenthema* in mm. 313–350 to be a first element that is "puzzling within the rondo-deformation context" [1992a p. 150]. After the third episode, Hepokoski claims, Strauss actually "shift genres" (or forms): from m. 457 onwards, he writes, "we hear a dominant intensification into what we may now interpret as the recapitulation of a breakthrough sonata deformation" [1992a p. 151]. The E-major recapitulation and the subsequent apotheosis of the *Heldenthema* confirm that "the rondo principle has been supplanted by that of the sonata," which in turn enables a retrospective reinterpretation of the preceding portions of the piece as having been part of a sonata form (or deformation) all along.

Hepokoski's virtuosic interpretation of *Don Juan* as a "rondo⇒sonata" form (or deformation) has much to commend it, but it remains ultimately unconvincing. The binary opposition between sonata and rondo form that lies at the basis of Hepokoski's reading sits uncomfortably with the much more continuum-like relationship between both formal types characteristic of his and Warren Darcy's Sonata Theory. Moreover, Hepokoski analyzes the beginning of *Don Juan* not as a rondo, but as a sonata rondo. Whereas the former implies a simple alternation of rondo-theme recurrences and contrasting episodes, the latter carries with it a much more elaborate succession of formal functions including main theme, transition, and subordinate theme.

The crucial difference between a rondo and a sonata rondo is the presence of a transition between the rondo theme and the first episode (or subordinate theme) in a sonata rondo (between mm. 1–39 and 90–148 in *Don Juan*). Admittedly, Hepokoski struggles to give mm. 40–89 a place in his rondo reading. He notes that mm. 46–65 (after the postcadential unit following the PAC in m. 40) initially appear to be an episode (which would suggest a simple rondo format), but adds that this interpretation is thwarted by the passage's "brevity and tonal instability and because of the incomplete appearance of DJ^{int} [the opening measures of the work] ... at its end, mm. 62–65." He thus finds it "not unreasonable" to relegate the passage to "the status of a transition (or 'transition episode') to the more stable B major of the following episode," which, he adds, is "preceded by a lengthy dominant" [1992a, pp. 144–145].

Recast in the terminology of Sonata Theory, Hepokoski's analysis amounts to that of the beginning of a "Type 4 sonata." Yet a defining characteristic of such a Type 4 sonata is precisely that it begins with "a first rotation [that] is structured as the exposition of a [Type 3] sonata" [Hepokoski & Darcy 2006, p. 404]. This means that for an informed listener who hears the opening portion of *Don Juan* for the first time, it is impossible to judge whether he or she is dealing with a sonata rondo or a sonata form (a "Type 4" or a "Type 3" sonata) on the basis of the sounding surface alone.

Hepokoski's motives for hearing the beginning of *Don Juan* as a (sonata) rondo must therefore lie beyond the work's mere score. The main reason for his so firmly holding to the rondo idea appears to be that "the libertine suggestions of the rondo structure" are very much in line with "what is normally taken to be the program [of *Don Juan*]" [Hepokoski 1992a, p. 147]. In the generic context of the symphonic poem, this argument is, of course, perfectly acceptable. As Hepokoski himself reminds us, "the explicit invitation ... to interpret the musical processes in light of the provided paratext-complex, ... is the defining feature of the symphonic poem as a genre" [1992a, p. 136]. Yet if the key to a successful interpretation of *Don Juan* really is that it begins as a rondo and then transforms into a sonata form, it is difficult to understand why the rondo elements in the piece are not articulated more unequivocally. Given its generic origins in the overture, the neutral horizon of expectation in a symphonic poem is that of a sonata form, to the extent that Hepokoski has recently deemed the rondo format "generically unavailable" to the symphonic poem [2006, pp. 29–30]. Even if it is true that the implications of the program of *Don Juan* favor a rondo interpretation, there is no point in changing the horizon of expectation if this change is not supported by the music.

It is not, in other words, that it is technically impossible to describe mm. 1–168 as the beginning of a sonata rondo; indeed, nothing that has happened in the form up to this point prevents a possible continuation of the piece as a "Type 4 sonata." But in the generic context of the tone poem, an interpretation as a sonata form simply appears much more plausible. This is all the more so since the further course of the form offers very little support for a rondo reading—a fact Hepokoski of course acknowledges: it is the crux of his reading. If, however, an interpretation as a rondo is only one of several possibilities in mm. 1–197, and, given the generic context, it is not even the most probable one, if that interpretation then gradually grows more improbable, and if it ultimately turns out to be untenable from m. 474

onwards, it seems misguided to regard *Don Juan* as a temporary rondo deformation in the first place.

Accordingly, Hepokoski has recently expressed reservations about his own interpretation of *Don Juan*, conceding that the "rondo impact of the work is perceptible primarily as an ongoing possibility" and that "the sonata deformation proves to be the governing factor" [2006, p. 31 n. 74]. In my view, this does not go far enough: given the generic background of the tone poem as well as the similarities in formal organization between *Don Juan* and other symphonic poems, I fail to see how a rondo would even be a real possibility at any point in the form.

The alternative is to hear *Don Juan* as a sonata form from the outset. Such a reading is straightforward enough in the initial stages of the form. The exposition begins with a main-theme complex comprising a thematic introduction (mm. 1–8) and a main theme proper. As example 10 illustrates, the main theme proper takes the form of a compound period—antecedent in mm. 9–20, extended consequent in mm. 21–39—and leads to a I:PAC main theme cadence in m. 40.

Even though it begins over a dominant pedal, the antecedent is fairly regular and takes the form of a hybrid of the "presentation + continuation" type.[5] The presentation is a so-called "evolving" presentation: a four-measure presentation that takes the form of a small-scale sentential pattern and in which the second measure is a (varied) repetition of the first and the last two measures belong together.[6] The continuation is expanded by a standing on the dominant that follows the HC in m. 17. The consequent begins with a compressed variant of the same evolving presentation and immediately leads to a cadential phrase that evades arrival on the tonic. Instead, it is repeated and dissolves into a four-measure fragmentation process. The consequent is further expanded by the interpolation of material from the thematic introduction that precedes the main theme proper. Only then is the main theme concluded by a PAC.

This cadence is elided with the beginning of the transition, which opens as a postcadential unit to the main theme but later confirms its transitional function by its increased looseness, its overall tonal trajectory from I to V/V, and the strong formal marker of an extended standing on the dominant of the new key in mm. 71–89. The subordinate theme, finally, takes the form of a period with an enormously expanded consequent that fails to bring a PAC in the new key but is instead elided with the arrival on the tonic minor that opens the development in m. 149. Nowhere in the initial 148 measures is a sonata-form hearing ever compromised, and with the off-tonic return of the main theme in mm. 169–196 the abstract possibility of a rondo hearing is definitively abandoned (I will come back to the intervening measures, mm. 149–168, below).

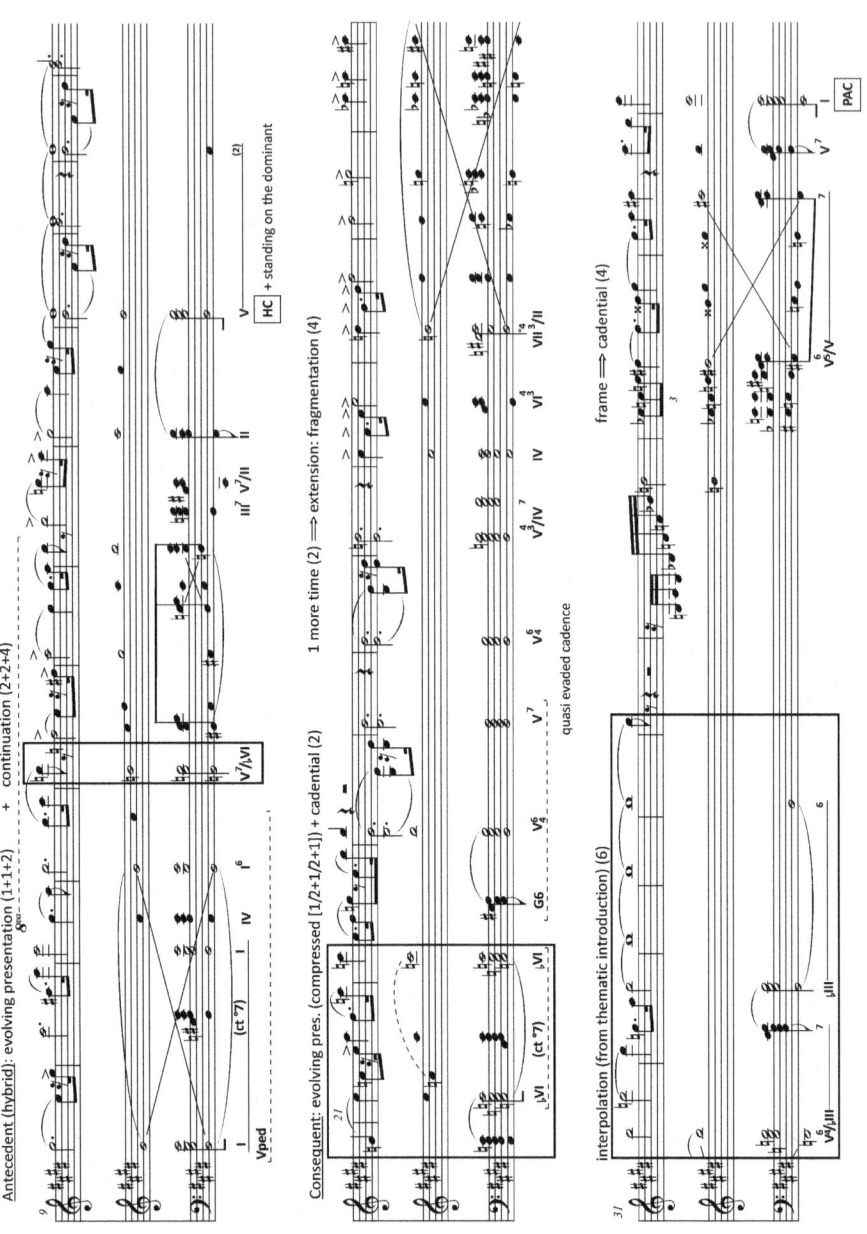

Example 10: Strauss, *Don Juan*: main theme, mm. 9-40

This is not to say that *Don Juan* is a sonata form pure and simple. Soon after the onset of the development, a sonata-form reading runs into serious trouble. Hepokoski singles out two major analytical difficulties [1992a, pp. 148–149]. The first is the presence of several "non-developmental episodes within the developmental space," which, according to Hepokoski, deny "the work, at least up to the moment of the reprise, the 'feel' of a standard sonata." The second is that in the recapitulation, "the exposition's 'transition' and 'second theme' [...] fail to reappear and are replaced instead by a grand statement of the seemingly post-expositional *Heldenthema*." Hepokoski considerably mitigates this second objection by placing *Don Juan* in his category of "breakthrough" sonata deformations, and he explains the presence of the various non-developmental segments in the development section by referring to the sonata deformation type with episodes in or as the development.

These peculiarities can also be explained when *Don Juan* is interpreted along the lines of a two-dimensional sonata form. In Strauss's tone poem, the sonata form is combined with numerous important elements from the sonata cycle—a possibility Hepokoski touches upon, but only very briefly.[7] The exposition and the beginning of the development in the overarching sonata form function as a complete first movement in the dimension of the sonata cycle. Not unlike *Die Ideale*, the off-tonic return of the main theme at the beginning of the development in the overarching sonata form functions as the recapitulation of the main theme in the local sonata form. To interpret the return of main-theme material early in a development as an indication of the presence of a local sonata form may seem a stretch, but it does explain the way this return is set up in mm. 160–168. Surely, the gradual regeneration of the main theme in conjunction with the emphatic dominant in E major in mm. 166–168 suggests an imminent recapitulation rather than the onset of a development. From this perspective, it even becomes possible to think of the unit in mm. 149–168, which is difficult to explain in the overarching sonata form, as the development of the local sonata form. Moreover, it seems hardly coincidental that the return of the main theme is in C major—a key that obviously refers back, if not to the main theme group as a whole, then at least to its opening sonority (I will return to the function of C major in the tonal plan of *Don Juan* below). Finally, it is very unusual for the development of a symphonic poem in the Liszt–Strauss tradition to refer so openly to main-theme material near the beginning of a development, except in those symphonic poems that are two-dimensional sonata forms.

From the perspective of two-dimensional sonata form, mm. 232–312—the second part of episode 2 in Hepokoski's rondo reading—can be understood as a fully-fledged interpolated slow movement that is even tonally and formally closed.

CHAPTER 4

After four introductory measures (mm. 232–235) comes a period of inflated proportions that consists of a sixteen-measure antecedent (mm. °236–251) and a hugely expanded consequent (mm. °252–295). The movement concludes with a coda over a tonic pedal (mm. 296–309) that is followed by a brief transition to the first appearance of the *Heldenthema* (mm. 310–312).

Although its status is significantly less clear than that of the slow movement, the final episode in the rondo reading (mm. 351–385) unmistakably bears the characteristics of a scherzo. In a reading of *Don Juan* as a two-dimensional sonata form, it is unsatisfactory to interpret it simply as an interpolation, since it is extremely short and closed neither formally nor tonally. Because of its initial thematic independence from the rest of the composition, however, it is not easily explained as a movement that is identified with part of the development either, as was possible with the scherzo of *Die Ideale*. It can most plausibly be described as an episode that gradually changes into the unequivocally developmental texture in m. 386. In any case, it functions as a second interior movement in the dimension of the cycle.

The finale of the sonata cycle is identified with the recapitulation and the coda of the overarching sonata form. Admittedly, the modifications mm. 476–555 have undergone in comparison to the exposition can also be explained as an attempt to solve the recapitulation problem outlined in Chapter 2. Yet since it is preceded by a first movement and two interior movements, has a strong climactic effect, and includes post-expositional thematic material, the recapitulation can also be understood as a finale. This is particularly so because this post-expositional material is related to the breakthrough that took place in the development. Walter Werbeck has even suggested that after the interpolated slow movement a new sonata form begins that consists of the "exposition, development, and concluding crowning recapitulation of the horn theme" ("Exposition, Durchführung und abschließende krönende Reprise des Hornthemas") [Werbeck 1996, p. 398]. Although Werbeck overstates the case, his interpretation does justice to the strong impact the *Heldenthema* has on the second half of the composition.

The two-dimensional sonata form of *Don Juan* is intimately related to a double-tonic complex E major/C major that governs the work's large-scale tonal organization. This double-tonic complex is first introduced at a local level not only by the aforementioned off-tonic opening, but also by the sudden shift to E:V^7/♭VI in m. 13 and by two striking digressions to E:♭VI and E:♭III in the main theme's consequent, both of which challenge the theme's E-major cadential structure (see example 10; the hints at C major as a shadow tonic are boxed). Later in *Don Juan*, C major clearly establishes itself as the tonic of the multi-movement cycle, while E major remains the tonic of the overarching sonata form. Example 11 interprets

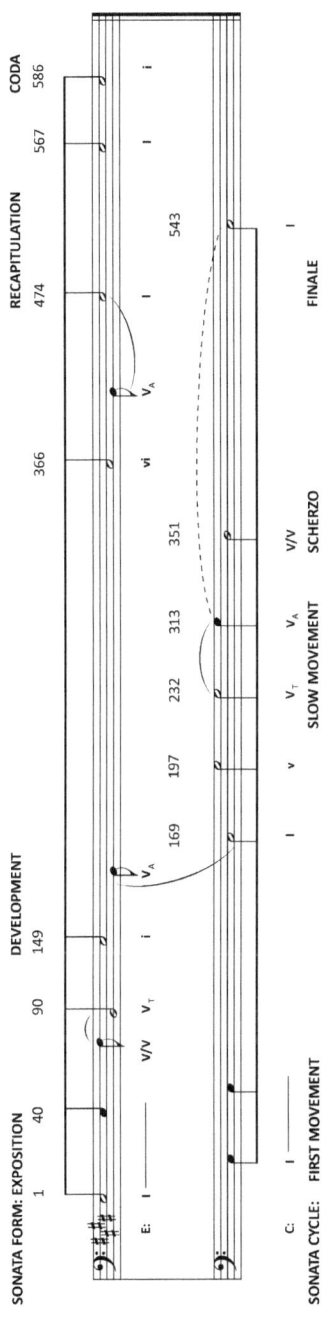

Example 11: Strauss, *Don Juan*: overview of the large-scale tonal organization

CHAPTER 4

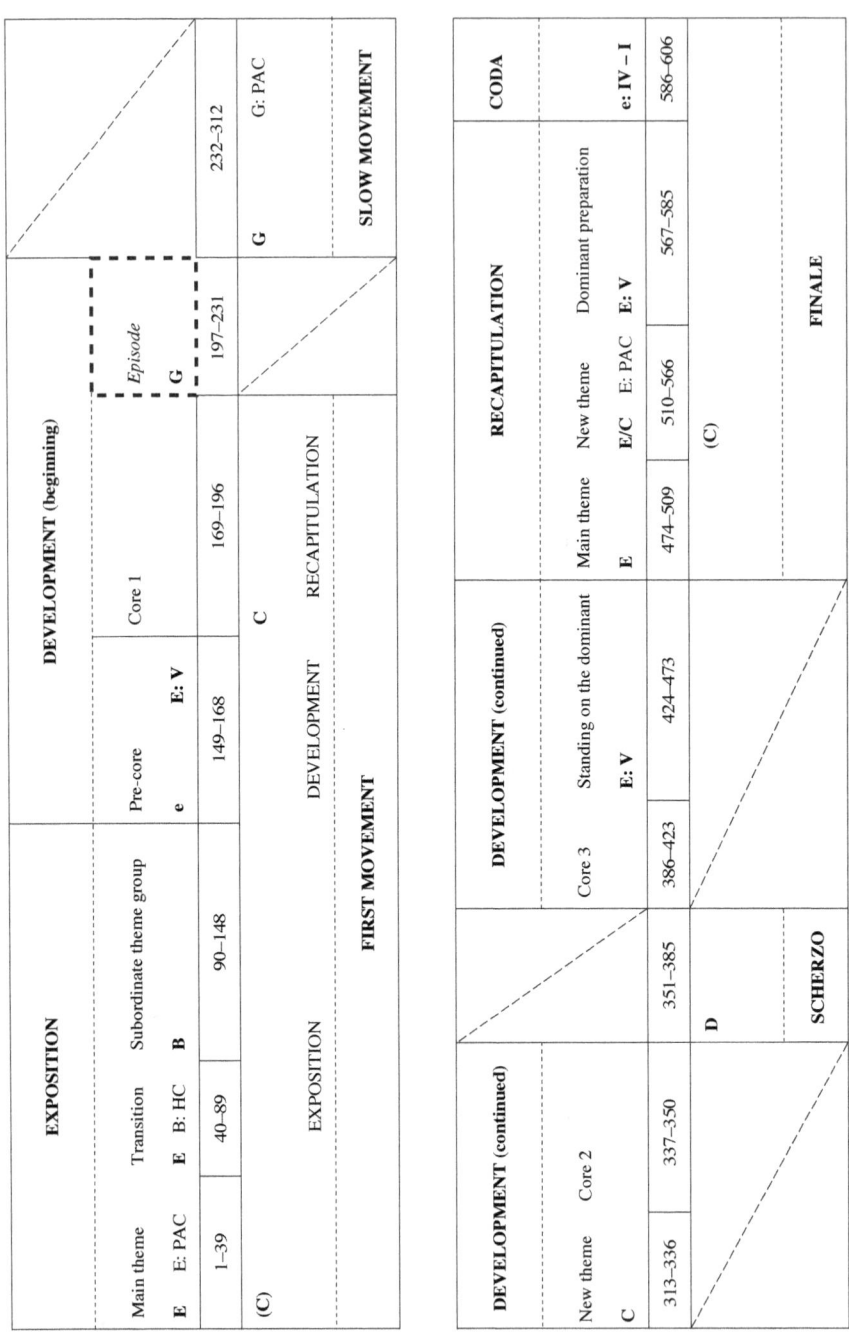

Figure 13: Strauss, *Don Juan*: form and cycle

significant tonal events in the form from this perspective. Except for the ♭VI inflections in the main theme and the transition, the exposition of the overarching sonata form is firmly rooted in E major, complete with the slightly old-fashioned move (by 1888 standards) to the dominant B major for the subordinate key. The same is true for the pre-core (E minor) and the final segment of the development (C♯ minor, then a standing on the dominant in E major), the beginning of the recapitulation (E major), and the coda (E minor).

The significance of C major as the tonic of the multi-movement cycle becomes clear not only when it appears as the key of the recapitulation of the sonata-form first movement (m. 169), but also in the interior movements of the sonata cycle, where G major and D major of the slow movement and the scherzo respectively conform to C major rather than to E major. Finally, the apotheosis of the *Heldenthema*—the major modification to the recapitulation, and the factor that points most clearly to its simultaneous function as a finale—conspicuously climaxes on a PAC in C major (m. 543).

Figure 13 gives an overview of the formal organization of *Don Juan*. It shows the first movement of the sonata cycle as identified with the exposition and the beginning of the development of the overarching sonata form, the slow movement as an interpolation in the development, the scherzo as a movement that begins as an interpolation but then merges into a more genuinely developmental unit, and the finale as identified with the recapitulation and the coda. The G-minor passage in mm. 197–231 seems to play no role in either the sonata form or the sonata cycle and can only be described as a (programmatic) episode. It is only thirty-four measures long and consists of a binary theme (mm. 197–202 and 203–207) and its varied and extended repetition (mm. 208–214 and 215–231). The varied repetition of the second part of the theme then becomes a transition to the subsequent slow movement. The unit can be considered tonally closed—it begins in G minor and ends on a tonic in G major that is elided with the beginning of the slow movement—and is thematically almost completely independent from the overarching sonata form, or at least no less independent than an interpolated movement. Nonetheless, it is unconvincing to interpret mm. 197–231 as an interpolated movement, both because of its brevity in comparison to the other movements of the cycle and because of its layout, which cannot be considered as a self-contained musical form at all.

It is important to delineate the two-dimensional sonata form of *Don Juan* from the sonata-deformation category with episodes in the development space that appears in several of Strauss's other tone poems and to which Hepokoski refers in his discussion of the work. Differences between the formal organization of *Don Juan* and that of the roughly contemporaneous *Macbeth*—one of Hepokoski's standard examples of the deformation with episodes—may seem to be minimal. According to Hepokoski, the exposition of *Macbeth* (mm. 1–122) is separated from its recapitulation (mm. 324–535) by two episodes (mm. 123–259 and 260–323) that "roughly correspond to a symphony's 'lyrical movement' (slow movement) and 'characteristic movement' (or scherzo)" [Hepokoski 1992b, p. 78]. One might take issue with Hepokoski's identification of two distinct episodes in *Macbeth* in the first place. It is beyond doubt that mm. 260–323 form a self-contained episode; they could even pass as an interpolated interior movement in a two-dimensional sonata form. The status of mm. 123–259 as an episode is, however, far less secure. This passage may prominently feature a lyrical idea, but it definitely does not constitute a homogeneously lyrical episode. The lyrical texture is repeatedly disturbed by the return of motivic material from mm. 20–24 of the main theme group, which generates a degree of conflict that is more typical of a development than of an episode. Moreover, the whole of mm. 123–259 turns out to be a build-up to the climactic return of the opening motto in m. 242, thus fulfilling an indispensable function in the overarching form rather than the kind of suspension of sonata-form activity characteristic of an episode. The least one can say is that both units Hepokoski calls episodes are very different in nature.

The same could, of course, be said about the interior movements of *Don Juan*. Nonetheless, it is possible to formulate a set of criteria that clearly distinguish two-dimensional sonata form from the sonata deformation with episodes in the development. First of all, a two-dimensional sonata form—at least in symphonic and chamber music—should contain a minimum of two units that can be interpreted as interior movements of the sonata cycle. Second, the character of the episodes or movements in question should clearly be that of a slow movement and a scherzo, and both of them should clearly contrast with each other. Third, surrounding the interior movements, there should be clear evidence of the presence of a first movement, a finale, or both; at least one of these outer movements should be present by more than mere implication.

These characteristics apply to *Don Juan*, but not to *Macbeth*. In the latter, the supposed episodes are only vaguely reminiscent of a slow movement and a scherzo; quite rightly, Hepokoski describes them first as a "lyrical" and a "characteristic" movement respectively, and only in the second instance as a "slow movement" and a "scherzo." More importantly, neither before nor after the episodes that might be perceived as interior movements is there any trace of the outer movements of a sonata cycle. The supposed first episode is preceded by a brief introduction and a two-block exposition, neither of which seems to function as more than just that. The recapitulation, for its part, is radically modified in comparison to the exposition, yet the modifications amount to a distortion of the recapitulation, and there is no suggestion at all of the climactic effect associated with a finale.

Ein Heldenleben Op. 40 (1897–98)

There is far more agreement among analysts about the form of *Ein Heldenleben* than about that of *Don Juan*. As Werbeck has pointed out, "not only the sonata elements, but also the correspondences to the symphonic *Mehrsätzigkeit* in *Ein Heldenleben* have never been disputed."[8] Yet it is also clear that the work contains several units that are difficult to align with either a sonata form or a sonata cycle: there seems to be a third dimension at work in *Ein Heldenleben*—that of the narrative. This third dimension is, of course, present in *Don Juan* as well. There, it nearly always coincides with the sonata form, the sonata cycle, or both. The single exception is the G-minor passage in mm. 197–231, which is an interpolated episode in the overarching sonata form but not a movement in the sonata cycle. In *Ein Heldenleben*, the autonomy of the narrative dimension appears more important, regularly giving rise to the presence of units—"programmatic episodes"—that are unaccounted for by either the overarching sonata form or the sonata cycle. These units interrupt or suspend both the form and the cycle and are solely, though sufficiently, legitimized by the extra-musical program.

The main theme group in the exposition of the overarching sonata form is itself organized as a sonata form.[9] The main theme of this small-scale sonata form (mm. 1–16) consists of an eight-measure antecedent and eight measures of continuation. It is concluded by a PAC in E♭ major that is elided with the onset of the transition in m. 17. The latter begins with a repetition of the opening four measures of the main theme—characteristically in a fuller texture—but suddenly breaks off. Without the slightest preparation, a subordinate theme enters in m. 21. Although it clearly begins in B major, it is anything but tonally stable. From a thematic point of view, however, the subordinate theme group strongly contrasts with the preceding twenty measures, presenting a number of new motives and not repeating a single one of those heard before. Similarly, mm. 45ff are defined as a development not by a further increase in tonal instability, but by the return of material from mm. 1–16 and its combination with material from the subordinate theme group. The development ends with a standing on the dominant in mm. 84–93, after which the return of the main theme in the tonic in m. 94 marks the beginning of the recapitulation. The upper half of figure 14 gives an overview of the small-scale sonata form in mm. 1–118.

CHAPTER 4

LOCAL SONATA FORM					
Main theme		Transition	Subordinate theme	Development	Recapitulation
E♭	E♭: PAC	E♭	B		E♭
1–16		17–20	21–44	45–93	94–118
E♭				E♭: PAC	E♭ E♭: HC
Main theme group					Transition
OVERARCHING SONATA FORM (beginning)					

Figure 14: Strauss, *Ein Heldenleben:* local sonata form (mm. 1–118) and beginning of the overarching sonata form

    The recapitulation does not repeat the actual main theme from the beginning, but the onset of the transition from mm. 17–20. This time, the passage also leads to an emphatic I:HC followed by eleven measures of standing on the dominant and a general pause that is difficult to mistake for something other than a medial caesura. As is indicated in the lower half of figure 14, mm. 94ff function as the transition in the overarching sonata form. One therefore expects the following unit to be a subordinate theme; and although the programmatic episode in mm. 118–136 does not immediately fulfill these expectations, mm. 137–170 do. They begin in G minor—not the most likely, but still a possible secondary key area in an E♭-major sonata form—and conclude with a clear PAC in the same key. Moreover, mm. 137–170 have a distinct thematic profile based on a lyrical transformation of the main theme's head and are organized as an eight-measure antecedent followed by an extended continuation of eighteen measures.

    A new transitional unit in mm. 171–191 leads to another HC in E♭ major, thus reverting to the situation at the end of the (previous) transition. The approach to the cadence is immediately repeated but eventually thwarted by the entry of the solo violin in m. 191. The lengthy, very heterogeneous, and tonally unstable dialogue between the orchestra and the solo violin that follows (mm. 192–287) is, though programmatically clear, form-functionally seemingly superfluous. The tonal instability and fragmented character of this episode suggest—if anything—a transitional function. Yet thematically it is closely related to the subsequent unit in G♭ major that doubtless belongs to a second subordinate theme group. This G♭ major unit, moreover, begins with a cadential passage (mm. 288–291) that seems to function as a conclusion. After the cadence in mm. 288–291 and the subsequent postcadential unit in mm. 292, the G♭ major passage is articulated by four more PACs (mm. 316, 327, 335, and 344), each concluding an increasingly short subordinate theme. The last PAC marks the end of the subordinate theme group and the beginning of the closing group (mm. 344–368). It is only with the onset of the G♭-major passage that the listener can be sure that the second subordinate theme group has definitely begun. Still, it remains possible to retrospectively reinterpret the entire programmatic episode from m. 192 as part of that second subordinate theme group.

From the perspective of the overarching sonata form, mm. 1–368 can be described as a three-key exposition, moving from E♭ major for the main theme group to G minor for the first subordinate theme group and G♭ major for the second. From the point of view of the sonata cycle, there is no doubt that the sonata form in mm. 1–117 functions as a first movement that is identified with the main theme group and transition of the overarching sonata form. The programmatic episode in mm. 118–136, the first subordinate theme in mm. 137–170, the transition towards the second programmatic episode (mm. 171–191), and the programmatic episode itself (mm. 192–287) are exocyclic. The cycle resumes with the G♭-major second subordinate theme group and the closing group, both of which are identified with the cycle's slow movement. In contrast to the first movement, this slow movement has no form of its own, although it is, of course, tonally closed.

The fanfares in mm. °369–377 and °392–395, the intermittent return of material from the first subordinate theme—and, by implication, the main theme—and its combination with material from the second subordinate theme group signal the beginning of the development of the overarching sonata form. This development can be divided in three large segments: mm. °369–433 and 434–615 are in effect equivalent to a pre-core and a (pseudo-)core, and mm. 616–630 (standing on the dominant) function as a retransition to the recapitulation. In the dimension of the cycle, the middle segment of the development functions as a scherzo. Like the slow movement, the scherzo has no form of its own, but merely lends its meter—and the initial tonal stability in C minor—to the core of the development.

The recapitulation in m. 631 is unmistakable. Correspondence to the exposition is, however, limited to its first twenty-eight measures. The recapitulation begins with a harmonized but otherwise only slightly modified reprise of the opening antecedent of the main theme, followed by a completely new continuation (mm. 639–652). As in the exposition, the cadence of this continuation is elided with the beginning of a repetition of the main theme, which is now combined with one of the motives from the subordinate theme group (mm. 653–656). The recapitulation of the overarching sonata form, in other words, borrows the main theme and the transition from the local sonata form. Also like that in the local sonata form, the transition in the recapitulation ends prematurely; after only four measures, the subordinate theme group abruptly enters.

CHAPTER 4

EXPOSITION

Main theme group		Transition		Episode		Subordinate theme 1		Transition		Episode	⇒	Subordinate themes 2–5		Closing group
E♭	E♭: PAC	E♭	E♭: HC	G		g	g: PAC	g	~~E♭: HC~~		G♭: PAC	G♭	G♭: PAC	G♭
1–93		94–117		118–136		137–170		171–191		192–291		292–343		344–368

E♭   G♭

FIRST MOVEMENT   **SLOW MOVEMENT**

DEVELOPEMENT

Pre-core		Core		Retransition	
				E♭: PAC	
369–433		434–615		616–630	

c

SCHERZO

RECAPITULATION

Main theme		Transition		Subordinate theme	
E♭	E♭: PAC	E♭		B	
631–652		653–656		657–658	

CODA

Series of episodes			E♭
B → E♭			
659–853			854–927

B → E♭

FINALE

Figure 15: Strauss, *Ein Heldenleben*: form and cycle

Yet the reprise of what was the subordinate theme group in the local sonata form is radically curtailed as well. After only two measures, the music takes a completely different direction. What follows is a seemingly rhapsodic succession of new thematic material, motives from the exposition and, most of all, self-quotations from all of Strauss's earlier tone poems, his opera *Guntram*, and a number of songs.[10] Every trace of a structural analogy to the exposition is missing. Although the coda (mm. 854–927), with its unfolding of one of the motives from the exposition's transition and its evanescent reminiscences of the development, is again more in line with conventional practice, there seems to be no possible way to come to terms with mm. 631–853 as part of a sonata form.

One way of interpreting mm. 659–853 is as another programmatic episode (or rather a series of episodes) that is interpolated between the recapitulation and the coda. There might, however, be an alternative way to explain this seemingly nonfunctional unit within the referential framework of two-dimensional sonata form. The new thematic material and the self-quotations may be understood as an original way of rendering the formal unit that functions as the recapitulation in the overarching sonata form sufficiently independent from the exposition to assume a simultaneous function as the finale in the dimension of the sonata cycle. Admittedly, there is no trace of the presence of a finale in the formal organization of mm. 631–853, and the character of the new formal units is not specifically linked to that of a finale. Thus, *Ein Heldenleben* relies heavily on the principle of cyclic completion: one is inclined to interpret the modified recapitulation (or at least the new music that follows the initial recapitulatory gesture) as a finale only because of the presence of a first movement, a slow movement, and a scherzo in the earlier portions of the composition.

Nonetheless, the relationship between sonata form and sonata cycle in *Ein Heldenleben* is remarkable, all four movements of the sonata cycle being identified with units of the sonata form. Interpolation is present only in the form of the two programmatic episodes (in mm. 118–136 and 192–287) that do not have a function in either the sonata form or sonata cycle. Neither the interior movements nor the finale exhibit an internal formal organization that is even remotely as elaborate and well-rounded as that of the first. The interior movements do not influence the formal course of the units with which they are identified; they merely lend them their tempo, character, and—in the case of the scherzo—meter: the slow movement lends its surface characteristics to the second subordinate theme group and the closing group of the exposition (mm. 288–368), the scherzo to the core of the development (mm. 434–615). Figure 15 gives a formal overview of *Ein Heldenleben*.

In spite of considerable differences between individual compositions, two-dimensional sonata form is clearly a governing principle in the formal organization of a number of Liszt's symphonic poems and Strauss's tone poems. Its function is to help realize the genre's symphonic aspirations. Not only does it increase the degree of formal complexity, it also problematizes the formal organization of these compositions, thus involving them in an approach to composition that is more typical of absolute genres than of programmatic instrumental music.

Both Liszt's and Strauss's symphonic poems play a role in the problem history of two-dimensional sonata form. In Liszt's symphonic poems, the focus is on different aspects of the relationship between the outer movements of a sonata cycle and the overarching sonata form. In *Tasso*, Liszt succeeds in identifying the finale with units of the overarching sonata form but does not articulate a separate first movement in the dimension of the cycle. In *Die Ideale*, the situation is reversed: the first movement is identified with the units of the overarching sonata form that precede the first interior movement, but the finale—identified with the whole of the recapitulation and the coda—is only moderately profiled.

The position of Strauss's *Don Juan* and *Ein Heldenleben* in the "Problemgeschichte" of two-dimensional sonata form is different. In *Don Juan*, a problem comes to the fore that had largely remained latent in earlier two-dimensional sonata forms: that of the relationship between an interpolated interior movement and the overarching sonata form. Because the interpolated slow movement in *Don Juan* includes a fully-fledged coda, it is difficult to resume the overarching sonata form afterwards. Strauss attempts to solve this problem with an unexpected insertion of the *Heldenthema*, which is unrelated to either the exposition of the overarching sonata form or, apart from a vague similarity to its main theme, the slow movement—a move that is as effective formally as it is programmatically. What this solution gains on one side, however, it loses on the other. The emphatic post-expositional introduction of the *Heldenthema* seriously endangers the integrity of the overarching sonata form—a central tenet in the Austro-German symphonic tradition—and with it of the composition as a whole.

It might seem that Strauss is very successful in integrating the dimension of the cycle with that of the form in *Ein Heldenleben*. All four movements of the sonata cycle are present, and each of them is identified with units of the overarching sonata form. Like *Don Juan*, *Ein Heldenleben* confronts the problem of reactivating the overarching sonata form after the slow movement, and here as well both this problem and the way it is solved are programmatically motivated. At the same time, *Ein Heldenleben* contains several episodes that seem to be merely programmatically motivated. Finally, it does not offer a solution for the problems of recapitulation and finale. Instead, the recapitulation of the main theme group is followed by a remarkable *coup de théâtre*. In contrast to the reactivation of the overarching sonata form after the slow movement—both in *Don Juan* and in *Ein Heldenleben*—this move seems to lack sufficient formal motivation. From a traditional nineteenth-century perspective on form, the main effect of the numerous quotations from other compositions that are unrelated to what precedes them is similar to that of the interpolated programmatic episodes: they imperil the integrity of the composition. All this does not necessarily lead to a negative evaluation, of course; Strauss's disinterest in a fully integrated musical form is one of the aspects that define him as a modernist. Still, it is something that sets him apart from some of his aesthetically more conservative contemporaries—most notably, as we will see, Arnold Schoenberg.

Notes

[1] This quotation first appears in the secondary literature in Steinitzer 1911, p. 60. The letter itself is, unfortunately, no longer extant.

[2] "Seite 32 'aber nicht nach Liszt' muß ein Irrtum sein. Ich erinnere mich nicht. Wenn schon, müßte es heißen: 'aber nach Liszt'" [Brosche 1977, p. 4].

[3] "Neue Gedanken müssen sich neue Formen suchen – dieses Lisztsche Grundprinzip seiner sinfonischen Werke, in denen tatsächlich die poetische Idee auch zugleich das formbildende Element war, wurde mir von da ab der Leitfaden für meine eigenen sinfonischen Dichtungen" [Strauss 1949, p. 168].

[4] "Ich habe mich von der f-moll-Sinfonie weg in einem allmählich immer größerem Widerspruch zwischen dem musikalisch-poetischen Inhalt, den ich mitteilen wollte, u[nd] der uns von den Klassikern überkommenen Form des dreiteiligen Sonatensatzes befunden" letter from Strauss to Hans von Bülow, 24–8–1888 [Strauss 1996, p. 83].

[5] On hybrid themes see Caplin 1998, pp. 59–63.

[6] I adopt the term "evolving presentation" from Mart Humal, who defines it as a presentation in which the "concluding two-bar unit arises as the result of a development *within* the *presentation*—a kind of twofold *swing*" [Humal 1999, p. 38].

[7] Another author who has argued in favor of an interpretation of *Don Juan*—and, indeed, all of Strauss's tone poems—as a form in which sections of sonata form and movements from the sonata cycle are combined at the same hierarchical level is Reinhard Gerlach [1966 & 1991].

[8] "In *Heldenleben* sind nicht nur die Sonatenelemente, sondern auch die Korrespondenzen zur symphonischen Mehrsätzigkeit nie bestritten worden" [Werbeck 1996, p. 444].

[9] See also Werbeck 1996, pp. 448–449. My analysis differs from Werbeck's in important ways.

[10] A complete list of the self-quotations is given in Kennedy 1984, pp. 46–47.

CHAPTER 5

SCHOENBERG'S *PELLEAS UND MELISANDE*

Before *Pelleas*

In 1949, looking back on his early period, Arnold Schoenberg recalled the musical situation in Vienna in the final years of the nineteenth century as follows [Schoenberg 1949d, p. 37]:

> Mahler and Strauss had appeared on the musical scene, and so fascinating was their advent, that every musician was immediately forced to take sides, pro or contra. Being then only 23 years of age, I was easily to catch fire, and to begin composing symphonic poems of one uninterrupted movement.

Evidently, Richard Strauss had already appeared on the musical scene by the early 1890s. By 1897—the year Schoenberg turned twenty-three—he had become the leading composer of his generation. Gustav Mahler, on the other hand, entered the Viennese musical scene in the final years of the nineteenth century mainly as a conductor. Having been appointed principal conductor of the Vienna court opera in April 1897, he became its director only a few months later. As Ulrich Thieme suggests, it may well be Mahler's breakthrough as a conductor (and not as a composer) that Schoenberg had in mind when writing in 1949 [Thieme 1979, pp. 150–151]. As Schoenberg recounts elsewhere, he became interested in Mahler's music only after his return from Berlin in 1903. In *My Evolution* he recalls [Schoenberg 1949c, p. 82]:

> [...] at this time [when composing *Verklärte Nacht*], I had already become an admirer of Richard Strauss, but not of Gustav Mahler, whom I began to understand only much later, at a time when his symphonic style could no longer exert its influence on me.

Somewhat surprisingly, then, not only Mahler's, but also Strauss's name remains conspicuously absent from the list of composers who influenced his works from around 1900 that Schoenberg gives in *My Evolution*. Apart from Brahms and Wagner, he only mentions "Liszt, Bruckner, and perhaps also Hugo Wolf" [1949c, p. 80]. The omission of Strauss from this list is, in all likelihood, the result of the rapidly deteriorating personal relationship between him and Schoenberg after 1914.[1]

CHAPTER 5

In any case, the increased influence of Strauss is unmistakable in Schoenberg's music written after 1897, the year in which he completed the D-major String Quartet (the final and most successful work of what Walter Frisch has called "Schoenberg's Brahmsian period" [Frisch 1993, p. 33]). In the realm of instrumental music, the earliest documents bearing proof of this influence are three incomplete programmatic compositions, all of which presumably date from 1898: two symphonic poems, *Hans im Glück* and *Frühlings Tod*, and a string sextet *Toter Winkel*. The fragments *Hans im Glück* and *Toter Winkel* break off after thirteen and thirty-four measures respectively, and are obviously too short to allow for any conclusions about their overall formal organization. Stylistically, however, *Hans im Glück* might reveal an early influence of Strauss. Walter Bailey has noted that the character of its opening measures is somewhat "reminiscent of Strauss's *Till Eulenspiegel*" [Bailey 1984, p. 44]. As for *Frühlings Tod*, both Thieme and Bailey conclude, on the basis of the 255-measure short score (135 measures of which are orchestrated), that it was intended to be a single-movement composition [Thieme 1979, p. 191 and Bailey 1984, pp. 47 & 49]. Bailey even goes one step further, interpreting the fragment as an introduction, an exposition, and part of a development, with a slow movement interpolated between the exposition and the development.

Schoenberg's first completed large-scale single-movement composition, the string sextet *Verklärte Nacht* Op. 4 (1899), has been analyzed as a rondo-like design paralleling the form of Richard Dehmel's eponymous five-strophe poem that inspired it, but also as a sonata form and even as a succession of two sonata forms.[2] None of these views is entirely satisfying. In the context of the present study, it is particularly important to retain that, although it is not a two-dimensional sonata form, *Verklärte Nacht* does contain something like an interpolated slow movement. In his analysis of the work as a sonata form, Wilhelm Pfannkuch has persuasively argued that mm. 229–369 can be understood as an interpolation separating the truncated recapitulation from the coda. Thus, *Verklärte Nacht* shows the young Schoenberg further assimilating the influence of Strauss, not only aesthetically, harmonically, or in the treatment of motives and themes, but also at the level of large-scale formal organization.

Pelleas und Melisande Op. 5 (1902–03)

In the years following the composition of *Verklärte Nacht*, Schoenberg's interest in Strauss seems only to have increased. In December of 1901, Schoenberg moved to Berlin—where Strauss was Kapellmeister at the court opera—to be appointed a conductor at Ernst von Wolzogen's *Überbrettl* theatre. In February of the next year, he received a letter from Zemlinsky, in which the latter writes:

> At the same time as you, I had the score—the large one—of Strauss's Heldenleben at my home for a couple of weeks. I studied it most carefully!³

This implies that late in 1901 or early in 1902, Schoenberg too had been studying *Ein Heldenleben*, and apparently wrote enthusiastically about it to Zemlinsky. This is the earliest documented instance of Schoenberg seriously engaging with a two-dimensional sonata form from the Liszt–Strauss tradition. Some weeks before, Zemlinsky had sent Schoenberg a letter of recommendation for Strauss: "He [Strauss] will have the impression," the accompanying note to Schoenberg reads, "that we are the most enthusiastic disciples of his muse."⁴ With this letter in hand, Schoenberg endeavored to get in touch with Strauss. The result was a regular professional contact between both composers, for Strauss hired Schoenberg to copy out the parts of his ballad for soloists, choir, and orchestra, *Taillefer* Op. 52 (1903).

Shortly after this encounter, Schoenberg started making sketches for his own symphonic poem *Pelleas und Melisande*. It is uncertain to what extent Strauss influenced Schoenberg's decision to begin composing this piece. For a long time, it was believed that Strauss was the one who drew Schoenberg's attention to Maurice Maeterlinck's play as a potential subject. In the editorial commentary accompanying their critical edition of *Pelleas und Melisande*, however, Nikos Kokkinis and Ralf Kwasny have firmly established that Schoenberg had become aware of Maeterlinck's play by 1900 at the latest [Kokkinis & Kwasny 1999, p. 206]. Schoenberg's original plan was, apparently, to turn Maeterlinck's play into an opera, but there is no reason to assume that it was Strauss who suggested that he do so, as is sometimes believed. Rather, Schoenberg may have decided to use the subject for a symphonic poem in response to Strauss's proposal of conducting such a work: it can be inferred from Schoenberg's correspondence that Strauss offered to perform an orchestral composition by Schoenberg if he would write one.⁵ Whether Schoenberg turned to Strauss for any technical advice when composing *Pelleas und Melisande* is hard to tell. All we know is that on one occasion Strauss "glanced through" the unfinished autograph score.⁶

In any case, *Pelleas und Melisande*, composed between July 1902 and February 1903, is generally considered to be the first composition in which Schoenberg seriously tried his hand at the integration of elements of a multi-movement cycle in a single-movement composition. The nature of this procedure initially seems to have eluded even Schoenberg's most dedicated students. Anton Webern in 1912, for instance, still thought that the piece had a rhapsodic form and wrote that "its construction is entirely free."[7] It was only Alban Berg's renowned analytical study of *Pelleas und Melisande* from 1920 that pointed explicitly in the direction of a two-dimensional sonata form.

No discussion of *Pelleas* can ignore Berg's analysis, which is summarized in figure 16.[8] According to Berg, mm. 1–160 constitute a first movement in sonata form without a development and with an abridged recapitulation. Mm. 1–43 function as an introduction and mm. 44–136 as an exposition comprising a main theme group (mm. 44–74), a transition (mm. 75–88), a subordinate theme group (mm. 89–123), and a closing group (mm. 124–136). This exposition is immediately followed by what Berg refers to as a "developmental recapitulation" (mm. 137–160). The second movement consists of a series of episodes or "scenes" (as Berg calls them), each of which corresponds to a scene from Maeterlinck's play: the scene at the fountain in the park (mm. 161–216), the scene at the castle tower (mm. 244–282), and the scene in the vaults beneath the castle (mm. 283–301). The second episode is separated from the first by a unit that Berg refers to as an epilogue (mm. 217–243).

The slow movement begins with what Berg describes as a "developmental introduction" (mm. 302–328) and continues with an extended adagio (mm. 329–460). The finale opens with a return of the introduction from the first movement (mm. °461–504) and continues with a recapitulation of the first movement's main theme (mm. 505–514) along with the theme from the slow movement (mm. 515–540). After another episode (mm. 541–565), the composition concludes with a substantial epilogue in ternary form (mm. 566–646).

The keystone of Berg's analysis is that the finale of the multi-movement sonata cycle is constructed as a sonata-form recapitulation. Thus, he argues, a large single-movement sonata form can be said to lie at the basis of the entire piece. From this perspective, the large units that precede the recapitulation, and which Berg initially describes as the movements of a sonata cycle, are retrospectively (and implicitly) reinterpreted as the introduction, exposition, and development of an overarching sonata form. It is easy to rephrase Berg's observations in the terminology developed in Chapter 1. He identifies the first movement of the sonata cycle with the introduction and exposition of the overarching sonata form, and the finale of the cycle with the recapitulation and coda of the form, while regarding both interior movements as interpolations in the overarching sonata form. In his view, the overarching sonata form does not contain any exocyclic units.

Although many analysts of *Pelleas* have taken Berg's interpretation as a starting point, few have wholeheartedly embraced it.[9] Critical comments on Berg's analysis in Schoenberg scholarship on both sides of the Atlantic have recently culminated in Ethan Haimo's plainly dismissive account in his 2006 book *Schoenberg's Transformation of Musical Language*. Haimo leaves little doubt as to what he thinks of Berg's analysis: "The analysis of *Pelleas und Melisande* as an abstract symphonic design is—to put it delicately—farcical. Everything about it is wrong" [Haimo 2006, p. 94]. Haimo also suspects a hidden agenda behind Berg's interpretation. Berg, he argues, invented an abstract and more or less traditional formal organization in order not to have to talk about the program. In trying to make a piece of program music look like a work of absolute music, Haimo continues, Berg attempted to mold *Pelleas und Melisande* to the aesthetic climate of the years following World War I, in which program music was considered one of the more questionable legacies of a long bygone nineteenth century. In doing so, Berg (still according to Haimo) was acting as a henchman for Schoenberg; Haimo even goes so far as to suggest that Berg operated as nothing less (or nothing more) than Schoenberg's ghostwriter [2006, p. 93].

```
° 1–160: FIRST MOVEMENT
    ° 1–43: INTRODUCTION (Im Walde)
    44–136: EXPOSITION
        44–74:    main theme group (Golo macht Melisanden zu seiner Frau
                  und bringt sie in das Schloß)
        75–88:    transition
        89–123:   subordinate theme group (Im Schlosse lernt Melisande
                  den jungen Stiefbruder Golos kennen)
        124–136:  closing group
    137–160: DEVELOPMENTAL RECAPITULATION

    161–301: SECOND MOVEMENT
    °161–216: [episode] (scherzo-like) (Szene am Springbrunnen)
    217–243: epilogue
    244–282: [episode] (Szene am Schloßturm)
    283–301: [episode] (Szene in den Gewölben unter dem Schlosse)

    302–460: SLOW MOVEMENT
    302–328: developmental introduction
    329–460: adagio (Abschieds- und Liebesszene zwischen Pelleas und Melisande)

° 461–646: FINALE – RECAPITULATION
    °461–504: recapitulation of introduction
    505–514: recapitulation of main theme group
    515–540: recapitulation of slow-movement theme
    541–565: [episode] (Das Sterbegemach Melisandens)
    566–646: epilogue (ternary)
```

Figure 16: formal overview of *Pelleas und Melisande* after Berg's analysis

CHAPTER 5

Berg's position is more nuanced than Haimo is willing to admit. Haimo conceives of the relationship between program and traditional musical form as a binary opposition: either *Pelleas und Melisande* is a piece of program music, or it has a symphonic design. The possibility that form and program interact is never considered. Haimo's decision to project this binary opposition onto Berg's analysis appears, however, somewhat forced. There is no denying that Berg has a hard time balancing form and program. Yet it is not that he ignores or even downplays the existence of the program. As the opening of the analytical portion of his essay illustrates (reproduced as figure 17), Berg's text is organized as a constant alternation of a limited number of different types of information: formal categories that are hierarchically organized (capitalized and in bold type); numbered references to music examples in the thematic table at the end of the booklet; analytical comments on these examples or programmatic labels for them; quotations from the German translation of Maeterlinck's play (in italics); and Berg's own narration of the story.

Berg rarely addresses the interaction between program and form in a direct way: both simply run parallel in his description. He does not, however, conceive of them as mutually exclusive. This becomes absolutely clear from his opening remarks:

> Schoenberg's music, based on the idea and the inner events of [Maeterlinck's] drama, reproduces its exterior action only in very broad terms. Never is the music purely descriptive; the symphonic form of absolute music is always maintained. ... How such a purely musical form nonetheless corresponds to Maeterlinck's drama, and how it depicts a limited number of scenes from the poem [sic], is shown in the following analysis.[10]

Berg does not say that the music is not determined by the drama—only that it is determined more by the drama's "inner events" than by its "exterior action"; he does not say that the music is not descriptive—only that it is not "purely descriptive"; and he does not say that *Pelleas* is first and foremost a piece of absolute music—only that Schoenberg has it both ways: a representation of Maeterlinck's drama and a symphonic design.

But how, then, is Haimo's seemingly unsympathetic stance towards Berg to be explained? I surmise that in accusing Berg of deliberately misrepresenting the aesthetic and analytical facts about *Pelleas*, Haimo is, paradoxically, trying to defend him. Haimo is not prepared to accept that Berg is sincere when he proposes an analysis that to him seems so utterly unconvincing. All speculations about ideological motivations concerning program and absolute music aside, there is no denying that a central concern throughout the reception history of *Pelleas*

Figure 17: first page of Berg's analysis of *Pelleas und Melisande* (reproduced from the original edition, Vienna 1920)

und Melisande has been that Berg's analysis simply fails to convince, as Derrick Puffett has amply illustrated [Puffett 1995].

In my view this is a problem of form more than of content. I believe Berg's central point about *Pelleas*—that the work combines a single-movement sonata form with a multi-movement sonata cycle—to be essentially justified. But his claim fails to convince for at least two reasons. Berg systematically neglects to justify his position by means of a detailed argumentation, and he only rarely comments on what current-day analysts find exceptional or requiring explanation. It is as if Berg's decision to analyze *Pelleas und Melisande* as a combination of a multi-movement sonata cycle and a single-movement sonata form automatically triggers the deployment of a host of terms in a fixed order, which are then attached to the nearest more or less appropriate formal unit, and that this operation requires

CHAPTER 5

no further justification. There can be little doubt that this style of analytical writing is partly dictated by the generic conventions of the concert guide for the general public. Yet this does not remove the semblance of arbitrariness from many of Berg's analytical decisions. In my view, this is what has caused the rather unfortunate reception history of his analysis.

All this is not to deny that many of the details of Berg's interpretation, regardless of his formulation, are highly debatable, nor to say that the combination of a sonata form and a sonata cycle is all that is noteworthy about the form of *Pelleas*. As Carl Dahlhaus pointed out more than thirty years ago, at least four things are going on simultaneously in *Pelleas*: a succession of musical scenes following the outlines of Maeterlinck's play, a leitmotivic organization reminiscent of music drama, a four-movement symphonic cycle, and a single-movement sonata form [Dahlhaus 1974, pp. 128–129]. Berg's critics have one-sidedly emphasized only two of these four processes: the succession of scenes and the leitmotivic organization.[11] In the following paragraphs, I want to restore the balance to a certain extent. I will move from the least to the most contested aspects of Berg's analysis—from his remarks on the interior movements to his reading of *Pelleas* in its entirety as a sonata form—complementing, refining, and correcting it where appropriate, and recasting it in the terminological and conceptual framework of two-dimensional sonata form.

Most authors agree that what Berg calls the beginning of the second movement indeed marks the onset of a new large formal unit. To be sure, its opening material is not completely new: Puffett has demonstrated that it begins with a largely diatonicized ornamental variation of the so-called "Melisande motive" (first heard in mm. °12–13) [Puffett 1995, p. 221]. Nonetheless, the motive appears here so radically transformed that it generates a complete contrast with the preceding formal unit in terms of character, tempo, meter, and key. Example 12 compares both versions of the motive.[12]

Example 12: Schoenberg, *Pelleas und Melisande*, "Melisande motive": (a) mm. °12–13; (b) mm. °161–163

One major corrective to Berg's analysis that several authors have proposed is to locate the division between the interior movements in m. 328 rather than in m. 301, thus severing Berg's "developmental introduction" from the rest of the slow movement. Admittedly, the contrast between mm. 302–328 and 329ff is not significantly stronger than that between mm. 302–328 and the unit that precedes it. Yet while this kind of contrast between relatively short units characterizes the entire passage between mm. 161 and 328, the slow movement from m. 329 onwards is far more homogeneous. If, moreover, mm. 302–328 are interpreted as part of the second movement, the latter becomes a succession of five episodes (mm. 161–222, 223–243, 244–282, 283–301, and 302–328). As Christian Martin Schmidt has observed, this succession is superseded by another five-part division—mm. 161–213, 214–243, 244–258, 259–301, and 302–328—that partly transgresses the borders of the episodes. "By elaborating certain motive groups," Schmidt writes, "expressive spheres are formed, which are ordered symmetrically: dance-like – dramatic – lyrical – dramatic – dance-like."[13]

Berg's claim that the unit between the end of the first movement and the beginning of the slow movement constitutes an actual movement nonetheless appears overstated. Although the first of the series of episodes has the stylistic characteristics of a scherzo, it cannot in itself be considered a movement. It begins in A major with what seems to be a period. Mm. 161–169 clearly form an antecedent (A: I→V), but while mm. 170–177 begin as the corresponding consequent, they end as a new antecedent, mm. 174–178 repeating mm. 165–169 up a minor second (A: I→B♭: V). Mm. 179–183 constitute yet another antecedent (B♭: I→V) that is not followed by a consequent. Instead, there follows a formal unit over a dominant pedal in B♭ major that suddenly shifts to a dominant in B major (mm. 184–189). This unit is repeated up a minor second (B: V→C: V) and followed by what is best described as a liquidation phase (mm. 196–213). The liquidation process reaches a climax in mm. 214–217, after which a transition to the next episode follows. This fragment cannot be considered an interpolated movement for the same reasons as the episode in mm. 197–231 in *Don Juan*: it is too short in comparison to the other movements of the cycle, its layout cannot be regarded as a form, and reshaping it into a potentially autonomous unit would require serious modifications. In addition to this, the fragment here is tonally open-ended. The entire passage up to and including m. 328 likewise does not amount to a full-blown scherzo movement. Unless one is willing to interpret the relatively loose juxtaposition of contrasting episodes as a characteristic of a scherzo, mm. 161–328 can at most be considered a placeholder for a movement in the sonata cycle.

The slow movement is of a completely different nature. It is much more homogeneous than the preceding series of episodes, even though it reveals no traditional formal plan. Although Frisch's comment that it is reminiscent of both a rondo and sonata form is not entirely unjustified, Frisch himself ultimately argues that any traditional formal pattern is "overridden to a large extent by an ongoing developmental process that builds toward successive climaxes" [Frisch 1993, p. 173]. The movement begins by presenting two contrasting themes, one in E major, the second modulating from E major to C♯ major (mm. 329–354). Thereupon the head motives of both themes are developed separately, each development leading to a climax (mm. 355–376 and 377–389). After a contrasting unit, a third development combines material from both themes and leads to the movement's ultimate climax (402–444), which is followed by a coda (mm. 445–460) (figure 18).

mm. 329–345	Theme A	→ E: HC
mm. 346–354	Theme B	→ C♯: HC
mm. 355–371	Development of A	(D♭ →)
mm. 372–376	Climax	
mm. 377–383	Development of B	
mm. 384–389	Climax	
mm. 390–401	Contrast	
mm. 402–420	Development of A and B	(F →)
mm. 421–444	Climax	
mm. 445–460	Coda	

Figure 18: Schoenberg, *Pelleas und Melisande*: overview of the slow movement

The slow movement offers superb examples of how well *Formenlehre* categories developed out of Schoenberg's theoretical work after his death apply to Schoenberg's own music. Its opening theme (theme A in figure 18 and shown in example 13) is a sixteen-measure hybrid of the antecedent + continuation type. The first four measures can be regarded as either a compound basic idea or a small-scale sentential gesture (a one-measure basic idea, its repetition, and two measures of continuation) that, by analogy to the "evolving presentation" discussed in relation to the main theme of Strauss's *Don Juan*, could be dubbed an "evolving basic idea." On a higher level, these four measures are complemented by the next

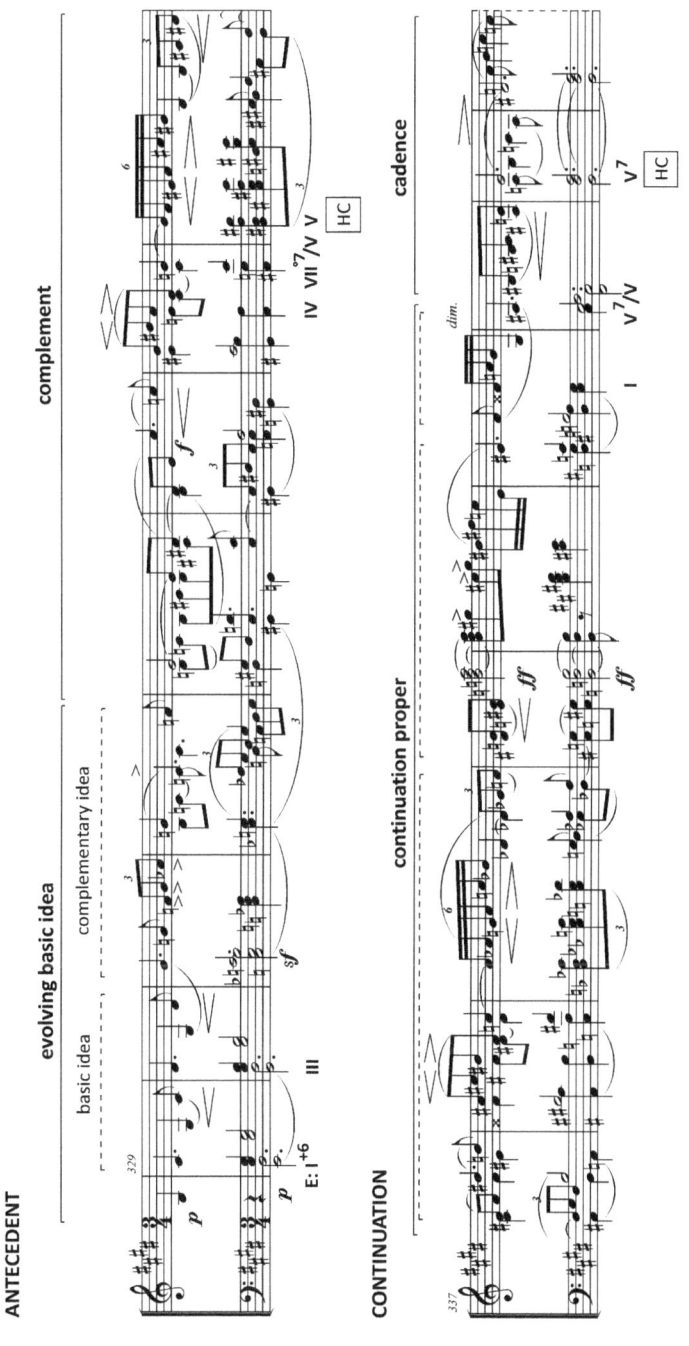

Example 13: Schoenberg, *Pelleas und Melisande*: slow movement, theme A (mm. 329–345)

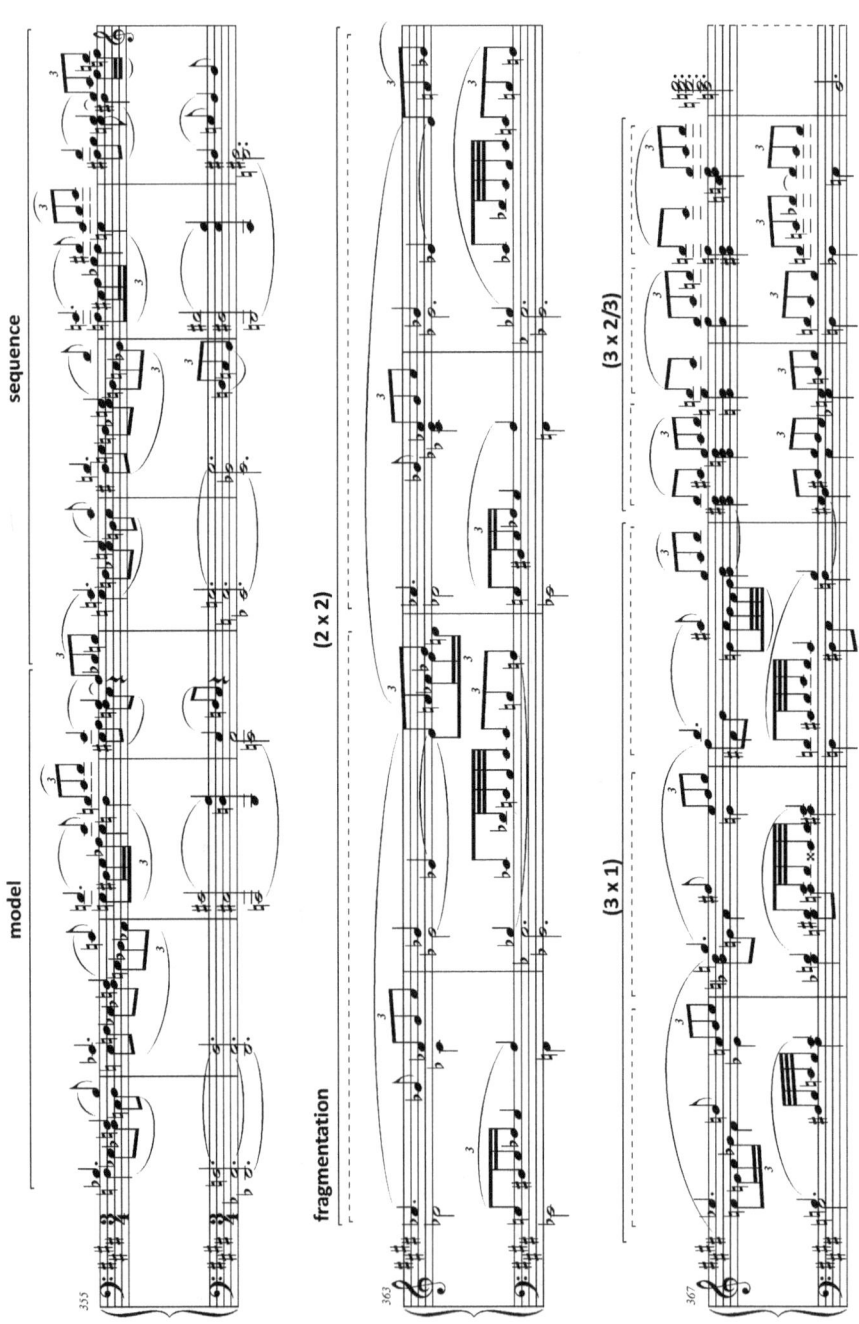

Example 14: Schoenberg, *Pelleas und Melisande*: slow movement: development (beginning), mm. 355–372

four measures to form an antecedent. The continuation begins with the isolation and immediate sequencing of the last three measures of the antecedent. This is followed by a further varied repetition of these three measures and an isolation of their final motive, after which the phrase comes to a rest on an HC.

Formenlehre categories are even more appropriate to describe the development of this theme, reproduced as example 14. Model-sequence-fragmentation technique is deployed here in an almost exemplary way. The process begins by presenting the four-measure basic idea from the antecedent as a model that the next four measures repeat up a major second. The isolation of the model's last two measures marks the beginning of a systematic fragmentation process: the two-measure starting point is first reduced to one measure and then compressed to two-thirds of a measure, while successive units of the same length group together into larger units of four, three, and two measures respectively.

Although the slow movement as a whole does not correspond to any standard pattern of formal organization, its constituent units consist of elements that are similar to the ones analysts working in the *Formenlehre* tradition have described in so much detail in instrumental music from the late eighteenth and early nineteenth centuries. Moreover, the interplay between these elements generates the contrast between tight-knit and looser units that articulates the movement's form. The theme, with its solid harmonic frame of an opening tonic chord and a concluding HC in E major, its balanced grouping structure, and developmental activity neatly contained in the continuation, is tight-knit; its development, characterized by tonal-harmonic openness, frequent sequencing, the forward-oriented gradual foreshortening of time-spans, and a concurrent liquidation process that spans the entire unit, is considerably looser.

From the perspective of two-dimensional sonata form, it is interesting to note that, like other interpolated movements I have discussed, this movement begins with material that strongly contrasts with its environment, but is then gradually integrated in the overarching form. Although Berg has derived the movement's opening theme from the opening gesture of the introduction [Berg 1994, p. 111], it initially gives the impression of being new. The integration process begins in m. 384, and from this point on the slow movement is infiltrated by material from the overarching sonata form. At the climax in mm. 384–389, the "Melisande motive" and the head of the subordinate theme are heard together, and both motives remain prominent in the entire subsequent unit (mm. 390–401), where they are joined by the motive first heard in mm. 124–127.

Berg's reading of the overall form of *Pelleas* as a sonata form has met with even greater resistance from later analysts than have his comments on the interior movements. Berg's most crucial analytical decision in this regard is to call m. 44

Example 15: Schoenberg, *Pelleas und Melisande*: sentential design in the main theme (mm. 44–54)

the beginning of the main theme ("Hauptsatz"). Not only does this decision relegate everything that came before to the status of an introduction, the use of the formal category "main theme" also is what triggers Berg's entire sonata-form reading. In the published version of his analysis, this claim appears unsubstantiated. In the more extended unpublished version, however, Berg points out that the theme, which was previously presented only as a leitmotiv, now takes a "symphonic shape" ("symphonischer Satzform") [1994, p. 101].

What Berg means becomes clear when we apply modern *Formenlehre* to the passage in question. The beginning of what he calls the main theme takes the form of a sentence, and it is the first formal unit in the piece to do so. As example 15 illustrates, the theme opens with a four-measure evolving basic idea and its sequential repetition and goes on with an abridged continuation of three measures that isolates the final measure of the model. Here, the sentential impetus (1+1+2) of the evolving basic idea becomes particularly relevant: the harmonic progression from the first to the second measure in the evolving basic idea (from I over VI^7 to II) is projected onto the presentation of the large sentence. Because of their sentential organization, these eleven measures are much more tight-knit than anything in the preceding forty-three measures. This stability is reinforced by the theme's harmonic vocabulary, which is tonally much more straightforward than the preceding portion of the piece.

The same tonal stability is, however, also the main objection to an interpretation of this theme as the beginning of an exposition. The apparent main theme is in the wrong key: it is in F major, whereas *Pelleas* as a whole is usually taken to be in D minor. Not surprisingly, it has even been argued that the theme behaves more like a subordinate theme than a main theme. But what *is* the tonic of this piece? Indications for D minor as a tonic are in fact extremely sparse in the opening portion of *Pelleas*. Before the entry of the F-major theme, no firm referential tonal centre has been established. If the opening of the introduction suggests any key at all, Haimo has noted, it suggests F (major/minor) and D (major/minor) in equal measure [Haimo 2006, p. 86]. Even though it is true that the few tonal clarifications present in the course of the introduction point to D rather than to F as a tonal centre, all of them remain so ephemeral that anything they might suggest is instantly overridden by the strong entry of F major in m. 44. Equally problematic is that this F major is itself very short-lived and never receives cadential confirmation. The supposed main theme modulates to A major after eleven measures, and this modulation is supported by a change in key signature. Since the unit Berg interprets as the subordinate theme group (mm. 89–123) begins in E major, A major may seem to be the governing key in the exposition.

Below, I will suggest why Schoenberg may have opted for this adventurous tonal strategy in light of the work's large-scale form. As for the more local level, suffice it to say that given the immense tonal instability in *Pelleas* as a whole and its first forty-three measures in particular, it might very well be that the establishment of long-term tonal stability—regardless of the key—is structurally more effective than the temporary confirmation of a specific key. Thus, the entry of the F-major theme in m. 44 undeniably generates a strong sense of stability. When this F-major passage is followed by a tonally stable passage in A major, this gives the large formal unit beginning in m. 44 a quality that is essentially different from that of the preceding unit. There can be little doubt that this is indeed the beginning of a main theme and, by consequence, of an exposition.

While Berg's interpretation of the F-major theme as a main theme is defensible, his interpretation of mm. 75–88 as a transition is far less so.[14] M. 80, the first measure of the second part of the transition, is an only slightly refashioned return of m. 67, which, in Berg's analysis, still belongs to the main theme group. Thus, it seems logical that mm. 67–74, at least, would belong to the transition as well. Another option is to let the transition begin in m. 55, with the varied repetition of the main theme in A major. In contrast to the original version of the theme in mm. 44–54, this repetition becomes increasingly interspersed with the "Melisande motive" from the introduction, especially from m. 57 onwards.

There is no question that the subordinate theme group begins in m. 89. Berg is not entirely clear about where it ends, but it seems safe to assume that he considers m. 113 as the beginning of the closing group.[15] In conjunction with the recombination of themes in the subsequent unit, the tempo change in m. 113 suggests that this is indeed the beginning of a new formal unit.[16] It is difficult to see, however, exactly why it would have to be a closing group. Not only do mm. 113–136 begin in yet another new key (F♯ minor, or d:♯III), they also contain numerous further modulations as well as two tempo changes. They even display an increasing, rather than a decreasing, thematic-motivic activity, so that they do not fulfill a closing function at all.

In view of Berg's interpretation of the following unit as a recapitulation, it seems more attractive to interpret mm. 113–136 as a development. To be sure, there is no sense of a development in any syntactic sense. But the various factors listed above—tempo changes, a combination of thematic material from various parts of the exposition, and a rather wayward modulatory trajectory—generate a loose texture that is more in line with what we expect of a development (possibly a pre-core of sorts) than with a closing group. As a result, the local sonata form in mm. 1–160 can be regarded as a complete sonata form, and no longer merely as a sonata form without development (as in Berg's analysis). It thus turns out to be much closer to what one would expect from a first movement of a symphonic cycle. Figure 19 illustrates the relationship between local and overarching sonata forms in mm. °1–160.

mm.	Overarching sonata form	Local sonata form
°1–43	Introduction	
44–54	Main theme group (F)	
55–88	Transition (A)	
89–112	Subordinate theme group (E)	
113–136	Development	Development
137–160	Development	Recapitulation (F)

Figure 19: identification of the local sonata form with the initial formal units of the overarching sonata form in *Pelleas und Melisande*

Several other objections have been raised against Berg's reading of the overarching sonata form. Matthias Schäfers, for instance, has pointed out the lack of a proper development section [Schäfers 1998, p. 389]. Although it is true that *Pelleas* does not contain one single large development section, a number of smaller units right after the exposition and right before the recapitulation (of the overarching sonata form) can be interpreted as developmental passages that frame the series of interpolated episodes and the slow movement. If, for instance, mm. 113–136 are interpreted as the development of the local sonata form rather than as the closing group of its exposition, there is no reason why they should not have the same function in the development in the overarching sonata form. The developmental traits of the recapitulation of the local sonata form (mm. 137–160) — the "developmental recapitulation" in Berg's terms — seem likewise to point in the direction of a simultaneous function as part of the development of the overarching sonata form. The main theme in this recapitulation is modified in several ways. As it is interspersed with the "Melisande motive," it is actually more closely related to the beginning of the transition from the exposition. Following the main theme is a unit that combines material from the exposition (the head of the subordinate theme) with material from the development of the local sonata form and completely new material (mm. 148–160). This unit has no equivalent in the exposition.

Also the return of the slow introduction after the slow movement's coda can be interpreted as a unit that occupies developmental space in the overarching sonata form rather than as one that initiates the recapitulation. A recapitulation that begins with a return of the introduction has, of course, its precedents in the nineteenth century. Yet interpreting mm. 460–481 as part of the recapitulation fails to explain why they are transposed down a minor second, why they are otherwise varied in comparison to their first appearance, or why they are separated from the recapitulation of the main theme group by an episode (mm. 482–504) that elaborates a motive added onto the return of the slow introduction. Moreover, this C♯-minor episode retrospectively clarifies the tonal position of the return of the introduction that precedes it. Together, both units operate as a large-scale dominant (or dominant substitute) preparation for the beginning of the recapitulation in m. 505. This becomes particularly clear when it ends on an augmented triad on V in D minor in m. 504.

Another objection to Berg's analysis that has been raised is that the tonal organization and thematic layout of mm. 505–565 are not those of a recapitulation. Not only is the main theme (mm. 505–514) recapitulated in a different key than that in the exposition (it is in D minor instead of F major now), it also appears in a heavily transformed and significantly less stable form. The further course of the recapitulation likewise differs radically from the exposition. In a manner reminiscent of *Tasso* and *Don Juan*, the subordinate theme group is substituted by the return of a theme that was first introduced after the exposition: in mm. 515–540, the abridged recapitulation of the main theme group is immediately followed by a transformation of the theme from the interpolated slow movement (the original and its transformation are shown in example 16), and the subordinate theme does not reappear later in the recapitulation. Mm. 541–565 constitute yet another episode, and m. 566 marks the beginning of the coda.

Example 16: Schoenberg, *Pelleas und Melisande*: (a) slow movement theme (mm. °329–332); (b) its transformation in the recapitulation (mm. 515–516)

It would be jumping to conclusions to infer from these differences between the recapitulation and the exposition that the recapitulation is identified with the finale. Certainly, the modifications to the recapitulation increase its independence

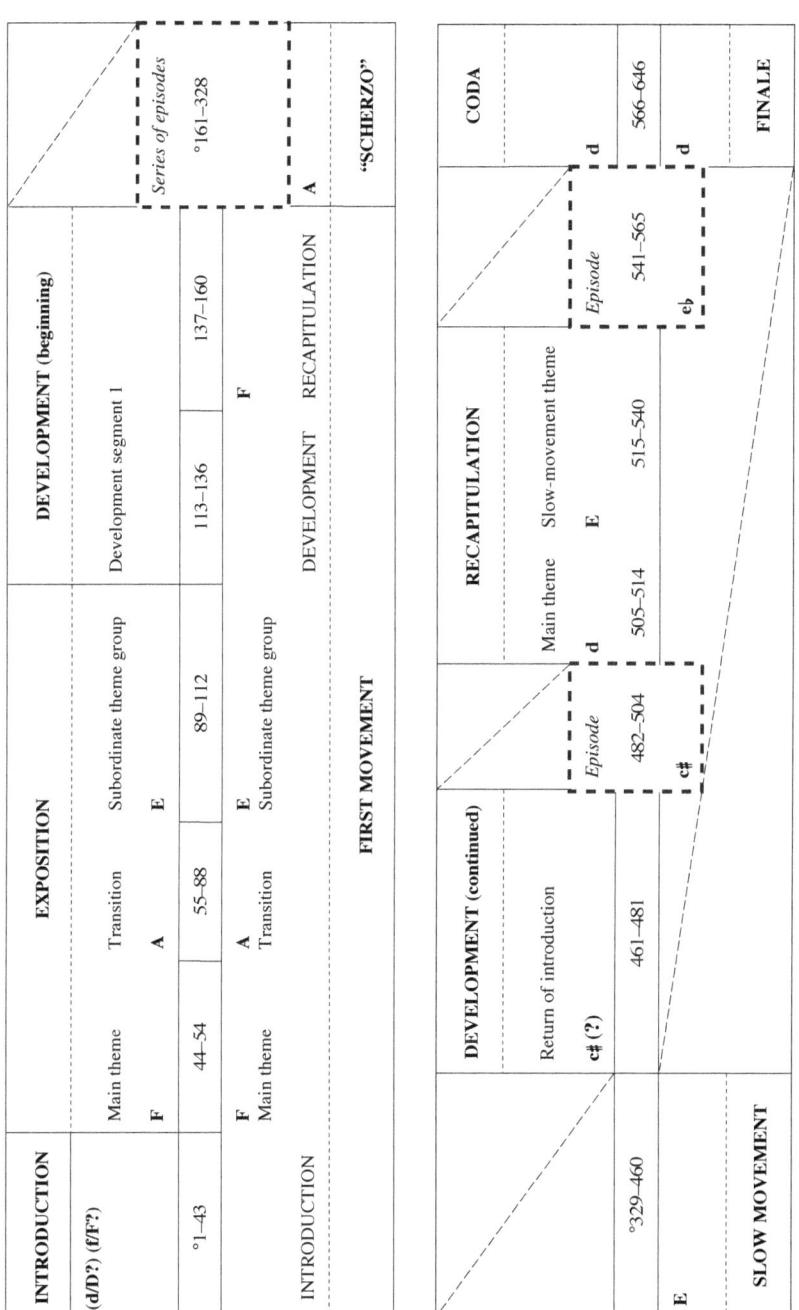

Figure 20: Schoenberg, *Pelleas und Melisande*: form and cycle

CHAPTER 5

from the exposition. They have, however, nothing to do with *Pelleas* being a two-dimensional sonata form. As has become clear in several of the preceding analyses, identifying the finale with the recapitulation is always precarious, because the modifications that articulate the finale can usually be explained without recourse to the dimension of the cycle. In *Pelleas und Melisande*, Schoenberg attempts to overcome this difficulty by dissociating the finale problem from the recapitulation problem: the finale begins only when the recapitulation is over. The recapitulation is, in other words, exocyclic, and the many modifications it contains merely serve to diminish its similarity to the exposition; the finale of the sonata cycle is identified only with the coda of the overarching sonata form.

Letting the finale begin only when the overarching sonata form is essentially over—the coda is, in Hepokoski and Darcy's terms, a "parageneric" space that lies outside "sonata space" [Hepokoski & Darcy 2006, p. 281]—has one significant advantage. In contrast to a recapitulation, the flexible formal conventions of a coda allow the finale to obtain a potentially autonomous formal organization. In *Pelleas*, the coda (and thus the finale) is a ternary form. Mm. 566–582 constitute a first section (A) that is firmly rooted in D minor and based exclusively on a new variant of the main theme. Mm. 583–610 function as a middle section (B), which has a more modulatory character and is more thematically heterogeneous, recalling thematic material from all three previous movements of the sonata cycle. An extended return of section A in mm. 611–634 is followed by the coda of the finale in mm. 635–646.

One might ask why the finale cannot be better interpreted as an interpolation. There are several reasons for this. First, it is difficult to accept that the final formal unit of a two-dimensional sonata form would not be part of the overarching sonata form. Second, the thematic dependence of the finale on the preceding units of the overarching sonata form is too strong to consider them an interpolated movement. Finally, it would be quite extraordinary for a sonata form of these proportions and from this tradition not to have a coda.

Figure 20 gives a complete overview of *Pelleas und Melisande*. The first movement of the sonata cycle is identified with the initial formal units of the overarching sonata form, a series of interpolated episodes takes the place of a second movement, the third movement is an interpolation, and the finale is identified with the coda. The final segments of the development and the entire recapitulation of the overarching sonata form are exocyclic.

The remarkable large-scale tonal organization of *Pelleas* warrants further reflection. One possible explanation for the recapitulation of the main theme being in D minor while its exposition is in F major is that it helps differentiate between the recapitulations of the local and the overarching sonata forms. Presenting the exposition's main theme in F major rather than in D minor allows Schoenberg to recapitulate the main theme in the local sonata form in its original key without having to write a recapitulation in the tonic so early in the piece. On the one hand, the return of the main theme in its original key guarantees that this return can be perceived as a recapitulation in the first place, rather than as a mere part of the development. On the other hand, writing an off-tonic local recapitulation clearly differentiates it from the recapitulation of the overarching sonata form, which is the first to bring the main theme back in the tonic.

At the same time, it becomes clear only in retrospect that the recapitulation of the overarching sonata form begins in the tonic. Nowhere before the onset of the recapitulation does D minor even begin to emerge as a tonic. After the tonally unstable introduction and initial stabilization in F major, the exposition decidedly veers towards A major as a tonic, with E major as a secondary key area. The shift to an A major tonic is further confirmed when the fifth relationship A–E is projected onto the tonal organization between the two interior movements. When D minor eventually appears at the beginning of the recapitulation, it is still very hazy, short-lived, and lacking cadential confirmation; in this respect, its status is weaker than that of F major at the beginning of the exposition. The recapitulation of the slow-movement theme in its original key even seems to pull the tonal plan back to E major. Only in the coda is D minor revealed to be the ultimate tonic of *Pelleas*. The emphasis on D minor in the coda retrospectively undermines the effect of the recapitulation as a formal event and heightens the significance of the finale as a movement in its own right. Example 17 provides an overview of the piece's large-scale tonal organization.

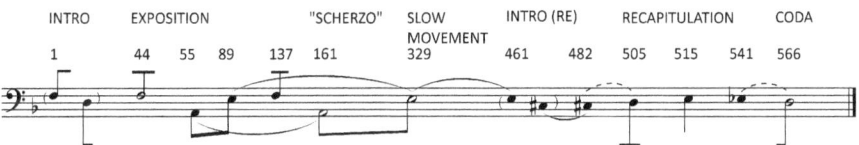

Example 17: large-scale tonal plan of *Pelleas und Melisande*

Like *Ein Heldenleben*, *Pelleas und Melisande* contains numerous episodes that appear to be motivated primarily by the program (they are, at least, more exclusively programmatic than the units that have a clear formal function in the sonata form or cycle). These include the series of episodes in mm. °161–328, the C♯-minor episode right before the recapitulation, and the E♭-minor episode immediately before the coda. In *Pelleas*, these episodes tend to assume some formal function. As we have seen, the series of episodes is subsumed under the scherzando character of the episode that opens it, occupying the position of a scherzo in the dimension of the cycle. The two other programmatic episodes (mm. 482–504 and 541–565) are given a function in the piece's large-scale tonal organization. They create a double chromatic approach to the tonic: from the lower chromatic neighbor at the beginning of the exposition, and from the upper chromatic neighbor at the beginning of the coda. Both chromatic neighbors are superimposed in the augmented-sixth sonority that precedes the tonic several times in the last twelve measures of the piece.

Pelleas und Melisande occupies a pivotal position in the history of two-dimensional sonata form. On the one hand, some of the strategies Schoenberg employs to combine form and cycle fit right into the problem history of two-dimensional sonata form in the Liszt–Strauss tradition. At the same time, *Pelleas* prefigures several of the procedures he would use in his later two-dimensional sonata forms. In order to identify the first movement of the sonata cycle with the initial units of the overarching sonata form, Schoenberg adopts the strategy used in *Die Ideale* and *Don Juan*: part of the first movement is identified with the development of the overarching sonata form. As in those pieces, the double-functionality is not immediately apparent. The slow introduction and the exposition are only latently double-functional, fulfilling the same function in both dimensions. A dimensional disconnection takes place only in m. 113: while mm. 113–136 function as part of the development in the dimension of the form, they constitute the entire development of the first movement in the dimension of the cycle. It is, however, only in m. 137—the beginning of the recapitulation of the local sonata form—that the listener might feel urged to reinterpret the preceding units. Only here does it begin to become clear that the introduction, the exposition, and the beginning of the development function not only within one large one-dimensional sonata form, but also within the first movement of a sonata cycle. This reinterpretation is confirmed with the beginning of the first interpolated movement in m. °161. As we will see in the next chapter, Schoenberg would adopt a very similar strategy in his First String Quartet Op. 7.

In addition, Schoenberg develops a completely new strategy for the relationship between the sonata cycle's finale and the overarching sonata form: rather than with the recapitulation, the finale is identified with the coda of the overarching sonata form. The resulting dissociation of the problems of recapitulation and finale sets *Pelleas und Melisande* apart from all two-dimensional sonata forms analyzed up to now. Not identifying the finale with the recapitulation of the overarching sonata form has two advantages. One is that it mitigates the finale problem. Since the finale is identified with the coda instead of the recapitulation, possibilities to provide it with a form of its own considerably increase. The other advantage of this strategy is that it allows Schoenberg to write a finale that, in Michael Talbot's terms, is not exclusively summative in character (compare Chapter 2). Although summative aspects do play a role (not least because of thematic recollections from earlier movements in the middle section), the finale of *Pelleas und Melisande* belongs first and foremost to the valedictory type. The dissociation of finale and recapitulation too is a strategy Schoenberg would return to, albeit in a modified version. As I will demonstrate in Chapter 7, Schoenberg realizes the relationship between the finale and the overarching sonata form in the First Chamber Symphony Op. 9 in a somewhat similar way.

Notes

[1] For a detailed account of the biographical relationship between Strauss and Schoenberg see Schäfers 2001.
[2] The rondo view was first advanced by Egon Wellesz [1921, p. 76] and adopted most notably by Carl Dahlhaus [1974, p. 127], Walter Bailey [1984, p.35], and—with reservations—Walter Frisch [1993, pp. 112–116]. A reading as a single sonata form has been proposed by Wilhelm Pfannkuch [1963] and one as a double sonata form by Richard Swift [1977]. A table comparing these and other approaches to the form of *Verklärte Nacht* is included in Dale 2000, pp. 57–58.
[3] "Zur gleichen Zeit wie du, hatte ich die Partitur – die Grosse – von Strauss' Heldenleben einige Wochen zu Hause. Ich studierte sie genauestens!" [Zemlinsky 1995, p. 8].
[4] "Er wird den Eindruck haben, dass wir die rührendsten Jünger seiner Muse sind." Letter from Zemlinsky to Schoenberg from 2-2-1902 [Zemlinsky 1995, p. 7].
[5] In a letter to the wife of his Viennese patron Carl Redlich (the dedicatee of the *Sechs Lieder* Op. 3), Schoenberg wrote: "Richard Strauss found my things very interesting; he wants to hear the Sextet [*Verklärte Nacht*] when it is played and said that if I have something for orchestra, I should take it to him [and] he will perform it." "Richard Strauß hat meine Sachen sehr interessant gefunden; er will sich das Sextett, wenn es gespielt wird anhören und sagte ich möge ihm wenn ich etwas für Orchester habe es bringen, er werde es aufführen" (letter from 2–4–1902 quoted in Kokkinis & Kwasny 1999, p. 206).
[6] In an unpublished text from 1944, Schoenberg wrote: "Strauß in 1902, after having glanced through the (then unfinished) scores of my 'Pelleas' and 'Gurrelieder' procured me the 'Liszt-Stiftung' for two years of a thousand Marks yearly." Koussewitsky – Toscanini,

Arnold Schönberg Center Signatur T 42.03, quoted in Kokkinis & Kwasny 1999, p. 207, n. 13.

7 "Sein Bau ist ganz frei" [Webern 1912, p. 27].

8 Apart from his so-called *Kleiner Pelleas-Führer*, published in 1920, Berg also wrote a *Großer Pelleas-Führer*, which was never printed during his lifetime. An edition of the manuscript has found its way into the *Alban Berg Gesamtausgabe*. Although it is impossible to say with certainty which version is the elder, there are reasons to assume that "the more elaborate version is the more recent one, and therefore an expansion of the original shorter one" [Stephan & Busch 1994, p. xxxi]. The *Großer Pelleas-Führer*, to which I will refer as Berg 1994, lacks the introductory remarks and the table of instruments included in the shorter published version. Apart from the many different formulations—most of them without intrinsic consequences—the large guide also differs from the small one in the increased attention to variants, elaborations, and derivations of themes and motives, and in the presence of more and often longer music examples. Only very occasionally does the large guide include additional information relevant to Berg's interpretation of the formal organization of the composition. A complete English translation—unfortunately not always equally reliable—of the short version of Berg's analysis is printed in Puffett 1995, pp. 250–264.

9 Analyses of *Pelleas und Melisande* with substantial discussions of Berg's interpretation include Schweizer 1970, Ackermann 1992, Frisch 1993, pp. 158–177, Puffett 1995, Schäfers 1998, Haimo 2006, pp. 66–111, and Cherlin 2007, pp. 68–154.

10 "Die Musik Schönbergs – getragen von der Idee und dem inneren Geschehnis dieses Dramas – gibt dessen äußere Handlung nur in ganz groben Zügen wieder. Nie ist die Musik rein beschreibend; immer wird die symphonische Form absoluter Musik gewahrt. …Wie sich dennoch eine solche rein musikalische Form mit dem Drama Maeterlincks deckt und wie innerhalb derer auch einige wenige Szenen der Dichtung zur Darstellung gelangen, zeigt die folgend Analyse" [Berg 1920, p. 85].

11 For a very detailed analysis of the treatment of leitmotivs in *Pelleas* see Cherlin 2007, pp. 68–154.

12 The number and diversity of transformations of the "Melisande motive" throughout the piece is stunning. After its first presentation in the introduction (mm. °12–13), it is transformed at the beginning of the transition, where it functions as a counterpart to the continuation of the transposed return of the main theme (m. 61). Later on, it forms the basis not only for the theme of the scherzando episode (shown in example 8), but also for the sonic field at the beginning of the second episode (mm. 244ff). It also returns at the end of the slow movement, in the course of the dominant preparation for the recapitulation, in the recapitulation itself, and finally in the coda. Although not all of these occurrences of the motive are equally unequivocal examples of thematic transformation as defined in Chapter 2, it is particularly striking that it reappears in one form or another in each large formal unit of the piece, thus forming a web that spans the entire composition.

13 "Durch Verarbeitung bestimmter Motivgruppen sind Ausdruckssphären geformt, die in Symmetrie angeordnet sind: tänzerisch – dramatisch – lyrisch – dramatisch – tänzerisch" [Schmidt 1978, p. 185].

14 On this point compare Puffett 1995, p. 219 and Schäfers 1998, p. 389.

[15] So assumes Frisch too [Frisch 1993, p. 161]. The cause of the uncertainty is that on the one hand Berg refers only to the theme first presented in mm. 124–127 as the "theme of the closing group," while on the other, his description suggests that mm. 124ff belong together with the unit starting in m. 113.

[16] In mm. 113–136, the first thematic idea from the subordinate theme group is combined with the "Melisande motive" and the motive that opens the slow introduction, as well as with what Berg calls the "theme of the closing group." This clearly contrasts with the subordinate theme group, which is much more restrictive in its use of thematic-motivic material.

Chapter 6

Schoenberg's First String Quartet

From program to absolute music

Schoenberg continued to use two-dimensional sonata form in his two large-scale instrumental works after *Pelleas und Melisande*: the First String Quartet Op. 7 (1904–05) and the First Chamber Symphony Op. 9 (1906). It is within this group of single-movement works that the transition in his oeuvre from program to absolute music takes place: after the completion of *Pelleas*, Schoenberg transplanted the concept of two-dimensional sonata form, which had resolutely migrated to program music after Liszt's B-minor Sonata, back to absolute music.[1]

The transition from program to absolute music in Schoenberg's early works took place gradually. *Pelleas und Melisande* is program music through and through. Its program plays both a poietic role in its composition process and an aesthetic one in its reception. As Schoenberg recalled in 1949, he "tried to mirror every detail of [Maeterlinck's wonderful drama] with only a few omissions and slight changes of the order of the scenes."[2] Three decades earlier, during preparations for a performance of *Pelleas und Melisande* in Prague in 1918, Zemlinsky had asked whether a program was to be distributed among the audience and whether Schoenberg could provide one. In his reply, Schoenberg outlined the program and said he had nothing against its distribution.[3]

In contrast, no program exists that was designated to play an aesthetic role for the First String Quartet. Schoenberg never published a program in any form, nor did he ever refer to one in any of his writings. In the *Notes on the Four String Quartets*, he even explicitly stated that after the completion of *Pelleas*, he "abandoned program-music and turned in a direction that was much more [his] own than all the preceding" [Schoenberg 1949d, p. 37]. In a composition class at the University of California at Los Angeles in 1940, however, Schoenberg is reported to have mentioned the existence of a program for his First String Quartet. His student Dika Newlin entered in her diary on March 6, 1940 [Newlin 1980, p. 193]:

> Today [Schoenberg] offered a tantalizing new sidelight on the work, one that I'd give anything to know more about. He said some of the extravagances of the form were because the piece was really a sort of "symphonic poem," and

> when [Leonard] Stein pressed him as to whether there was a definite program to it or not, he replied promptly, "Oh yes, very definite—but private!"

Schoenberg famously refused to enter into detail—"One does not tell such things anymore"—so Newlin concluded that "the great secret will remain forever unrevealed" [Newlin 1980, p. 193].

In the 1980s, however, Christian Martin Schmidt discovered a "private" program on a leaf glued to the back of the sketchbook Schoenberg used when writing his First String Quartet [see Schmidt 1986b].[4] This program is not a continuous text, but an ordered collection of isolated phrases and single words, definitely not intended for publication. Certain phrases can easily be related to moments in the composition, but for others any attribution to what happens in the score remains hypothetical or even problematic. Although there is little doubt that this program has played a role in the genesis of the piece, it is not clear to what extent it did so. Mark Benson has argued that the program was sketched out, at the earliest, four and a half months after the beginning of the composition [Benson 1993, pp. 380–382], and it is not clear whether Schoenberg continued working with it throughout the completion of the quartet. Given the discrepancy between the artistic merits of the program and those of the composition, it is understandable that Schoenberg decided not to publish the program. For the same reason, the attention it has recently received seems misplaced, or at least exaggerated.

For the First Chamber Symphony, finally, no program appears to exist at all. Schoenberg never referred to one—whether officially or casually—and there is no material indication that there has ever been anything that comes remotely close to a program for this composition. The Chamber Symphony is Schoenberg's first instrumental composition with an opus number never to have included programmatic elements at any point in its genesis or reception.

□

The formal organization of Schoenberg's First String Quartet has received ample attention in Schoenberg scholarship in the late twentieth and early twenty-first centuries.[5] Today, there is by and large a consensus that it comprises an exposition and a development (mm. 1–398), a scherzo (mm. 399–783), further development (mm. 784–908), a recapitulation of the main theme group (mm. 909–951), a slow movement (mm. °952–1067), a transition (mm. 1068–1081), a recapitulation of the subordinate theme group (mm. 1082–1121), a finale (mm. 1122–1260), a transition (1261–1269), and a coda (mm. 1270–1320). The first movement of the sonata cycle is identified with the first 398 measures of the overarching sonata form, while the scherzo, the slow movement, and the finale are interpolated. Figure

21 gives a formal overview of the work. The second development, recapitulation, and coda of the overarching sonata form are exocyclic units.

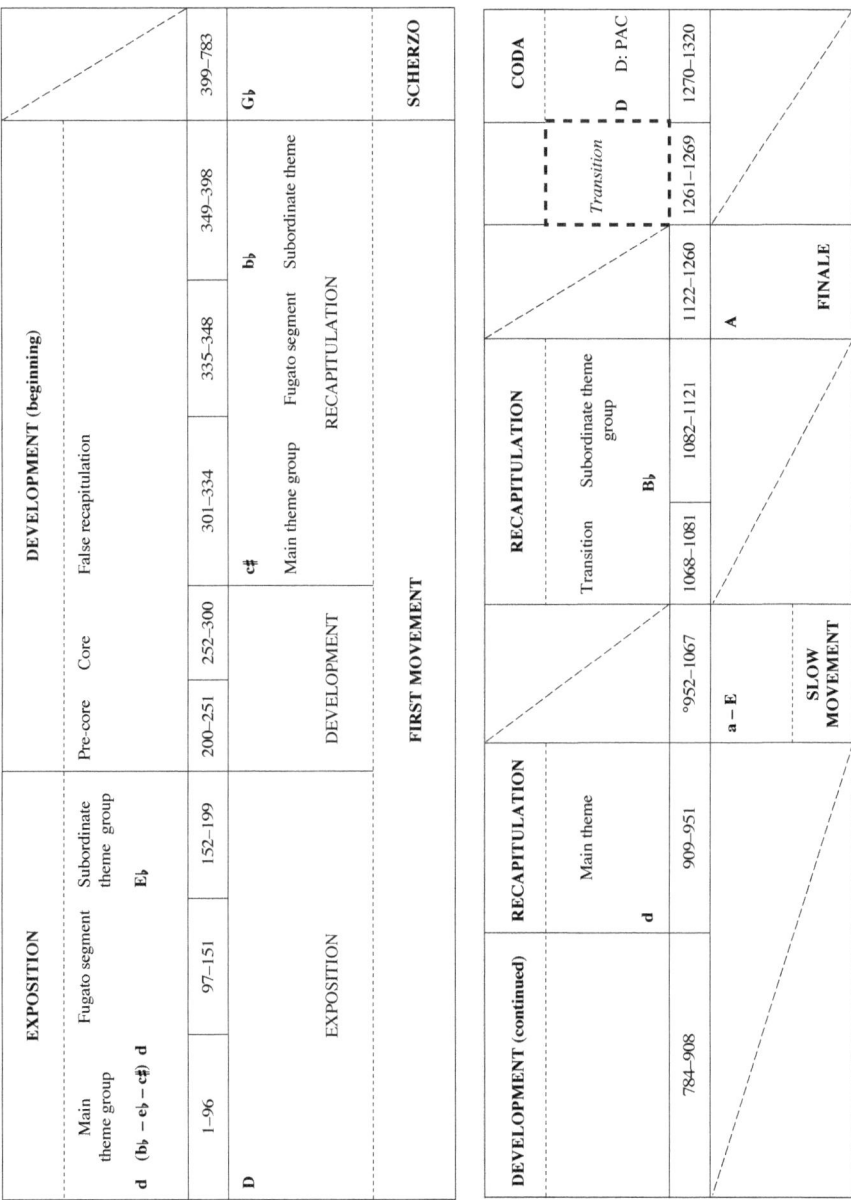

Figure 21: Schoenberg, First String Quartet: form and cycle

CHAPTER 6

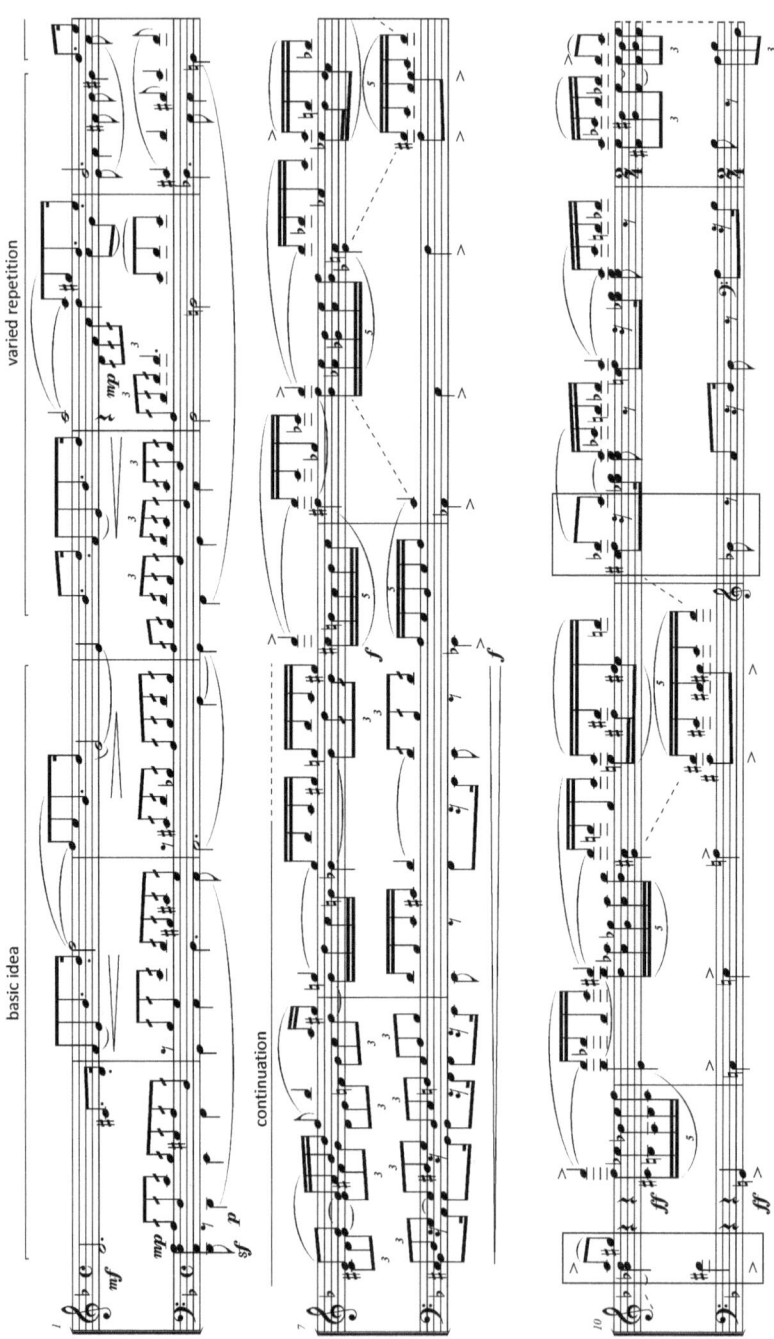

Example 18: Schoenberg, First String Quartet: main theme (beginning) (mm. 1–13)

In this chapter, I first offer an analysis of the exposition and the beginning of the development of the overarching sonata form. I then go on to show how the first movement of the sonata cycle is identified with these units. Next, I focus on the three interpolated movements, paying particular attention to the manifold ways in which they are integrated into the overarching sonata form. I conclude the chapter with a number of remarks on the overall formal and tonal organization of the piece.

Issues of form in the overarching sonata form

The main theme group in Schoenberg's First String Quartet extends from mm. 1 to 96 and has an intricate formal organization. Its opening thirteen measures, shown in example 18, have a sentential design, with a basic idea in mm. 1–3, a varied repetition of the basic idea in mm. 3–6, and a continuation in mm. °7–13. In the repetition of the basic idea, the melody (but not the basic idea as a whole) shifts metrical position by condensing its opening note from three beats to one. Alternatively, and as Walter Frisch has proposed, one could hear an overlap between the last note of the melody in the basic idea and the first of its repetition [Frisch 1993, p. 194]. The continuation does not lead to a recognizable cadence, but it does achieve closure through an arrival on two interlocking whole-tone tetrachords in mm. 10 (f♯-d-b♭-g♯) and 12 (b♭-e-f♯-c), the last one followed by what may be dubbed a "standing on the arrival chord."

The next unit, which relates to the former by the principle of "contrasting derivation" ("kontrastierende Ableitung"),[6] has a sentential design as well: mm. 14–15 are a basic idea, mm. 16–17 its varied repetition, and mm. 18–23 a continuation. Mm. 24–29 provide closure to the first part of the main theme group.

In its internal fabric, this opening unit differs considerably from the idiom of Schoenberg's earlier compositions, and, indeed, from all nineteenth-century two-dimensional sonata forms discussed in the previous chapters. Along with the very intense and almost systematic thematic-motivic relationships that pervade the entire quartet, this is the most palpable manifestation of Schoenberg's move back in the direction of the Beethoven–Brahms tradition. In its combination of musical prose (the asymmetrical relationship between the basic idea and its repetition in mm. 1–6), developing variation (the twofold varied repetition of the basic idea in mm. 3–6 and at the beginning of the continuation in mm. 6–8), and contrasting derivation between mm. 1ff and mm. 14ff, mm. 1–29 offer a textbook example of how much Schoenberg's instrumental music from this period owes to Brahms.

On the largest scale, the main theme group has a ternary organization.[7] Mm. 1–29 constitute an exposition (A), mm. 30–64 a very developmental contrasting middle (B), and mm. 65–96 begin as a recapitulation (A'). In spite of the complex foreground harmonies, the main theme group's underlying tonal plan is very clear: as example 19 illustrates, its exposition and recapitulation begin in D minor, while the middle tonicizes E♭ minor and C♯ minor respectively—the chromatic neighbors to D minor (the tonicization of both chromatic neighbors, incidentally, echoes aspects of the tonal organization of *Pelleas und Melisande*). The transition from D minor to E♭ minor is mediated through B♭ minor. B♭ minor functions as a key centre in the second half of the exposition, which leads to an HC in E♭ minor. B♭ minor, E♭ minor, and C♯ minor will play a role later in the composition: E♭ major (instead of minor) is the key of the subordinate theme group in the exposition and C♯ minor that of the recapitulation of the local sonata form. B♭ minor returns as the subordinate key in the recapitulation of the local sonata form, while its parallel major operates as the subordinate key in the recapitulation of the overarching sonata form.

Example 19: Schoenberg, First String Quartet: tonal organization of the main theme group

As Lynn Cavanagh has demonstrated, the contrasting middle develops motivic material from the exposition in the order in which it originally appeared [Cavanagh 1996, p. 95]. Mm. 30–44 develop material from mm. 1–8, mm. 45–53 from mm. °9–13, and mm. 54–64 combine material from mm. 14–23 with material from mm. 1–8. This parallelism seems no sufficient reason, however, to limit the main theme group to mm. 1–64 and follow Cavanagh's interpretation of mm. 1–29 and 30–64 as the antecedent and consequent of a large and freely organized period. The relationship between both units is that of exposition and development; in no way—tonally, phrase-structurally, or texturally—do mm. 30–64 create a sense of balance in relation to mm. 1–30. Balance is achieved only in m. 65, with the varied return of part A in the original key.

At the same time, there is some truth to Cavanagh's assertion that m. 65 "marks the beginning of the transition process" [1996, p. 95]. Yet mm. 65ff are not merely a transition: they are at the same time an integral part of the main theme group. The recapitulation of the small ternary, in other words, *becomes* the transition. The transitional function becomes apparent only after several measures, but urges a retrospective reinterpretation of the function of the entire unit—without, however, completely overriding its original function as the recapitulation of the small ternary main theme group. By analogy to the period with dissolving consequent, one might call this phenomenon a small ternary with dissolving recapitulation.[8] It is not a particularly unique strategy, of course: examples from the core repertoire of *Formenlehre* include the main themes from the finale of Beethoven's Piano Sonata in C major Op. 2 no. 3 and from the first movement of Schubert's last Piano Sonata in B♭ major (D960).

In m. 97, the main theme gives way to a fugato on a seven-measure subject that will dominate the next large segment of the composition. The subject is stated in full for the first time at the second entry (violin 2, mm. °99–105), which is shown in example 20.

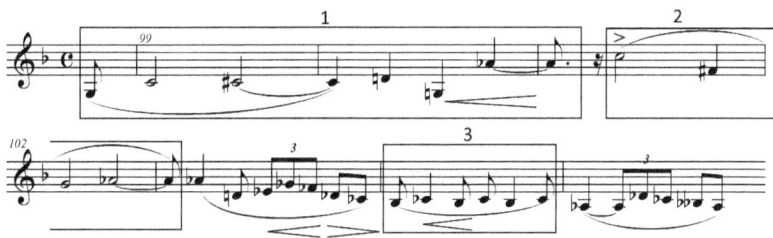

Example 20: Schoenberg, First String Quartet: motivic components in the fugato subject (mm. °99–105)

Each of the three distinct motivic components bracketed in example 20 return separately in the further course of the form. Traditionally, the fugato is assigned the formal function of a transition. Arguments for this interpretation are, however, rarely given, with the exception of the implicit argument of its position between the main theme group and what is obviously a subordinate theme group (from m. 152 onwards). Admittedly, the extreme tonal instability of this entire passage, which has been described as "one of the least tonally oriented passages in ... Schoenberg's music up to this point" [Frisch 1993, p. 189], might be thought of as being characteristic of a transition. Yet it is exactly because of its quasi-atonality that the fugato starkly contrasts with the tonally relatively stable units surrounding it. As a result, it does not exert a transitional function at all, but rather stands on its own. This is all the more true because it is itself preceded by a unit that already functions as a transition. It seems plausible, therefore, to consider mm. 97–151 as the second segment of an exposition that comprises three segments: the main theme group, the fugato segment, and the subordinate theme group. Although it is no less thematic than the main and subordinate theme groups, I will continue to refer to this second segment of the exposition as the "fugato segment" rather than as a "first subordinate theme group," not only to distinguish it from the third segment (the actual subordinate theme group), but also to emphasize its very different nature from the two segments that surround it.

The subordinate theme group, beginning in m. 152, consists of three thematic ideas, which are first presented in mm. 152–156, 157–158, and 159–166 respectively and then developed, varied, and recombined in various ways. Example 21 gives the opening measures of the subordinate theme; the different thematic ideas are bracketed.

Example 21: Schoenberg, First String Quartet: three thematic ideas in the subordinate theme (mm. 152–162)

The elaboration of these three ideas starts immediately after their presentation. Mm. 167–177 are based on a transformation of the second thematic idea, and mm. 178–187 combine a transformation of the first thematic idea with diminutions and inversions (sometimes both at the same time) of the second thematic idea. The subordinate theme group clearly begins in E♭ major; secondary key centers that receive some emphasis are C major (m. 167), G major (m. 172), and A♭ major (m. 178).

The return of E♭ major along with the first thematic idea of the subordinate theme group in its original shape (but in counterpoint with the third thematic idea) strongly suggests that mm. 188–199 conclude the subordinate theme group and, perhaps, the exposition as a whole. There is no doubt that the development is underway by m. 234. For the first time in the composition, material from all three different segments of the exposition is directly superimposed. While the violins continue to play subordinate-theme material, the bass line from the main theme appears in the viola, and the cello plays the head of the fugato subject. The next formal unit, starting in m. °253, has all the characteristics of a developmental core: mm. °253–258 present a six-measure model combining material from the main theme, the transition, and the subordinate theme. This model is repeated, up a perfect fifth, in mm. 259–264, and from m. 265 onwards it is subject to a fragmentation process. In mm. 276–280 a new model is developed organically from the preceding one by combining the motive resulting from the fragmentation process with the subordinate theme group's second idea. This new model is repeated, up a minor second, in mm. 281–285, and in m. 286 a liquidation process starts in which the second idea from the subordinate theme group is combined with a rhythmic figure that undoubtedly originates in the main theme. But what about mm. 200–233? It is difficult to determine whether they are still part of the exposition or whether they mark the beginning of the development. Their exclusive dependence on subordinate-theme material suggests that they still belong to the subordinate theme group, yet their unstable tempo as well as the preceding recapitulatory unit suggest that they do not. Moreover, mm. 200–207 are very closely related to the model presented at the beginning of the core, both in tempo and in the melodic content of the first violin's part (doubled in mm. 200–207 by the cello). All things considered, the most plausible option is probably to include mm. 200–233 in the development where, together with mm. 234–252, they occupy the position of a pre-core.

Each of the three segments of the exposition is connected to the next by a transition. The transitional function of mm. 65ff — connecting the main theme group to the fugato segment — becomes especially clear after the climax in m. 79, which marks the beginning of a liquidation of thematic material from the main theme. On the fourth beat of m. 85, an intervallic preparation of the fugato subject begins. Example 22 gives the crucial measures of this process. First, the viola ostentatiously brings an isolated diminished fifth into play, an interval that plays an important role in the main theme itself but has been absent in the last few measures. This diminished fifth remains prominent in the next few measures and becomes part of a motive derived from the main theme in the second violin from m. 90 onwards. In the mean time (from m. 88 onwards), the first violin introduces the interval of a perfect fourth, initially in a pizzicato figure linking two perfect fourths by a major third. After their temporary combination in m. 92, when the

Chapter 6

Example 22: Schoenberg, First String Quartet: transition from the main theme group to the fugato segment (mm. 84–100)

first violin links two perfect fourths by an augmented fourth, both intervals acquire the gestural characteristics, as well as the exact pitches, that they will have at the beginning of motivic components 1 and 2 in the fugato subject.

A comparable relationship exists between the end of the second and the beginning of the third segments of the exposition. The "oscillating" minor second from the end of the fugato subject is isolated and rhythmically augmented in the first violin from m. 146 onwards (as if to demonstrate its origin more clearly, the augmentation is directly confronted with the original shape in the second violin). In mm. 153–154, the augmented figure—now based on a major second—returns at the head of the first thematic idea of the subordinate theme group. As Frisch has noted, a second correspondence between both segments is that the first four notes of the second component of the fugato return in the lower parts at the very beginning of the subordinate theme group (mm. 152–153) [Frisch 1993, p. 190].

Identification

In Schoenberg's First Quartet, the first movement of the sonata cycle is identified with the exposition and with the beginning of the development of the overarching sonata form: each unit in mm. 1–398 fulfills a function in both the dimension of the cycle and that of the form. Initially, this double-functionality remains latent. In mm. 1–199, the presence of two dimensions is practically unnoticeable because they coincide completely, the exposition of the local sonata form being identical to the exposition of the overarching sonata form. The double-functionality temporarily becomes somewhat more palpable in the fugato segment. Since part of the fugato subject adumbrates the scherzo's main theme (see below), one of its functions in the dimension of the cycle is to announce the second movement. This function obviously remains meaningless in the dimension of the form and does not entail a structural difference between the two dimensions.

The first segments of the development of the overarching sonata form—a pre-core in mm. 200–252 and a core beginning in m. °253—have the same function in both dimensions as well. It is not until m. 301 that dimensions are really disconnected, since mm. 301–398 are the first formal unit to fulfill two completely different functions simultaneously. While in the dimension of the form they are yet another unit in the development section, they function as the recapitulation of the first movement in the dimension of the cycle. This conflict between non-identical functions sheds new light on the preceding portion of the composition, revealing that there were two different dimensions at work all along. Only here is the listener urged to reconsider what he or she has heard before and to interpret it not only as the exposition and the beginning of the development in one sonata form, but also as the exposition and the entire development in another, smaller-scale sonata form.⁹

In mm. 301–398 the opposing functions the same formal unit has to fulfill in the different dimensions can no longer easily be reconciled. As the recapitulation of the first movement in the dimension of the cycle, mm. 301–398 are required to have a stabilizing function and to have a layout that more or less parallels that of the exposition; in a one-dimensional sonata form, the recapitulation of the main theme would induce a sense of tonal and thematic return, and that of the subordinate theme group would resolve the tonal conflict established in the exposition. If, on the other hand, the same formal unit has to function as part of the development section of the overarching sonata form, its main tasks consist of the working out of the material presented in the exposition as well as the generation or prolongation of an overall instability.

Mm. 301–398 exemplify in a particularly eloquent way how the opposing demands of both dimensions can be dealt with, and how the tension between them can be kept under control at a point at which it threatens to become most problematic. The clearest indication of their function as the recapitulation of the local sonata form is, quite obviously, the return of the three thematic groups from the exposition in the original order: the main theme group in mm. 301–334, the fugato segment in mm. °335–348, and the subordinate theme group in mm. 349–379.

At the same time, a number of important changes have been made to each of these groups in order to allow them to meet some of the main requirements of a development section. It is from this perspective, for instance, that one can understand why the recapitulation starts in C♯ minor instead of D minor, and why each of its segments is radically abridged and recomposed. The restoration of tonal stability is avoided, and although thematic material from the exposition is clearly recapitulated, it is subject to developmental treatment by means of reorganization, recombination, variation, and elaboration.

The original formal organization of the main theme group, for example, has completely disappeared. At the beginning of the theme, the original upper voice still survives, but it has moved to the bass. The other voices have been replaced by the obstinate repetition of a rhythmic figure from the cello part in m. 7 of the main theme, a change in texture that has been prepared by the same rhythmic figure in the immediately preceding unit of the development (mm. 286–300). Phrase-structurally, only the first six measures of the theme (the basic idea and its repetition) are identical to the exposition. From the onset of the continuation, the recapitulation follows a completely new path. In mm. 307–308, the variant of the main theme's head motive that opens the continuation in the exposition is replaced by a return of the original head motive. This is followed by the related motive familiar from m. °9, so that the recapitulation actually refers to part A' of the original main theme group rather than to part A itself. A systematic liquidation process starting in the second half of m. 309 (2 + 1,5 + (4x1) + (4x½) + (4x¼) measures) leads to a new formal unit in mm. 320–329. This unit is based on the upper voice of m. 81 from the exposition, but develops in a completely different way. Finally, a short concluding unit follows in mm. 330–334. Although very clearly derived from the basic idea of the main theme, it does not as such occur in the exposition.

The fugato segment in the recapitulation of the local sonata form is even more radically recomposed than the main theme group. Unlike its counterpart in the exposition, it retains, and even increases (*Viel rascher*), the momentum of the main theme group, starting as a kind of stretto on a slightly expanded version of the head of the fugato subject. In m. °342, the fourth, fifth, and sixth notes of this first component are isolated to build an ostinato. Once this ostinato is tonally stabilized in B♭ minor (m. 349), it serves as the accompaniment to a transformed version of the head motive of the first thematic idea from the subordinate theme group. Smoother versions of the same ostinato accompany the return of a portion of the second thematic idea in D major (mm. 360–362) and, after a brief interruption, the beginning of the third idea (starting in F major, mm. 366–371). Somewhat surprisingly, this idea is joined by the original bass line of the main theme. The presence of this bass line here is, however, mediated by a motivic relationship. As example 23 illustrates, both the second thematic idea of the subordinate theme group and the bass line of the main theme begin with two groups of three adjacent notes in the same direction that even share the same rhythm.

Example 23: Schoenberg, First String Quartet: motivic relationships between (a) the third thematic idea from the subordinate theme group (mm. 340–342) and (b) the bass line of the main theme in the recapitulation of the local sonata form (mm. 366–368)

The recapitulation of the third thematic idea continues with the first and only quasi-literal transposition of a fragment from the exposition (mm. °371–372 correspond to mm. °163–164). This quotation serves as the model for a short liquidation process that leads to a return of the first thematic idea (in the variant first presented in mm. 178–179). Mm. 380–383 are clearly reminiscent of mm. 24–28 from the exposition and thus suggest closing function. The last measure of this unit is elided with the first measure of the transition to the second movement (mm. 383–398).

Needless to say, the tension between both dimensions in mm. 301–398 remains unresolved. It is impossible to meet all of the opposing requirements of a development and a recapitulation in one single formal unit. Rather, each dimension can realize only those functions it absolutely requires in order to continue functioning, and realizes them in such a way that they do not prohibit the other dimension from functioning. This explains why there is no "double return" (of both tonic and main theme) at the beginning of the recapitulation of the local sonata form, but only a thematic one. Obviously, some kind of return at this point is an indispensable requirement of the dimension of the cycle. A double return would, however, have rendered the remainder of the overarching sonata form superfluous. Not surprisingly, then, the double return is postponed until the recapitulation of the overarching sonata form in m. 909.

But why is the single return a thematic rather than a tonal one? No doubt, this is partly due to the undeniable predominance that the thematic aspect of a sonata form had acquired over its tonal-harmonic aspect in the years around 1900.[10] In the tonally unstable idiom of Schoenberg's First String Quartet, a mere tonal recapitulation that is not supported by a thematic one would hardly succeed in creating the effect of a recapitulation at all. This does not mean, however, that in this music tonality has lost every structural potential. It continues to play a structural role on the large scale, and it is for this reason that the tonal return is exclusively associated with the largest-scale recapitulation—that of the overarching sonata form. The recapitulation in m. 301 is, in other words, a single return to allow the overarching sonata form to continue functioning; it is a thematic return not only to allow it to function properly within the local sonata form, but also to differentiate between the scale of both recapitulations—that of the local and that of the overarching sonata form. It is not difficult to imagine why exactly the recapitulation of the local sonata form is in C♯ minor. Not only is it one of the keys touched upon in the second subsegment of the main theme group, it is also enharmonically equivalent to the dominant minor of G♭ major (the key of the interpolated scherzo) and thus operates as a long-range tonal preparation of this first interpolated movement.

It may be clear that the lack of tonal closure can sufficiently temper the recapitulatory function of mm. 301–398 for this passage to function simultaneously as a development. Yet it is harder to see how the recapitulation itself can continue functioning when it is not only tonally, but also thematically so radically altered in comparison to the exposition. The liquidation in the main theme group (mm. 309–319), the stretto at the beginning of the fugato segment (mm. 335–342), and the liquidation at the end of the subordinate theme group (mm. 372–377)—all of which are absent in the exposition—are procedures typical of a development section. It appears as if the developmental features in mm. 301–398 prevail in every respect, and the return of the material groups from the exposition in their original order seems hardly able to compensate for that. Yet unlike similar units in a proper development, the larger formal units in mm. 301–398 (which, in the dimension of the cycle, are the segments of the recapitulation) are not part of an overarching developmental process. Instead, every single one of them retains a certain degree of independence, not least because the final units of both the main and the subordinate theme groups suggest a closing function. Rather than that the segments of the recapitulation are subsumed under a larger-scale development, small-scale developmental processes intrude into the recapitulation.

Interpolation and integration

Schoenberg's First String Quartet is a veritable compendium of strategies that isolate and integrate movements that are interpolated in the overarching sonata form. Each of its three interpolated movements begins by establishing a marked contrast to its environment and goes on to develop its own more or less self-contained form. As mentioned before and as illustrated in example 24, the scherzo's main theme is derived from the head of the fugato subject presented in the exposition (mm. °99–103). In the scherzo, the latter gains a distinctly new quality that largely depends on a thematic transformation involving changes in tempo, meter, and rhythm.

Example 24: Schoenberg, First String Quartet: (a) head of the fugato subject (mm. °99–101) and (b) beginning of the scherzo (mm. °399–402)

The slow movement, by contrast, begins with a theme that cannot be deduced from the overarching sonata form; it is shown in example 25a. The opening material of the finale, shown in example 25b, is also unrelated to that of the overarching sonata form; in fact, it is a transformation of the slow movement's main theme (example 25b).

Example 25: Schoenberg, First String Quartet: (a) main theme of the slow movement (beginning) (mm. °952–959); (b) main theme of the finale (beginning) (mm. °1122–1127)

The scherzo is a good example of an interpolated movement with its own fully-fledged traditional form. Its overall form is ternary and consists of a scherzo (mm. °399–531), a trio (mm. 532–705), and a modified recapitulation of the scherzo (mm. °706–783). The scherzo section also has a ternary design, with segment A in mm. °399–448, segment B in mm. °449–503, and an abridged return of segment A in mm. 504–531. The finale (mm. 1122–1260) displays a similarly traditional pattern of formal organization. Although it has been described as a rondo, it might more effectively be heard as a ternary form. Figure 22 summarizes this reading. The opening section in mm. °1122–1180 has a ternary design that consists of a first segment in A major (mm. °1122–1142), a contrasting middle segment (mm. °1143–1168, beginning in C♯ major but ending standing on the dominant in A), and a recapitulation of the first segment in mm. °1169–1180. Mm. 1181–1247 form a substantial developmental middle section, and mm. °1248–1260 constitute a recapitulation of the opening section, now restricted to a variant of its opening segment.

The formal organization of the slow movement is more elusive. Consensus on its interpretation is limited to the broad outlines: almost all authors observe caesurae in mm. 1003 and 1031 and regard mm. 1054–1067 as a transition back to the overarching sonata form. To interpret the three sections that thus appear as a large ternary form is no less thorny than to regard them as a sonata form.[11] The main objection to the first interpretation is that from m. 1031 onwards—the supposed return of section A—the texture is dominated by material from the middle section rather than from the exposition; after m. 1047, material from the middle

CHAPTER 6

section even completely disappears. Objections can also be raised against the sonata form interpretation that sees a main theme in mm. 952–1002, a subordinate theme in mm. 1003–1030, a development in mm. 1031–1047, and a recapitulation in mm. 1048–1053. Only the subordinate theme returns in the recapitulation, where it occurs in the same key as in the exposition (E major, the dominant of the movement).

```
               FINALE (mm. 1122–1260)
A (mm. °1122–1180)
     a (mm. °1122–1142)    A
     b (mm. °1143–1168)    c♯ → A: V
     a' (mm. °1169–1180)   A
B (mm. 1181–1247)
A' (mm. °1248–1260)        A
```

Figure 22: Schoenberg, First String Quartet: overview of the finale

Simultaneous to the establishment of a certain degree of independence, the interpolated movements are also very strongly integrated in the overarching sonata form. Integration sometimes takes place in the units that frame a particular interpolated movement. The scherzo, for instance, is preceded by a thematically preparatory transition. Mm. 380–383 bring a varied return of mm. 24–28, the closing portion of the main theme group's part A. It is transposed down a semitone to D minor, as if to conclude the development section and lead to the recapitulation of the main theme in the tonic. The phrase breaks off before its penultimate chord (which would have arrived in m. 384), making way for a superposition of the head of the main theme's bass line and the first component of the fugato segment. The following measures generate a renewed energy that leads to a first goal in m. 389, where the first component of the fugato segment is definitively transformed into the scherzo theme.

In a similar way, the resumption of the overarching sonata form after the interpolated scherzo is prepared in that movement itself. The recapitulation of the scherzo section is radically modified. Recapitulating material from segment A, its formal organization does not correspond to that of the first scherzo section at all. Its texture, moreover, is unexpectedly unstable and developmental. While both the first scherzo section and the trio are unequivocally closed—not least because their final cadences confirm their opening keys (G♭ major and E major respectively)—

this is not the case for the scherzo as a whole, which remains tonally open-ended. To be sure, the return of the closing figures from mm. 522–531 suggests a sense of closure, but neither the start nor the end of the scherzo's recapitulation is in the movement's home key. Because of the developmental texture and the lack of closure in the scherzo's recapitulation, moreover, the resumption of the development of the overarching sonata form in m. 784 can happen almost unnoticed. In fact, mm. 784ff are identifiable as the resumption of the overarching sonata form mainly because of the renewed presence of material from the main theme.

Further integration of the interpolated movements is achieved by thematic means. In most cases, this integration is indirect, i.e., it operates through the detour of thematic integration within the dimension of the cycle, as explained in Chapter 1. The transformation of the fugato subject from the exposition into the head of the scherzo's main theme is only the most obvious example; there are many more later in the scherzo. From its return in m. °424 onwards, the scherzo theme is combined with the bass line from the beginning of the main theme (mm. 1–3) in a variant familiar from the beginning of the development section (mm. 234–236). This figure returns several times—partly or entirely—in the introduction to the trio (mm. 553–560 and 564–575), as well as in the trio itself (mm. 596–600 and 611–645). In the introduction to the trio, it is joined by a variant of the third thematic idea from the subordinate theme group (mm. 560–566) that has been rhythmically adapted to the scherzo and trio themes; the thematic idea from the subordinate theme group is repeated in a broadened version in mm. 567–577. The third thematic idea from the subordinate theme group plays an important role in the trio itself too, not only in the easily recognizable shape it acquires in mm. 594–610 and 646–650, but also in a more radically varied shape seen in mm. 611–617, 622–628, and 636–645. Still in the trio, two more motives have their origins in the exposition. The entry of the first violin in mm. °615–621 is clearly derived from mm. 14–15. It is taken up briefly in mm. °621 and °632 by the cello, as well as, in a more extended way, in mm. °626–632 by the viola. Finally, a motive from mm. 8–9 returns as a continuation of the trio theme in mm. 581–586 and 656–663. References to the overarching sonata form in the scherzo's recapitulation are much less numerous. The only exceptions are two more varied returns of the third thematic idea from the subordinate theme group in mm. 719–721 and 721–722.

While the scherzo is more or less equally strongly related to each segment of the exposition, the slow movement is primarily associated with the subordinate theme group. It is infiltrated by the latter's first and second thematic ideas, the very ideas from the subordinate theme group that remain absent in the scherzo. More broadly, the material from the exposition used to integrate the slow movement is different from that recollected in the scherzo: no theme from the exposition that returns in the scherzo does so in the slow movement. The first theme from the overarching sonata form to return in the slow movement is the first thematic idea from the subordinate theme group. It first appears in mm. 965–969 and returns wholly or partially in mm. 969–971, 989–992, 993–997, and 1035–1045, as well as in mm. 1065–1066 and 1067–1068 in the transition. The second thematic idea from the subordinate theme group first appears in the slow movement in mm. 969–970, and returns in one form or another in mm. 975–976, 981–982, 993–995, 1023, 1029–1030, 1035–1036, and 1041–1044. As it is related to the accompaniment in mm. 213ff, finally, the accompanying figure in mm. 1000ff refers to the beginning of the development.

Similarly to what happened in the scherzo, the material from the exposition that returns in the slow movement is usually adapted to and given a function in its new context. In contrast to the scherzo, however, the slow movement contains one real quotation: in mm. 1016–1017, the viola plays a figure that is closely related to the beginning of the main theme of the overarching sonata form and that initially remains isolated from its new context. Only a few measures later, in mm. 1024–1025, the quotation is integrated in the slow movement through its association with the variant of the second thematic idea from the subordinate theme group played in m. 1023.

In contrast to the scherzo and slow movement, both of which recall thematic material from the first movement only, the finale incorporates material from all three preceding movements. Thus, it contains examples of ordinary cyclic integration—referring to material that has previously occurred only in the interpolated movements—alongside thematic references that integrate the interpolated finale in the dimension of the form. Moreover, the finale does not introduce any new thematic material at all, but is entirely based on transformations of material previously heard in the composition. Figure 23 gives a list of thematic recollections in the finale.

Instances of direct integration—thematic relationships between interpolated movements and exocyclic units of the overarching sonata form—are rarer. This should not come as a surprise. Since all motivic-thematic material in the overarching sonata form is first introduced in the formal units that coincide with the first movement of the sonata cycle, it is impossible to refer to it without simultaneously referring to that movement itself. As a result, direct integration in Schoenberg's First String Quartet is always retrospective: exocyclic units of the overarching sonata form refer back to the preceding interpolated movements. The first exocyclic unit to do so is the second development of the overarching sonata form. When the overarching sonata form resumes in m. 784, it is set apart from the preceding recapitulation of the scherzo primarily by the renewed prominence

	mm.	instrument	theme
a	°1122–1127	violin 1	theme A from slow movement
	1131–1134	violin 1	first thematic idea from subordinate theme group
	1133–1136	cello	first thematic idea from subordinate theme group
	1136–1139	viola	main theme (basic idea)
	1137–1140	violin 1 – cello	main theme (continuation)
	1141–1143	violin 2	main theme (basic idea)
	°1143–1146	violin 1	theme A from slow movement
	1143–1146	cello	main theme (continuation)
b	1147–1149	cello	main theme (basic idea – quasi inversion)
	1147–1150	viola	theme B from slow movement
	1150–1153	violin 1	theme B from slow movement
	1153–1158	viola	theme B from slow movement
	1158–1165	violin 1	third thematic idea from subordinate theme group
a'	°1169–1178	violin 1	theme A from slow movement
	1178–1180	violin 1	first thematic idea from subordinate theme group
B	°1181–1184	viola	fugato theme (scherzo theme)
	1183–1186	cello	first thematic idea from subordinate theme group
	°1189–1193	violin 1	fugato theme (scherzo theme) (inversion)
	°1195–1198	cello	fugato theme (scherzo theme)
	1197–1199	violin 1	first thematic idea from subordinate theme group
	°1202–1206	violin 1	fugato theme (scherzo theme)
	1202–1205	cello	fugato theme (scherzo theme) (inversion)
	1205–1208	cello	first thematic idea from subordinate theme group
	1208–1211	viola	main theme (basic idea)
	1209–1211	violin 1 – 2	main theme (continuation)
	1213–1214	violin 2	main theme (basic idea)
	°1215–1219	violin 1	theme A from slow movement
	1219–1222	viola	theme B from slow movement
	°1222–1225	violin 1	theme A from slow movement
	1226–1233	viola	theme B from slow movement
	1228–1233	cello	second thematic idea from subordinate theme group
	1231–1233	violin 1 – 2	first thematic idea from subordinate theme group
	1234–1239	violin 1	theme B from slow movement
	1236–1241	cello	second thematic idea from subordinate theme group
	1237–1242	violin 2	second thematic idea from subordinate theme group
	1241–1244	violin 1 – viola	first thematic idea from subordinate theme group
	1242–1244	cello	first thematic idea from subordinate theme group
	1243–1244	violin 2	first thematic idea from subordinate theme group
	1245–1247	violin 1 – 2	theme B from slow movement
A'	1248–1259	violin 1	theme A from slow movement
	1248–1259	viola – cello	theme B from slow movement

Figure 23: Schoenberg, First String Quartet: thematic recollections in the finale

of material from the main and subordinate theme groups of the exposition, which had remained almost completely absent from the recapitulation of the scherzo. At the same time, this development is contaminated by elements from the scherzo, which thus integrate that movement into the overarching sonata form. The most prominent among them is the three-note figure from the scherzo's final measures (mm. 782–783). This figure is derived from the scherzo theme—more exactly from its fourth, fifth, and sixth notes—near the end of the movement. In the development, it recurs in mm. 784–793 and 826–837.[12] A second remnant from the scherzo is the arpeggiated triad in mm. 788–792, 823–825, 832–835, and 904–905, originating in the final part of the first scherzo section (mm. 522–525) and restated twice at the end of the scherzo's recapitulation (mm. 772–775 and 779–782). Finally, there are the sixteenth-note runs in mm. 803–809, 847–853, and 868–872 that come from the trio of the scherzo (mm. 587–592 and 667–669) and are incorporated here in the third thematic idea from the subordinate theme group.

No material from the interpolated movements appears in the recapitulation of the main theme group in mm. 909–951. The recapitulation of the subordinate theme group (mm. 1082–1121), by contrast, contains three fragments from the interpolated slow movement. In mm. 1100–1103 and 1111–1114, the second violin plays the beginning of theme B from the slow movement. The first time, this is followed by a further motive from that theme in mm. 1103–1104, which is echoed by the first violin one measure later.

The very tight web of thematic interrelations integrating the different movements and the two dimensions in Schoenberg's First String Quartet is summarized in figure 24.

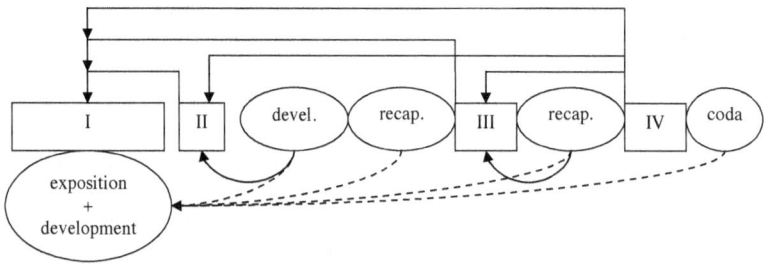

Figure 24: Schoenberg, First String Quartet: thematic integration

Michael Cherlin has addressed similar aspects of Schoenberg's Quartet [Cherlin 2007, pp. 155–172].[13] While Cherlin's interest is in motive and memory in Schoenberg's Quartet in general, and thus in any kind of anticipation and recollection in any formal unit of the composition, this figure is limited to three categories of thematic integration: thematic relationships within the cycle, thematic relationships within the overarching sonata form, and thematic relationships between movements of the cycle and sections of the overarching sonata form.[14] Movements in the sonata cycle are shown in squares and sections of the overarching sonata form in ovals. The arrows on the upper side of the figure show how all subsequent movements depend on the first—which simultaneously functions as the exposition and the beginning of the development of the overarching sonata form—and how the finale integrates material from all movements that precede it. The discontinuous arrows on the lower side indicate the (obvious) dependence of the sections of the overarching sonata form on the exposition, whereas the continuous arrows show which sections of the overarching sonata form recollect material from a preceding interpolated movement.

Overall form and tonal plan

From the point of view of the local sonata form, the internal proportions of mm. 1–398 are surprising. The exposition comprises 233 measures, the development 67, and the recapitulation (including the transition to the scherzo) 98. In performance time, the exposition takes up more than half, the recapitulation approximately a quarter, and the development the remainder of the total duration of the local sonata form.[15] The exposition is, in other words, disproportionately long in comparison to both other sections. Of almost equal size themselves, the development and the recapitulation are so much shorter than the exposition that they seem to be of the same order as the segments of the exposition, which comprise 96, 55, and 82 measures respectively.

The exposition of the local sonata form rather matches the proportions of the overarching sonata form. Of the 1320 measures of the composition as a whole, 671 are proper to the overarching sonata form, while the remainder are interpolated. Of those 671 measures, 290 belong to the development (mm. 234–398 and 784–908), 97 to the recapitulation (mm. 909–951 and 1068–1121), and 51 to the coda (mm. 1270–1320). In performance time, the exposition and the development each take up approximately one third of the total duration of the overarching sonata form, while the recapitulation and coda each last for approximately one sixth (the recapitulation slightly longer). Here it may initially seem that the recapitulation is disproportionately short (that the coda is shorter than the preceding units is less remarkable). This is compensated for by the recapitulation's close association with the interpolated slow movement. Not only is the slow movement interpolated into the middle of the recapitulation, but, as was shown in the previous section, the slow movement also prominently incorporates material from the subordinate theme group. At the same time, the recapitulation of the subordinate theme group assimilates thematic material from the slow introduction. The effect is that the slow movement enhances the proportional weight of the recapitulation in the overall form. The overarching sonata form thus consists of three more or less balanced blocks (exposition/development/recapitulation including slow movement) that are followed by a coda. The point to retain is that mm. 1–233 are first and foremost the exposition of the overarching sonata form. Only in the second instance do they function as the exposition of the local sonata form, which borrows its exposition from the other dimension.

A second remarkable characteristic of Schoenberg's First String Quartet is that the segments of the recapitulation sit on different sides of the second interior movement. This means that two of the four movements in the dimension of the cycle come after the double return of main theme and tonic at the beginning of the recapitulation in the dimension of the form—potentially a first major point of structural resolution. In order to sustain momentum after the beginning of the recapitulation and prevent the form from collapsing, the unusually long portion of the composition that comes after the beginning of the recapitulation must be made to appear meaningful.

Schoenberg achieves this in three ways. First, the weight of the recapitulation itself is literally reduced. The main theme group in the recapitulation is considerably shorter than its counterpart in the exposition (43 instead of 96 measures), the fugato segment is not recapitulated at all, and the recapitulation of the subordinate theme group is slightly abridged (40 instead of 48 measures). Second, the significance of the recapitulation as a formal event is undermined by its interruption by the interpolated slow movement. Because of the reciprocal rapprochement between the slow movement and the recapitulation's transition and subordinate theme group, both latter units tend to be absorbed into the sphere of the slow movement. The original fugato segment from the exposition or its variant from the recapitulation of the local sonata form is replaced by a genuine transition which, although based on main-theme material, is much more lyrical, thus continuing the texture of the slow movement until the beginning of the equally lyrical subordinate theme group. Third, both the interpolated slow movement and the finale are involved in the large-scale tonal plan of the overarching sonata form even though they are interpolations. Every return of main-theme material with an explicit recapitulatory character, up to and including the recapitulation of the overarching sonata form, conspicuously avoids an approach from a strong dominant in D minor or major. This is true for the recapitulation of the small ternary in the main theme group, for the recapitulation of the local sonata form (in C♯ minor instead of D minor), and for the recapitulation of the overarching sonata form (which is preceded by a dominant chord, but not in root position). After the recapitulation of the main theme group, however, A, both as a key and as a pitch in the lower register, suddenly becomes omnipresent. The slow movement is in A minor, the finale in A major, and at the beginning of the latter's recapitulation (mm. °1248ff), the bass emphatically introduces a pedal tone A that is immediately coloured as a dominant in D by the g♮ in the viola and cello. The A disappears from the bass part for most of the recapitulation and the transition between the finale and the coda, moving to the upper voice instead. Still, there is no doubt that it functions as a dominant preparation for the tonic major in the coda. Thus, the apex of the form shifts from the beginning of the recapitulation to the coda. Tonal resolution is postponed, so that the large-scale tonal trajectory of the piece is achieved only here, as is emphasized by the long tonic pedal at the end of the coda (mm. 1288–1320). Even this tonic pedal is not approached from a regular dominant, but from an applied French sixth chord similar to the closing progression in *Pelleas*. Only the very last approach to the tonic, in m. 1308, is from a dominant chord. Example 26 summarizes the large-scale organization of the piece.

A final noteworthy aspect of the large-scale formal organization of Schoenberg's First String Quartet is a process of thematic transformation that spans the entire composition and involves the first component of the fugato subject (first heard in mm. °99–101). This component reappears in various transformations all over the piece, but its first occurrences after the beginning of a new large formal unit (the first movement, the scherzo, the development, and the finale)[16] and its final occurrence towards the end of the coda are especially notable. Comparing these transformations, it becomes immediately clear that each of them differs considerably from the others, as appears from example 27. Moreover, the differences between the transformations shown in this example are more significant than those between different transformations within the same large units. For instance, the 300 measures separating the first presentation of the fugato subject from the transformation at the beginning of the scherzo are bridged by intermediate shapes in mm. °236ff, °335ff, 383ff, and 389ff. Rhythmically, all of them are more closely related to the first transformation than to the original shape; the shape in mm. °236ff is even rhythmically identical to the head of the scherzo theme. In terms of interval content, however, the original shape starts to transform into the scherzo theme only in the actual transition to the scherzo.

CHAPTER 6

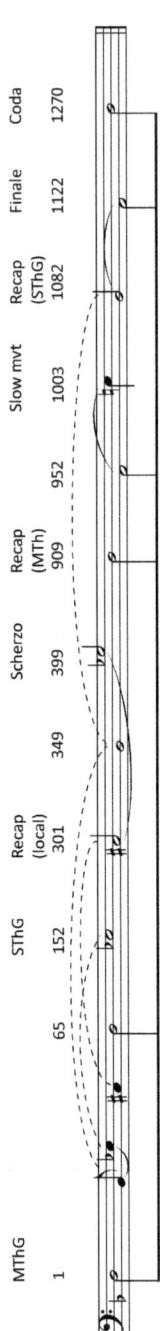

Example 26: large-scale tonal relationships in Schoenberg's First String Quartet

Example 27: Schoenberg, First String Quartet: first component of the fugato subject and four transformations; (a) mm. °99–101, (b) mm. °399–402, (c) mm. 880–882, (d) mm. °1181–1182, (e) mm. °1302–1304

At first glance, all these versions of the head of the fugato subject are related by a simple process of thematic transformation, fully in keeping with the criteria outlined in Chapter 2. The thematic contour of the model remains intact, but tempo, rhythm, and meter change with every new transformation. Furthermore, it is immediately obvious that the final transformation is very similar to the original shape, that the first and third transformations are somewhat alike, and that the second transformation is quite different from all others. When the interval structures of the different shapes are compared, an interesting additional feature comes to light. In each new transformation, the interval constellation is modified according to a very systematic pattern. As shown in figure 25, the first and fourth intervals—a rising perfect fourth and a falling perfect fifth respectively—never change. In the first, second, and third transformations the second and third intervals are augmented—a major instead of a minor second—and in the first and third transformations the final interval, a minor ninth, is diminished to an octave. Only the fourth transformation has an interval constellation that is identical to that of the original shape. Thus, the relationships that are established by means of changes in tempo, rhythm, and meter (original and transformation 4 on the one hand, transformations 1 and 3 on the other) are reflected in the shapes' interval constellations. Moreover, the arrangement of the different shapes follows a symmetrical pattern.

CHAPTER 6

original (first movement):	+5	+1	+1	-7	+13
transformation 1 (scherzo):	+5	+2	+2	-7	+12
transformation 2 (development):	+5	+2	+2	-7	+13
transformation 3 (finale):	+5	+2	+2	-7	+12
transformation 4 (coda):	+5	+1	+1	-7	+13

Figure 25: Schoenberg, First String Quartet: interval structure of the first component of the fugato subject and four of its transformations

In his First String Quartet, Schoenberg impressively tackles the three fundamental problems of two-dimensional sonata form: the identification of the sonata cycle's first movement with part of the overarching sonata form, the integration of interpolated movements into the overarching sonata form, and the relationship between the recapitulation of the overarching sonata form and the finale of the sonata cycle. In identifying the first movement of the sonata cycle with the exposition and the initial segments of the development of the overarching sonata form, he perpetuates the strategy used by Liszt in *Die Ideale* and by Strauss in *Don Juan*, and which he had adopted in *Pelleas und Melisande*.

The decision not to identify the finale of the sonata cycle with the recapitulation or coda of the overarching sonata form allows him to deal with the finale problem in a very elegant way. The result of this decision is not only that the finale acquires a form of its own; it is, to return once more to Michael Talbot's three basic types of finales, also an opportunity to avoid an exclusively summative finale. Of course, Schoenberg's finale is summative in that it recalls themes from all previous movements. Yet in overall character, it is predominantly relaxant. A valedictory aspect—Talbot's third type of finale—is overwhelmingly present in the coda that follows the shift back to the dimension of the form.

The difficulties associated with the technique of interpolation occupy a more central position in Schoenberg's First String Quartet than in any previous two-dimensional sonata form. In most two-dimensional sonata forms, shifts to and from interpolated movements are concealed by transitions that smooth over the contrast between units of the overarching sonata form and interpolated movements. Obscuring the boundaries between neighboring formal units of different dimensions, they distract attention from the actual shift to a new dimensional situation.

Even when those boundaries are highlighted by thematic material that returns at all major formal junctions, the recurrence of the same thematic material near every dimensional shift contributes to a unity at a higher level.

This is not the case in Schoenberg's First String Quartet. Here, the transitions towards and away from the slow movement and finale are not only highlighted as transitions, but denounced as an artificial means of relating both dimensions. Before the beginning of the slow movement, the recapitulation of the main theme group almost literally gets stuck. It ends on a long general pause, explicitly marked *sehr lange Haltung*. Although it is possible to relate the rhythm of the violin's first motive in the slow movement to the cello's motive immediately preceding it, the slow movement begins as a complete *non sequitur*. The transition back from the slow movement to the overarching sonata form is no less remarkable. Instead of realizing a gradual change towards the new texture, it contrasts starkly with its environment, especially in timbre, all four string instruments playing *sul ponticello*.

Although the finale is preceded by a lead-in (mm. 1118–1121), this hardly functions as a transition. The beginning of the lead-in contrasts too strongly with the end of the preceding unit of the overarching sonata form, and the transition from this unit to the beginning of the finale would have been far more fluent if the lead-in had not been there. The unit that leads back from the finale to the overarching sonata form is very similar in nature to that between the slow movement and the resumption of the overarching sonata form. It too contrasts strongly with both the end of the finale and the beginning of the coda, thus highlighting the dimensional shift rather than concealing it.

The form of Schoenberg's First String Quartet thus obtains a reflexive quality, expressing, as it were, its own impossibility, or at least the impossibility of achieving a complete integration of both dimensions of a two-dimensional sonata form. This new approach to form probably has everything to do with the transfer of the concept of two-dimensional sonata form from the public sphere of the symphonic poem to the rather more intellectual genre of the string quartet. It might also be related to the return of Brahms as an influence on Schoenberg's music that was mentioned earlier in this chapter: although the large-scale pattern of formal organization itself has its origins in the New German School, its content is of a much more Brahmsian nature.

Notes

1. To be sure, various programmatic interpretations of Liszt's B-minor Sonata have appeared in print (for a brief overview see Hamilton 1996, pp. 28–31). As there is no indication whatsoever that a program for Liszt's Sonata ever existed, and given that Liszt did not usually work with hidden programs, the conclusion must remain that the Sonata is absolute music.
2. Schoenberg, *Analysis of Pelleas and Melisande*, cited after Bailey 1984, p. 61. Schoenberg's originally English text has been published in its entirety only in German translation. This translation is listed in the bibliography as Schoenberg 1949b.
3. Letters from Zemlinsky to Schoenberg (17-2-1918) and from Schoenberg to Zemlinsky (20-2-1918) [Zemlinsky 1995, pp. 185 & 189]. Incidentally, Erwin Stein's edition of selected letters by Schoenberg includes only part of this letter (erroneously dated 23-3-1918), the passage concerning the program being omitted [Schoenberg 1958, pp. 52–54]. Stein's decision to leave out this particular passage is, so it seems, not without relevance to the position of some of Schoenberg's disciples in regard to the programmatic nature of their master's early work.
4. A transcription of this "secret program" has been published in Schmidt 1986a, p. 111. An English translation appears in Benson 1993, p. 379.
5. An excellent survey of the relevant analytical literature up to 1992 is included in Claus-Steffen Mahnkopf's published dissertation on Schoenberg's First Chamber Symphony. More recent publications Mahnkopf was unable to take into account include a monograph on Schoenberg's early chamber music by Rainer Boestfleisch [1990], the chapter on the First String Quartet from Walter Frisch's book on Schoenberg's early works [1993, pp. 181–219], Lynn Cavanagh's dissertation on the harmonic and tonal organization of the First String Quartet [1996], and essays or chapters by Michael Cherlin [2007, pp. 155–172], Ralf-Alexander Kohler and Markus Böggeman [2002], and Ethan Haimo [2006, pp. 112–142].
6. The term "kontrastierende Ableitung" was coined by Arnold Schmitz, who originally applied it to Beethoven's instrumental music [Schmitz 1923].
7. On this point compare Frisch 1993, p. 193.
8. Caplin discusses the common procedure of a transition in the form of a dissolving consequent, but does not name it. In a footnote, he refers to A.B. Marx's concept of the "Periode mit aufgebrochenem Nachsatz" [Caplin 1998, pp. 127–128]. Hepokoski and Darcy make more prominent use of the term "dissolving consequent," defining it as "a parallel consequent that is diverted before long into transitional processes" [Hepokoski & Darcy 2006, pp. 101–102].
9. Strictly speaking, there is one minor difference between the roles mm. 234–300 play in the overarching and the local sonata forms. While they constitute the entire development in the latter, they are only part of it in the former. This difference does not, however, imply opposing functional requirements.
10. As Dahlhaus famously wrote: "During the nineteenth century, thematic structure gradually usurped the preeminence of tonal structure, ... [and] in the twentieth century, with Schoenberg, the ultimate consequence of the primacy of thematicism proved to be the paradox of atonal sonata form" ("Im 19. Jahrhundert ist allmählich die thematische statt der tonalen Struktur in den Vordergrund gerückt [...], und im 20. Jahrhundert, bei Arnold

Schönberg, wurde als extreme Konsequenz des Vorrangs der Thematik das Paradox einer Sonatenform unter den Bedingungen der Atonalität möglich") [Dahlhaus, 1987, pp. 133–134; English cited after the translation by Mary Whittall, p. 98].

[11] Interpretations as a large ternary form can be found in Hattesen 1990 (p. 301) and Frisch 1993 (p. 188), readings as a sonata form in Dahlhaus 1988 (p. 212) and Mahnkopf 1993 (p. 34).

[12] From m. 828 onwards, the original rhythmic shape of the figure is replaced by a new variant.

[13] Cherlin also gives a convenient table of "Thematic Recollections of Sonata themes outside of 'Sonata space'" (p. 171).

[14] Figure 24 only shows the relationship between the return of a theme or theme fragment and its first appearance. It goes without saying that when a theme or theme fragment returns several times and in several formal units, those formal units will be related not only to the units in which this thematic material originates, but also to all other formal units in which it appears. The most obvious example is the return of the first component of the fugato subject from the exposition in sections of the overarching sonata form that come after the scherzo, notably in mm. 880–896 of the development and in the coda. They relate these sections not only to the exposition, but, because of the dependence of the scherzo theme on the beginning of the fugato subject, also to the scherzo.

[15] Performance times are approximations based on a comparison of recordings by the Lasalle (1971, Deutsche Grammophon), Prazak (1997, Praga Digitals), and Arditti (1993, Naïve) quartets.

[16] The only large formal unit where this component does not reappear is the one comprising the recapitulation and the slow movement.

CHAPTER 7

SCHOENBERG'S FIRST CHAMBER SYMPHONY

Overview

In 1949 Schoenberg wrote [Schoenberg 1949a, p. 440]:

> The *Chamber Symphony*, composed in 1906, is the last work of my first period which consists of only one uninterrupted movement. It still has a certain similarity with my *First String Quartet Op. 7*, which also combines the four types of movements of the sonata form and in some respect with the symphonic poems [sic] *Verklärte Nacht Op. 4* and *Pelleas und Melisande Op. 5*, which, disregarding the conventional order of the movements, bring about types resembling the contrasting effect of independent movements.

The First Chamber Symphony Op. 9 indeed testifies to Schoenberg's continued involvement with the combination of movements of a sonata cycle and sections of a sonata form in a single-movement composition. Compared to his previous two-dimensional sonata forms, the formal organization of the Chamber Symphony is generally considered to be less complex. Reinhold Brinkmann, for instance, has briefly compared it to that of the First String Quartet:

> The comparison of both dispositions shows the clear segmentation of the Chamber Symphony in contrast to the string quartet. [In the former,] the sharp thematic delineation corresponds to that of the formal units, while in the quartet, both the formal units and the thematic interrelations are often intertwined.[1]

This impression is confirmed by Schoenberg's own analysis, which was produced to go with a recording of the piece. According to his description, the Chamber Symphony consists of five large units: an "allegro first movement," a "scherzo," a "main development section," an "adagio," and a "recapitulation and finale" [Schoenberg 1949a, p. 441]. Figure 26 gives a somewhat more detailed overview of Schoenberg's reading. In the first movement, a short introduction (mm. 1–9) precedes the exposition, which consists of a main theme group (mm. °10–67), a transition (mm. 68–83), a subordinate theme group (mm. 84–122), and a closing group (mm. 123–135). In mm. 136–159, a brief recapitulation of the main theme group rapidly turns into a transition to the scherzo. Schoenberg parses this second movement into a scherzo section proper (mm. 160–199), a trio (mm. 200–226), a brief development (mm. 227–248), and a recapitulation in which material from the scherzo and trio is superposed (mm. 249–273). A brief transition (mm. 274–279) leads to the lengthy main development section (mm. 280–367). This is followed by an "interlude" (mm. 368–377) that functions as a transition to the slow movement, the latter consisting of a "first section" (mm. 378–414) and a "subordinate theme" (mm. 415–434). The return of the transition in mm. 435–447 marks the beginning of the recapitulation, which continues with the reprise of the subordinate theme group (mm. 448–471) and the main theme group (mm. 472). Only with the recapitulation of the main theme group, Schoenberg says, does the finale begin.

First movement	1–9	Introduction
	10–67	Main theme group
	68–83	Transition
	84–122	Subordinate theme group
	123–135	Closing group
	136–159	Recapitulation ⇒ Transition
Scherzo	160–199	Scherzo
	200–226	Trio
	227–248	Development
	249–273	Recapitulation (combining Scherzo and Trio)
Transition	274–279	
Development	280–367	
Interlude = Transition	368–377	
Slow movement	378–414	First section
	415–434	Subordinate theme
Recapitulation and Finale	435–447	Transition
	448–471	Subordinate theme
	472–…	Main theme = Finale
Coda ("Schlußstretta"?)		

Figure 26: Schoenberg, Chamber Symphony: overview of Schoenberg's own analysis

Schoenberg keeps his analytical comments very terse and does not address the Chamber Symphony's tonal organization at all; in this sense, his analysis resembles Berg's analysis of *Pelleas und Melisande*. Admittedly, the absence of a discussion of key centers might be more to the point here than in an analysis of the earlier work. As Ethan Haimo has demonstrated, tonality as an organizing force pushes against its limits in the Chamber Symphony. Long-range key centers are even rarer than in *Pelleas*, and both the overall tonic and many of the subsidiary keys are, although still recognizable, often weakly articulated [Haimo 2006, pp. 166–176].[2]

Schoenberg also neglects to address the Chamber Symphony's famous motto: the fanfare-like ascending fourths that are first presented by the first horn in mm. °5–6. It bears stressing that this motto plays an important clarifying role in the work's large-scale formal organization. Variants of it almost systematically reappear near the borders of movements: in mm. °279–280 in the transition from the scherzo to the development, in mm. °355–373 at the end of the development and the beginning of the slow movement, and in mm. 473–474 before the recapitulation of the main theme. Only the beginning of the scherzo is not explicitly marked by the motto. Nonetheless, this passage too is indirectly (and retrospectively) related to it: the dotted-rhythm motive from the transition to the scherzo (first played by the viola in m. 148) returns in conjunction with the motto just before the slow movement (mm. 364–367). Finally, we will see that the return of the motto in mm. 407–410 (according to Schoenberg's reading in the middle of the slow movement) also marks an important formal event, even though this is not apparent from Schoenberg's own analysis. The effectiveness of the motto as a formal articulator is enhanced by its immediate recognizability. To be sure, it sometimes occurs in shapes that evidently differ from its original shape: it can be verticalized, inverted, or stripped of its rhythmic contour. Yet none of these shapes contributes to even a small-scale variational or developmental process, and none of them affects the motto's pitch structure. Whatever form it assumes, the motto always remains directly linked to its original shape.

As a formal overview, Schoenberg's analysis is relatively complete, at least as far as the largest formal units are concerned. The only unit Schoenberg fails to specify is the coda. He mentions a "Schlußstretta" but neglects to say where exactly it begins or whether it is equivalent to a coda. When it comes to explaining exactly how the Chamber Symphony's form works, Schoenberg's analysis is significantly less helpful. Much like Berg's analysis of *Pelleas und Melisande*, most of Schoenberg's description of the Chamber Symphony is two-dimensional only in the sense that it moves back and forth between the dimension of the cycle and that of the form. Only when discussing the finale and the recapitulation of the main theme does he state that both dimensions coincide. For all other units, the relation between both dimensions remains unspecified: Schoenberg calls mm. 10–159 a "sonata-allegro" first movement, but analyzes them almost exclusively

CHAPTER 7

as a sonata-form exposition; he does not comment on the relationship between the interior movements and the overarching sonata form, and he does not explain how exactly the finale relates to the recapitulation.

The following paragraphs will address each of the questions Schoenberg's analysis leaves unanswered. I will argue that the first movement of the sonata cycle is identified with the exposition and the beginning of the development of the overarching sonata form, that the scherzo is interpolated in the overarching sonata form, that the slow movement begins as an interpolated movement but then merges into the development of the overarching sonata form, and that the finale is identified with the end of the recapitulation and the coda of the overarching sonata form.

Identification

Walter Frisch has interpreted the overarching sonata form's exposition not as a single exposition, but as a "*double* exposition, or pair of expositions." The recapitulation, analogously, he considers to be a "double recapitulation" [Frisch 1993, pp. 221–224 & 227–229]. According to Frisch, the first of this pair of expositions consists of an E-major main theme in mm. °10–15, a transition-like unit in mm. 16–31, and an F-minor subordinate theme in mm. 32–49. Mm. 50–57 function as a transition to the second exposition that begins in m. °58. The main theme of the second exposition (mm. °58–67) varies that of the first, but its transition (mm. 68–83) as well as its subordinate theme and key (mm. 84–105) are new. A transition in mm. 106–112 connects the second exposition to a closing group in mm. 113–132. Figure 27 gives an overview of Frisch's analysis.[3]

Frisch's analysis is highly imaginative but ultimately untenable. I see three problems with it. First, the key point in Frisch's reading is that both expositions share the same main theme—or, more precisely, that the main theme of the second exposition is a variant of that of the first. His analysis does not, however, account for the fact that the main theme from the first exposition (mm. °10–15) is not the only unit to return in the second: the formal unit that immediately follows the main theme (mm. 16–31) does so as well. The concrete realization and the size of both units are quite different, but materially mm. 62–67 clearly correspond to mm. 16–31; there is no doubt that mm. 62–67 constitute a compressed variant of mm. 16–31. Although there is no reason to presume that the relationship between these two formal units differs from that between mm. 58–61 and 10–15, Frisch nonetheless ascribes the same function (that of a main theme) in both expositions only to mm. 10–15 and 58–61. Mm. 16–31 and 62–67, by contrast, each have a

Introduction	slow introduction (mm. 1–4)	
	horn motto (mm. °5–6)	
	cadential figure (mm. °7–9)	
Exposition 1	main theme (mm. °10–15)	**E major**
	transition-like unit (mm. 16–31)	
		[f: HC]
	subordinate theme (mm. 32–49)	F minor
Transition (mm. 50–57)		
Exposition 2	main theme (mm. °58–67)	**E major**
		[E: PAC]
	transition (mm. 68–83)	
	subordinate theme (mm. 84–105)	**A major**
Transition (mm. 106–112)		
Closing group (mm. 113–132)		**A major**

Figure 27: Frisch's analysis of the exposition of Schoenberg's Chamber Symphony

different function in his analysis. Mm. 16–31 are interpreted as a transition, whereas mm. 62–67 have slipped through his analytical net, apparently being nothing more than an anonymous extension of the second exposition's main theme. For Frisch, the transition of the second exposition begins only in m. 68. It is difficult to see, however, how mm. 16–31 can be the transition of the first exposition while mm. 62–67 are not the transition of the second one, given that one is a variant of the other and both occupy parallel positions in the two expositions.

A second problem is that the internal proportions of the two consecutive expositions appear somewhat odd. In the first exposition, the main theme comprises six measures, the transition sixteen, and the subordinate theme eighteen; the main theme group of the second exposition comprises ten measures, its transition sixteen, and its subordinate theme twenty-nine. In either case, the main theme is the shortest of all three segments, and each time, the subordinate theme is no less than three times the length of the main theme. Since the transition is based on main theme group material in neither of the expositions, an interpretation that implies this kind of proportions appears counterintuitive.

A final important objection to Frisch's analysis is that the most emphatic cadence of the exposition, the quasi-PAC in E major in m. 68, is in the middle of the alleged second exposition. The import of this cadence can hardly be overestimated. It is the only rhetorically reinforced cadential gesture in the exposition—and one of the very few in the entire piece—and the first time E major/minor is unequivocally

CHAPTER 7

confirmed as a tonic. It is hardly probable that the main theme of the second exposition would be rounded off this emphatically when the end of the entire first exposition is much less so. This strong cadence is a clear signal that a first major formal unit has come to an end and that mm. °10–67 should be regarded as one entity.

In my view, the cadence in m. 68 is a main theme cadence and therefore leaves little doubt that the preceding unit has to be understood as the main theme group. This main theme group has a ternary form: mm. °10–31 are an exposition that modulates from the tonic E major to an HC in the minor Neapolitan F minor, mm. 32–57 function as a contrasting middle in F minor, and mm. 58–67 constitute a recapitulation that concludes with the PAC in m. 68. Interpreting mm. °5–132 as a single exposition with mm. °10–67 as its main theme group has the additional advantage that it balances the internal proportions of the exposition. It begins with a five-measure extended motto[4] (which I, along with Frisch but in contrast to Schoenberg, include in the exposition rather than in the introduction), and continues with a complex main theme group of fifty-eight measures. This is followed by a sixteen-measure transition, a twenty-nine-measure subordinate theme group, and a closing group of twenty measures.

In spite of these objections, Frisch's analysis contains valuable ideas, particularly in regard to the exposition's simultaneous function as the first movement of a sonata cycle. After all, the formal unit Frisch calls "first exposition" does have a number of important traits in common with a complete sonata-form exposition. Mm. °10–31 can be considered a main theme merging into a transition that even ends on an HC in the new key (a medial-caesura effect), mm. 32–49 do not defy an interpretation as a subordinate theme, and mm. 50–57 have at least the character of a closing group. Moreover, they are followed by a transitional unit that might very well have led back to an exposition repeat from m. 10 onwards. It is tempting, therefore, to retain Frisch's interpretation of mm. °10–57 as "an" exposition.

Since it has proven problematic to combine the exposition in mm. °10–57 with a second exposition in the dimension of the form, however, I propose to regard it as an exposition only in the dimension of the cycle, more exactly as the exposition of a local sonata form that is identified with the initial units of the overarching sonata form. If mm. °10–57 constitute the exposition of the local sonata form, then mm. 136–147, a false exposition repeat between the exposition and the interpolated scherzo in the dimension of the form, clearly function as its (abridged) recapitulation.[5] What role mm. °58–135 play in the local sonata form is, however, far less obvious. Standing between the exposition and the recapitulation, they seem to occupy the position of a development; beginning with a variant of the main theme, moreover, they echo a standard procedure for opening a development section. Nonetheless, it is difficult to interpret mm. °58–135 as a development in their entirety. Not only is it unusual for a development to start in the exposition's home key, as is the case here, it is also problematic that the only emphatic tonic cadence in the entire exposition of the overarching sonata form (mm. 67–68) should occur in the middle of the supposed development of the local sonata form.

Both problems disappear when mm. °58–67 are interpreted as an abridged exposition repeat in the local sonata form rather than as part of the development. The formal unit that opens the development in this reading starts after the cadence in m. 68, and although it begins in E major, it rapidly modulates away from it. Moreover, as the transition of the overarching sonata form, mm. 68–83 are likely to function as the development of the local sonata form in light of the analogies examined in Chapter 1. The beginning of the overarching sonata form's subordinate theme group is less easily interpreted as part of a development. Its first measures (up to m. 95) are among the most thematic and stable in the entire exposition. In the continuation of the subordinate theme group, however, developmental activity rapidly increases; consider, for instance, mm. °100–105. In mm. 106–112, the subordinate theme is even combined with elements from the main theme group.[6]

It is clear that the double function of mm. 67–135 as the development of the local sonata form and as the transition, subordinate theme group, and closing group of the overarching sonata form generates important tensions. Many of the singularities described above can be explained only as concessions Schoenberg has to make in order to balance the opposing demands of the two different dimensions. The majority of these concessions is at the expense of the dimension of the cycle.[7] The presence in the local sonata form of an abridged exposition repeat that is restricted to the main theme group and does not modulate away from the home key (with the result that the development begins in the tonic), for instance, is clearly anomalous in the dimension of the cycle. It is a concession to the demands of the dimension of the form, the ternary main theme of which cannot do without a recapitulation that ends in the tonic. Also the thematic and stable nature of the beginning of the subordinate theme group is an indispensable requirement of the overarching sonata form, and thus an equally unsurprising anomaly in the dimension of the cycle. Finally, it is clearly a concession in the dimension of the cycle that its recapitulation is abridged and incomplete. Had this recapitulation occupied more space and solved all the exposition's conflicts, it would not only have rounded off the local sonata form, but also have deprived the overarching sonata form of every reason to continue. In general, the dimension of the form clearly is the most fundamental layer of formal organization in the first 159 measures of the Chamber Symphony. The underlying tonal plan, underarticulated though it may be, is that of a sonata-form exposition. In the design of this exposition, however, Schoenberg

CHAPTER 7

INTRODUCTION	EXPOSITION (beginning)			
	Motto	Main theme group		
		A → f: HC	B f	A' E: PAC
		E		E
1–4	°5–9	10–31	32–49	50–57	58–67
		E	f	E
		Main theme	Subordinate theme	Closing group	Main theme
	INTRODUCTION	EXPOSITION		ABRIDGED EXPOSITION REPEAT

EXPOSITION (continued)			FALSE EXPOSITION REPEAT
Transition	Subordinate theme group	Closing group	Retransition	
	A			E
68–83	84–112	113–132	133–135	136–141
				E
	DEVELOPMENT			ABRIDGED RECAPITULATION

Figure 28: Schoenberg, Chamber Symphony: identification of the local sonata form with the initial formal units of the overarching sonata form

makes choices that enable it to accommodate the presence of a simultaneous complete sonata form and infuses it with a number of additional rhetorical gestures that point in the same direction. Figure 28 summarizes my reading of mm. 1–141.

The dimensional disconnection in Schoenberg's First Chamber Symphony takes place far less abruptly than in his First String Quartet. Up to m. 134, there is no reason to challenge the initial interpretation of the composition as a one-dimensional sonata form. The first serious indication of a local sonata form is the false exposition repeat from m. 135 onwards. As part of a one-dimensional sonata form, it would seem curiously out of place in the very dense idiom of this composition. Even so, it is only at the beginning of the first interpolated movement—when the false exposition repeat turns out not to function as the beginning of a development section—that a reinterpretation of mm. 1–141 as a local sonata form becomes unavoidable.

Interpolation

The scherzo of Schoenberg's Chamber Symphony (mm. 160–279) displays all of the characteristics of an interpolated movement. It is formally closed and in many respects contrasts with the environment in which it is interpolated. At the same time, the movement is prepared motivically in the transition that immediately precedes it and retrospectively integrated in the further course of the overarching sonata form.

There is no question that the scherzo is formally closed. Expanding on Schoenberg's own description of the movement as a ternary form with a development between the trio and the recapitulation of the scherzo, Frisch has interpreted mm. 160 and 220 as the beginning of two contrasting themes rather than as the beginning of a scherzo and a trio. "The way in which the two themes are introduced and developed," he points out, "gives the scherzo a shape closer to sonata form than to the tripartite scherzo plan" [Frisch 1993, p. 224]. In this sonata-form reading, mm. 160–183 constitute the main theme (in C minor), mm. 184–199 the transition, and mm. 200–214 the subordinate theme (in A♭ minor). Mm. 215–248 can be interpreted as a development, and mm. 249–273 as a recapitulation—a "synthesizing reprise," in Haimo's words [Haimo 2006, p. 162]—in which both themes are superimposed. Figure 29 gives an overview of the scherzo.

Exposition	main theme (mm. 160–183)	c
	transition (mm. 184–199)	
	subordinate theme (mm. 200–214)	a♭
Development (mm. 215–248)		
Recapitulation (mm. 249–273)	main theme + subordinate theme	
Transition to overarching sonata form (mm. 274–279)		

Figure 29: Schoenberg, Chamber Symphony: formal overview of the scherzo

The scherzo contrasts with the overarching sonata form in thematic content, keys and key signatures, tempo, and meter. The most important contrasting feature is that all of its thematic material is new. Although its main theme can be derived from the ascending chromatic line played by the second violin in mm. 2–4,[8] its novel quality is never threatened. In the remainder of the scherzo, there is no trace of any thematic material from the preceding exposition. In the tonally underdefined sound world of the Chamber Symphony, it would be an exaggeration to claim that the main key areas of the scherzo (C minor and A♭ minor) effect a significant contrast with the E-major home key of the overarching sonata form. More important than the specific keys of the scherzo, however, is that the movement has a key signature of its own, which visually emphasizes its distance from the exposition of the overarching sonata form. Also the tempo change adds to the contrasting character of the scherzo. With a metronome marking of 276–288 to the quarter note, it is considerably faster than the exposition of the overarching sonata form, which has 208 to the quarter note. This contrast is heightened by a slowing down at the beginning of the transition immediately before the scherzo (*etwas ruhiger* in m. 142 and *noch ruhiger* in m. 148). Although there is an accelerando from m. 152 onwards, Schoenberg indicates that the dotted half note at the beginning of the scherzo should be faster still than the half notes of the measures immediately preceding it. The metrical contrast between the scherzo and the preceding units of the overarching sonata form is, finally, quite obvious. The metrical complications in the scherzo, with its irregular alternation of ternary and binary meters, are very different from the straightforward common time in the overarching sonata form.

At the same time, the contrast between the scherzo and its environment is mitigated in several ways. Thematically, the accompanying figure of the scherzo's main theme is prepared in the course of the transition that precedes the movement; later, the same figure turns out to be a prefiguration of the scherzo's subordinate theme. In terms of key relationships, C minor and A♭ minor are symmetrically third-related to the overarching sonata form's tonic, and the scherzo's initial C minor is, to a certain extent, prepared in the transition that precedes it.

Further integration of the scherzo takes place later in the overarching sonata form. In the development that follows it, the scherzo is integrated directly into the overarching sonata form by means of two overlapping motivic processes. The first two segments of the development (mm. 280–311 and 312–334) exclusively use material that stems from the exposition of the overarching sonata form. In the third segment (mm. °335–367), this material is temporarily joined by the second motive from the scherzo theme (from mm. °163–164) in rhythmic diminution. As example 28 illustrates, this motive is gradually modified by infusing it with structural characteristics of the overarching sonata form's main theme. Example 28a reproduces the beginning of the scherzo's main theme in its original shape. The entry of the first violin in m. °335 (example 28b) restates a fragment from this theme at pitch and leaves its interval content intact. The second entry (viola, mm. 335–336; example 28c) transposes the same fragment down a major second but alters its last interval. The third statement (m. °336, first violin, example 28d), finally, develops a new variant. It retains only the rhythm of the motive (still in diminution), while the original pitch content is substituted by fragments of a chromatic and a whole-tone scale (for the first two and the rest of the intervals respectively). In the measures that follow (mm. 336–345), this new variant is used next to, and on equal terms with, the original shape, after which the motives from the scherzo disappear and all attention once again goes to material from the overarching sonata form.

Example 28: Schoenberg, Chamber Symphony: (a) scherzo main theme (mm. 160–164),
(b) and (c) rhythmic diminutions in the development (mm. °335 and 335–336),
(d) whole-tone variant (m. °336)

The whole-tone content (that is, apart from the upbeat) of the resultant motive of the process outlined in example 28 clearly relates it to the overarching sonata form's main theme, which is developed simultaneously with the phrase from the scherzo theme. This relationship is made explicit by a new derivation of the main theme from m. 345 onwards, shown in example 29.

Example 29: Schoenberg, Chamber Symphony: (a) main theme (beginning) (mm. °10–12); (b) development, m. 345; (c) development, m. 348

Example 29a shows the beginning of the original main theme, indicating its three main rhythmic motivic elements as well as its underlying whole-tone structure. Throughout the third segment of the development, the main theme—particularly its incipit—remains conspicuously present. New motive forms are derived from the main theme from m. 345 onwards. Example 29b shows a motive form played by the flute and oboe in m. 345. It combines motives c and b, but inverts their direction. In a further variant (example 29c, played by the flute and English horn in m. 348), the original direction of b is restored, and the pitch content of both motives is filled out with a whole-tone scale, the pitch framework of the original main theme. The resultant motive of this process is very similar to the final version of the phrase from the scherzo theme (compare example 29c with 28d).

The slow movement (mm. 378–409) is separated from the overarching sonata form's development by a transition that combines the motto with elements from the slow introduction (mm. 368–377).[9] In his *Structural Functions of Harmony*, Schoenberg lists mm. °386–390 as an example of a "contrasting middle section" [Schoenberg 1954, p. 124]. He does not comment on the rest of the ternary pattern to which this middle belongs, apart from indicating that m. °391 is the beginning of "(a')". Although it obviously contradicts Schoenberg's analysis quoted at the beginning of this chapter, this reading is plausible. Following four introductory measures, mm. °382–385 can be interpreted as the exposition, mm. °386–390 as the contrasting middle (elaborating on a motive from the end of the exposition), and mm. °391–397 as the recapitulation of a small ternary. Somewhat surprisingly, the recapitulation opens up in m. 395 and leads to an expanded return of the introduction, which marks the climax of the movement (mm. 398–404). A reminiscence of the exposition follows in mm. °405–406 (figure 30).

> Introduction (mm. 378–381)
> Main theme (small ternary) (mm. °382–397)
>   exposition (mm. °382–385)
>   contrasting middle (mm. °386–390)
>   recapitulation (mm. °391–397)
> Climax (mm. 398–404)
> Reminiscence (mm. °405–406)
> Transition (mm. 407–414)

Figure 30: Schoenberg, First Chamber Symphony: form of section A of the slow movement

In spite of their very chromatic nature, mm. 378–406 never really leave the key of G major. This is one of the reasons why they do not have the appearance of a movement, but rather that of a first section of a (possibly ternary) movement. After a brief transition (mm. 407–414), they are indeed followed by a unit that has the appearance of a middle section (mm. 415–434). Thematically, this middle section is derived from the preceding unit: as has often been observed, the entry of the first horn in mm. 430–431 is derived from the beginning of section A (m. °382). It has, however, gone largely unnoticed that the entire formal unit in mm. 415–434 is based on this thematic idea, and that mm. 430–431 is only the place where this correspondence is made most explicit.[10] Example 30 shows the head of the slow-movement theme and a number of its variants from mm. 415–434, changing the order in which they appear to highlights their connectedness through a process of developing variation.

Instead of leading to the expected recapitulation of section A, mm. 415–434 are followed by a return of the transition from the overarching sonata form's exposition. It seems wise, therefore, to interpret mm. 415–434 not merely as the middle section of the slow movement, but as a double-functional unit that simultaneously acts as a resumption of the development of the overarching sonata form. The latter function is emphasized by the presence of a transitional unit in mm. 405–414. Based on the motto, this unit separates mm. 415–434 from the rest of the slow movement in very much the same way that the beginning of the slow movement was separated from the preceding development by mm. 368–377. As will become clear later in this chapter, the absence of a recapitulation in the slow movement is compensated for later in the composition.

Example 30: Schoenberg, Chamber Symphony: (a) m. °382, (b) mm. 430–431, (c) m. °426, (d) mm. 424–425, (e) mm. 415–416

Beginning as an interpolated movement and evolving into a unit that is identified with the development of the overarching sonata form, the status of the slow movement is very unstable. Interestingly, Schoenberg appears to have had serious doubts about mm. 415–434; he even entertained the idea of cutting them completely [Frisch 1993, pp. 231–232]. Nonetheless, identifying the final unit of an incomplete and initially interpolated movement with the resumption of the overarching sonata form is a subtle way of shifting back from that interpolated movement to the overarching sonata form. Only when the middle section of the slow movement is not followed by that movement's own recapitulation but by that of the overarching sonata form does it become clear that we have left the dimension of the cycle.

Recapitulation, coda, and finale

Schoenberg's 1949 analysis identifies the return of the transition and the E-major key signature in m. 435 as the beginning of the recapitulation. All subsequent analysts of the Chamber Symphony have followed this reading.[11] It is, however, problematic, not so much because it is not the main theme that returns here, but rather because mm. 435–447 are, in spite of the change in key signature, not in E major, but in its dominant B major. A return of E major is postponed until the return of the subordinate theme group in m. 448. It is difficult to see, then, how mm. 435–447 could function as the beginning of a recapitulation when they lack both a tonal and a thematic return.

A much more plausible option is to interpret mm. 435–447 as the final segment of the development, which functions as a dominant preparation for the recapitulation. This is what the change of key signature in m. 435 indicates: it does not signal the beginning of the recapitulation, but the change in status of B major from a relatively independent tonal region within the development to the dominant of the tonic E major.[12] The recapitulation begins only in m. 448 with a structurally unaltered transposition of the beginning of the subordinate theme in the tonic. From m. 455 onwards, the course of the subordinate theme is changed, leading to a return of the motto from mm. °5–6 (at pitch), in m. 472. This is followed by a varied recapitulation of the first part of the main theme that is concluded with a (quasi-)PAC in m. 497. Beginning with a clear thematic restatement in the tonic, incorporating both contrasting themes from the exposition, and concluding with a tonic PAC, mm. 448–496 satisfy all the necessary requirements of a sonata-form recapitulation. Moreover, the absence of three other important thematic ideas from the exposition—the main theme's middle, the transition, and the closing group—is compensated for by their reappearance in the units framing the recapitulation: material from the transition returns in the final segment of the development, material from the main theme's middle and the closing group, as we will see, in the coda. One could say, then, that the recapitulatory function is not limited to the recapitulation as a formal unit (as delineated by the form's tonal and cadential structure), but spills over to adjacent formal units before and after the recapitulation.

A recapitulation mirroring the theme order from the exposition of course has precedents.[13] A classical example is the first movement of Mozart's Piano Sonata in D major K311. There, the final part of the transition returns at the end of the development (mm. °75–78), and the recapitulation starts with the subordinate theme (mm. °79–98), ends with the main theme (mm. 99–108), and is followed by a closing group in mm. 109–112. Even more relevant because of its greater chronological proximity to Schoenberg's Chamber Symphony is the finale of Brahms's Third Violin Sonata in D minor Op. 108 (1886). Brahms's movement is not a straightforward sonata form, but a sonata rondo of sorts. Nonetheless, the analogy between the transition from development to recapitulation in this composition and that in Schoenberg's Chamber Symphony is striking. In Brahms's sonata, the transition comes back in its entirety at the end of the development and functions as a dominant preparation for the recapitulation (mm. 194–217).[14] The recapitulation itself starts with the subordinate theme group (mm. 218–282) and the closing group (mm. 283–286). Subsequently, a transition leads to the recapitulation of the main theme (mm. 293–310) in the same way that it led, at the end of the exposition, to the restatement of the main theme at the beginning of the development.

The demarcation of the beginning of the recapitulation is not the only elusive aspect of the later portions of Schoenberg's Chamber Symphony; so too is the exact location of the coda. In his analysis of the Chamber Symphony, Berg gives m. °497 as the beginning of the coda [Berg 1918, p. 129]. In Frisch's and Mahnkopf's analyses, by contrast, the coda begins only in m. 555 [Frisch 1993, pp. 228–229; Mahnkopf 1994, pp. 37–38]. Frisch even engages in a discussion with Berg, arguing that "Berg's coda seems unusually and disproportionately long." It is true that Berg has to admit the presence of an "Endkoda" (mm. 555ff) after his "Koda," yet so in fact does Frisch when he says that "coda I," starting in m. 555, is followed by "coda II" in m. °576. The only real objection Frisch raises against Berg considering the coda to begin in m. 497 is its disproportionate size. The actual content of the passage does not preclude an interpretation as a coda. All of a sudden, the music, which is elsewhere of a highly dynamic and teleological physiognomy, comes to a halt (consider the eight-measure tonic pedal on E in mm. 497–504). From m. 497 onwards, some of the thematic material is presented in a new perspective; "the composer," to borrow Schoenberg's own description of the function of a coda, "wants to say something more" [Schoenberg 1967, p. 185].

What exactly is the relationship between the recapitulation and coda of the overarching sonata form and the finale of the sonata cycle? For Mahnkopf, the finale is identified with the recapitulation, which in his view stretches from m. 435 to m. 554. Although he admits that mm. 435ff lack the thematic independence of a finale, he argues that a number of factors nonetheless strongly suggest its presence. He particularly emphasizes the different order of the material in the recapitulation, the presence of material that does not stem from the exposition, the extent to which returning material is varied, and the overall character of the passage [Mahnkopf 1994, pp. 152–153]. Mahnkopf's arguments are somewhat weakened by the consideration that a recapitulation mirroring the order of the themes from the exposition has its precedents in movements in which there is no reason whatsoever for the recapitulation to function simultaneously as the finale. Moreover, Mahnkopf himself recognizes that for a composer like Schoenberg the recapitulation is an eminently problematic formal unit [1994, p. 151]. This implies that the modifications the recapitulation has undergone in comparison to the exposition may primarily be an attempt to solve the recapitulation problem and can thus be explained without recourse to the dimension of the cycle.

One option could be to proceed along the lines of the previous analyses of Liszt's B-minor Sonata, *Die Ideale*, and Strauss's *Don Juan*, and to understand these modifications as indications of the presence of a finale in light of the principle of cyclic completion. In Schoenberg's Chamber Symphony, there is an alternative possibility, one related to the unexpected size of the coda. In my view, only the end of the recapitulation and the coda are identified with the finale: only with the return of the motto in m. 473 and the subsequent intensified recapitulation of the main theme does the recapitulation attain the character of a finale. This is what Schoenberg's 1949 formal overview suggests.

Moreover, although Schoenberg himself remains vague about the finale's internal organization, it is possible to discern the traits of a sonata form in mm. 473–593. Mm. 473–515 allow for an unproblematic interpretation as the exposition of a small-scale sonata form, in which the return of the motto in mm. 473–476 functions as an introduction and the recapitulation of the main theme in mm. °477–496 as, obviously, the main theme. The PAC in m. 497 (the beginning of the coda in the overarching sonata form) marks the end of the finale's main theme group and the beginning of its transition, and the return of part A from the slow movement in mm. 508–515 functions as a subordinate theme (in the dominant B major). M. °516 marks the beginning of the finale's development, which combines thematic material from various parts of the form. In mm. °516–534, the preceding subordinate theme is developed and combined with motives from the transition of the overarching sonata form's exposition. The climax of the slow movement returns in mm. °535–540, the contrasting middle of the overarching sonata form's main theme in mm. 541–554, and mm. 562–569 comprise a return of material from the exposition's closing group. The development culminates in a standing on the dominant in mm. 573–575, which includes a return of the motto. This is followed by a return of the main theme in E major that does not defy an interpretation as an abridged recapitulation.

The overarching sonata form's coda has a compensatory function in both the dimension of the cycle and that of the form. In the dimension of the form, the return of the middle of the main theme in mm. 541–554 and of material from the exposition's closing group in mm. 562–569 compensates for their absence from the recapitulation. In the dimension of the cycle, the return of the theme and the climax from the slow movement in mm. 508–515 and °535–540—linked, moreover, by a passage that develops the theme from the slow movement—compensate for the absence of a recapitulation in that movement itself. Figure 31 summarizes the relationship between the final units of the overarching sonata form and the sonata cycle's slow movement and finale.

	DEVELOPMENT			RECAPITULATION (beginning)
			Retransition	Subordinate theme
			B	E
378–414	415–434		435–447	448–472
G	"B"			
EXPOSITION	MIDDLE			
SLOW MOVEMENT				

RECAPITULATION (cont.)			CODA			
Motto	Main theme					
	E E: PAC	E				
473–476	477–496	497–508	509–515	516–575		576–593
	E	E	b			E
	M Th	Tr	S Th			
INTRODUCTION	EXPOSITION			DEVELOPMENT		RECAPITULATION
FINALE						

Figure 31: Schoenberg, Chamber Symphony: identification of the finale with the final formal units of the overarching sonata form

After the reflexive First String Quartet, Schoenberg's First Chamber Symphony constitutes a renewed attempt to solve the problems of two-dimensional sonata form. Not only is its first movement identified with units of the overarching sonata form, but also, and particularly successfully, its finale. As with *Pelleas und Melisande* and the First String Quartet, the problems of recapitulation and finale are dissociated. But the strategy Schoenberg develops in the Chamber Symphony is unique. Unlike the First String Quartet, the finale is not interpolated between the recapitulation and the coda, and unlike *Pelleas und Melisande*, it is identified not only with the coda of the overarching sonata form, but with both the final segment of the recapitulation and the coda. As a result, Schoenberg manages to combine the summative aspect of a finale—by beginning at the recapitulation of the motto and the main theme group—with the formal freedom guaranteed by identifying most of the finale with the coda.

Equally remarkable is the way in which the interpolated slow movement is integrated in the overarching sonata form. Its middle section is identified with the resumption of the overarching sonata form. This is followed not by its recapitulation, but by a further developmental segment, which eventually leads to the recapitulation of the overarching sonata form. Only the coda of the overarching sonata form compensates for the lack of a recapitulation in the interpolated slow movement.

Notes

[1] "Der Vergleich beider Dispositionen zeigt die – gegenüber dem Streichquartett – klare Gliederung der Form in der Kammersinfonie, wo der scharfen thematischen Abgrenzung die der Formteile korrespondiert, während diese im Quartett – wie dort auch die thematischen Bezüge – vielfältig ineinander verschränkt sind" [Brinkmann 1977, p. 143].

[2] Another discussion of the harmonic and tonal language of the Chamber Symphony, grounded in Schoenberg's own theoretical thought, can be found in Dale 2000, pp. 20–52.

[3] In order not to complicate matters, I have made some minor changes to Frisch's terminology that do not affect the content of his analysis. The formal units I call transition, for example, he simply calls "themes," at the same time admitting that they "definitely have the character of a modulatory transition" [Frisch 1993, p. 224]. In two instances, I have merged two formal units that appear separate in Frisch's analysis: mm. 68–83, which fall apart into mm. 68–74 and 75–83, and mm. 113–132, which Frisch subdivides into mm. 113–126 and 127–132.

[4] I use the term "extended motto" to distinguish the entire five-measure unit from the motto as such, which is limited to the seven-note horn call.

[5] On this point compare Mahnkopf 1994, p. 36.

[6] Haimo too hears mm. 68–135 as a development, even though he interprets the first movement as a rondo [2006, p. 162].

[7] The only concession in the dimension of the form is that mm. 50–57 (the closing group of the local sonata form's exposition) appear unusual as the end of the middle of the main theme group in the overarching sonata form.

[8] The e♭ – e – f in mm. 2–4 corresponds to the a♭ – a – b♭ head of the scherzo theme. See Frisch 1993, p. 225.

9 Needless to say, the motto was a transposed horizontalization of the opening fourth chord from the introduction all along.
10 On this point compare Frisch 1993, p. 227.
11 Frisch errs when he claims that "Berg places the start of the recapitulation at m. 410" [Frisch 1993, p. 228]. Berg's comments are unequivocal:"The construction of the first part of this free recapitulation of the first part of the symphony first brings the 'transition' of that first part" ("Der Bau der ersten Partie dieser [...] freien Reprise des 1. Symphonie-Teiles bringt vorerst [...] die "Überleitung" dieses I. Teiles") [Berg 1918, p. 129].
12 An additional advantage of interpreting mm. 435–447 as part of the development is that it accounts for the repeated intrusion of material from mm. 415–434 (the preceding double-functional segment of the development).
13 See also Jackson 1997. In Hepokoski and Darcy's classification of sonata types, the Chamber Symphony's overarching sonata form would probably qualify as a "Type 2 Sonata."
14 An additional complication in the Brahms movement is that the recapitulation starts in III (a fifth-transposition of the ♭III of V in which the subordinate theme in the exposition begins) and reaches the tonic only considerably later.

CHAPTER 8

ZEMLINSKY'S SECOND STRING QUARTET

First approach

Alexander Zemlinsky wrote his Second String Quartet Op. 15 between 1913 and 1915. The earliest reference to it appears in a letter to Schoenberg of 20 July 1913, in which Zemlinsky informed the latter that he was "working steadily on a—string quartet!!" On a postcard a few days later, Zemlinsky revealed that the quartet was to be in "only one movement, that is to say four parts in one movement" and was "seemingly in F♯ minor."[1] Almost eighteen months later, on New Year's Eve 1914, he announced that he intended to dedicate it to Schoenberg [Zemlinsky 1995, p. 127]. The combination of its formal organization, its key, and its dedicatee strongly suggests that Zemlinsky's Second String Quartet is closely related to some of Schoenberg's instrumental music. It shares its key with Schoenberg's Second String Quartet Op. 10, while its formal organization is similar to that of Schoenberg's *Pelleas und Melisande*, his First String Quartet, and his First Chamber Symphony.

A formal analysis of Zemlinsky's Second String Quartet is complicated by a number of factors: the tendency of formal units to merge, the abundant thematic interrelations between different units, the paucity of cadential articulations, and the absence of clear tonal centers over long stretches of music.[2] These difficulties crop up right from the beginning. Rudolf Stephan and Werner Loll have described the quartet's remarkably fluid opening ten measures as a motto [Stephan 1976, p. 130 & Loll 1990, p. 159].[3] This motto, reproduced in example 31, does not precede the exposition (as if it were some kind of introduction), but is an integral part of it. It occurs, in different guises, twice more in the further course of the exposition—more specifically within the main theme group and immediately before the subordinate theme—and it begins the recapitulation. As we will see, it fulfills a form-articulating function that gains importance in the absence of other clarifying factors. At the same time, mm. 1–10 have a distinct thematic quality. Formally, they are organized as a sentence. Mm. 1–2 present a basic idea, m. 3 contains its compressed repetition, and mm. 4–10 constitute a continuation. The continuation itself also has a sentential structure, with mm. 4–5 as a basic idea, mm. 6–7 as its repetition, and mm. 8–10 as the continuation.

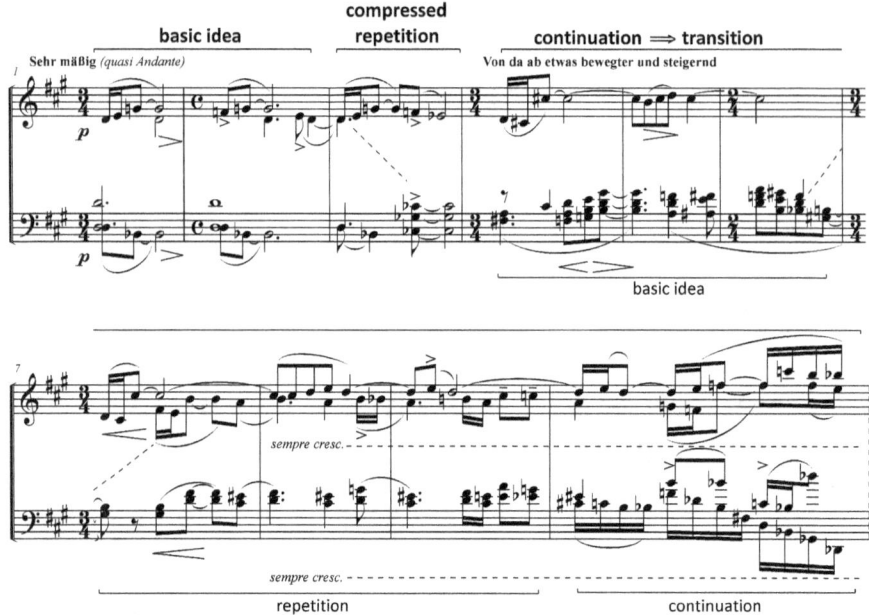

Example 31: Zemlinsky, Second String Quartet: mm. 1–10

This thematic quality entails a thematic treatment of the opening material later in the composition. Unlike that in Schoenberg's Chamber Symphony, the motto in Zemlinsky's Quartet does not merely reappear in relatively unaltered forms. For this reason, it seems appropriate to refer to mm. 1–10 not just as a motto, but as a "motto theme." If one insists on distinguishing a concisely formulated motto, it may be possible to consider mm. 1–3 (the presentation phrase of the sentence) as the actual motto. In this case, however, one must realize that when the motto returns in the further course of the composition—as often as not under the guise of a new variant—mm. 4–10 can be repeated or varied independently, i.e. without a preceding statement of mm. 1–3, thus functioning as a substitute for the actual motto.

The continuation in mm. 4–10 becomes a transition that leads to a (temporarily) steady fast tempo in m. 11. Along with new thematic material and the arrival on D in the bass—highlighted by the very characteristic sonority of D minor with added augmented fourth g♯ on top of it[4]—this marks the beginning of the main theme group (mm. 11–49). The main theme group consists of a binary theme (mm. 11–15 and 16–18) that is separated from a variant of its second part (mm. 25–39) by the first of the aforementioned returns of the motto theme. A linking unit (mm. 40–49), which is thematically related to the motto, leads to a relatively extensive transition that begins with a return of the main theme's head motive, now harmonized in F minor (mm. 50–104). This transition can be divided into three parts: a first in mm. 50–82, a second in mm. 83–90, and a third (standing on the dominant) in mm. 91–104. The subordinate theme group (mm. 123–160) enters after a second return of the motto theme (mm. 105–122). It begins with a ternary unit (mm. 123–136, 137–146, and 147–155) and concludes with a transformation of the main theme's second part in combination with a motive from the middle part of the subordinate theme group (mm. 156–160).

Mm. 161–245 are a theme (mm. 161–179) followed by five variations (mm. 180–198, 199–215, 216–225, °226–239, and 240–245). Only the theme itself (mm. 161–179) ends on a tonic chord in D major, the key of the subordinate theme group. The variations, in contrast, all end on the far less stable chord of D minor with added augmented fourth g♯ (the sonority that opened the main theme group). On this basis, it seems plausible to interpret mm. 161–179 as the exposition's closing group and m. 180 as the beginning of the development, which is thus initiated by an elaboration of the material from the closing group.

The development does not last very long. In mm. 246–253, the motto is reconstructed stepwise, and its actual return in mm. °254–263 soon becomes a transition to an interpolated slow movement (mm. 264–360). This slow movement is immediately followed by an interpolated scherzo (mm. 361–744) that culminates in the return of the motto theme (mm. 745–756). This return marks the beginning of the abridged and varied recapitulation, where the main and subordinate theme groups have changed positions: the subordinate theme group (mm. 757–781) follows the return of the motto theme, and the main theme group (mm. 801–823) is separated from the subordinate theme group by a transition (mm. 782–800). Based on the motto and material from the closing group, this transition is completely different from the one in the exposition. From m. 814 onwards, the recapitulation of the main theme group turns into a transition to the interpolated finale that starts in m. 824. In m. 1137, finally, the coda begins, summarizing the most important thematic material of the composition. Figure 32 gives a first overview of my reading of the piece's formal organization.

The following paragraphs follow a by now familiar trajectory. First I will investigate the manner in which the local sonata form is identified with the exposition of the overarching sonata form. Then I will focus on the interpolated movements, discussing first their formal organization and then the ways in which they are integrated into the overarching sonata form. The chapter concludes with a number of observations on the position of Zemlinsky's Second String Quartet in relation to Schoenberg's two-dimensional sonata forms on the one hand and the broader tradition of two-dimensional sonata form since Liszt on the other.

CHAPTER 8

FIRST MOVEMENT

EXPOSITION

Motto theme ("f♯")	Main theme group	Link	Transition	Motto theme	Subordinate theme	Closing group
	d				D	D
1–10	11–39	40–49	50–104	105–122	123–160	161–179

DEVELOPMENT

Variations	Regeneration of motto
180–253	254–263

SLOW MOVEMENT

d
264–360

SCHERZO

361–744

RECAPITULATION

Motto theme	Subordinate theme	Transition	Main theme
	D		?
745–756	757–781	782–800	801–823

FINALE

F♯
824–1136

CODA

D
1137–1221

Figure 32: Zemlinsky, Second String Quartet: form and cycle

Identification

Although both Horst Weber and Werner Loll maintain that the beginning of Zemlinsky's Second String Quartet functions as both the exposition of a sonata form and the first movement of a sonata cycle, neither of them actually mentions how and why it does so [Weber 1977, p. 99 and Loll 1990, pp. 159–160].[5] Still, indications that mm. 1–179 are double-functional lie there for the taking, and it is in fact Weber's analysis that holds the key to their successful interpretation. Comparing Zemlinsky's Quartet with Schoenberg's two-dimensional sonata forms, Weber notes that Schoenberg tends to reduce the number of developmental units: whereas he wrote two separate development sections in his First String Quartet, he wrote only one in the Chamber Symphony.[6] Zemlinsky, Weber argues, takes the opposite path: in his Quartet, every segment of the overarching sonata form is followed by its own development [Weber 1977, p. 99].

One such unit is mm. 50–104, which Weber hears as the development of the main theme group that immediately precedes them. This interpretation might at first seem surprising. Given their position between the formal units Weber analyses as the main and subordinate theme groups respectively (mm. 1–49 and 105–263) it seems more plausible to interpret mm. 50–104 as a transition. Yet there is some truth in Weber's assertion. As I have argued in Chapter 1, the analogy between the sections of a sonata form and the segments of a sonata form's exposition nowhere becomes more obvious than between a development and a transition. As a consequence, it is a valid analytical option to interpret mm. 50–104 not only, because of their position, as a transition, but also, because of their size, the degree of developmental activity, and the energy they generate, as a development. Weber considers the development in mm. 50–104 to be part of the dimension of the form. Together with other developmental fragments scattered over the composition, he argues, it operates as a substitute for a single central development section.

I suggest an alternative interpretation: the transition of the exposition in the overarching sonata form simultaneously functions as the development of the local sonata form in the dimension of the cycle. Arguments abound for an interpretation of mm. 1–179 as a local sonata form with mm. 50–104 as a development. A first centers on the internal organization of the main theme group. Syntactically, the main theme group consists of two parts, the second of which is a lyrical and slower transformation of the first part's second phrase. The six measures between the first and the second part are entirely derived from the motto theme as presented at the very beginning of the composition; in mm. 21–24, the upper voice from mm. 1–3 even returns virtually unchanged. The intricate formal organization of the main theme group is reflected by its tonal structure. Whereas its first part begins in D minor, its second part starts in E major/minor, ends on a dominant in F major/minor, and is followed by a harmonically unstable link to the transition. It is not hard to see how, in the overarching sonata form's main theme group, the outlines of a complete sonata-form exposition shine through, with mm. 11–18 as a main theme, mm. 19–24 as a transition, mm. 25–39 as a subordinate theme that contrasts harmonically as well as in character, and mm. 40–49 as a transition to the next formal unit. From this perspective, mm. 1–49 can be regarded as the exposition of the local sonata form, with mm. 50–104 functioning as the development.

A second argument is the tonal organization of the overarching sonata form's exposition. The subordinate theme group (from m. 123 onwards) is in D major. Since the main theme group started in D minor, this is, of course, highly unusual. One could argue that the beginning of the exposition is not in D minor, but—given the key signature—in F♯ minor. Yet F♯ minor is a shadow tonic at most; as mentioned earlier, Zemlinsky himself described the quartet as being only "seemingly in F♯ minor." Although there is an unmistakable F♯-minor triad in m. 4, this key is never firmly established in the overarching sonata form and plays a role only in the interpolated F♯-major finale. The main theme group's opening sonority clearly hints at D minor, and even though the rest of its harmonic organization is quite fitful, nothing indicates that it should be heard in F♯ minor rather than in D minor. The hypothesis that D is the tonic gains strength in view of the further tonal organization of the overarching sonata form: its recapitulation is in D minor (here, the key signature is the appropriate single flat) and the quartet ends in D major.

The tonal relationship between mm. 105–160 and 11–49 becomes less idiosyncratic if it is not regarded exclusively as that between a main and subordinate theme, but also as that between a recapitulation and exposition. The overall harmonic organization of mm. 1–179 indeed is that of a sonata form rather than of a sonata form's exposition, and in that sonata form the subordinate theme group functions as a recapitulation. The recapitulatory function of the subordinate theme group is, moreover, not realized solely through the large-scale tonal relationship between an exposition in the tonic minor and a recapitulation in the tonic major, but is also supported thematically. To be sure, the subordinate theme itself (mm. 123–160) cannot possibly be regarded as a thematic recapitulation. It genuinely incorporates the thematic contrast it is expected to generate in an exposition, thus fulfilling one of the essential and indispensable requirements of a subordinate theme in the dimension of the form. The effect of a thematic return in the dimension of the cycle is, however, realized not by the subordinate theme itself, but by a restatement of the motto theme at pitch that immediately precedes it. This restatement clearly refers back to the opening measures of the exposition, mm. 105–109 being quasi-identical to mm. 3–4.[7] Identifying the first movement of the sonata cycle with the exposition of the overarching sonata form, Zemlinsky thus very carefully balances the opposing requirements of both dimensions: given the demands of the dimension of the form, the thematic return necessary in the dimension of the cycle could not possibly have been realized as a return of the main theme within the formal unit that functions as the overarching sonata form's subordinate theme. Instead, Zemlinsky transfers the thematic recapitulation from the subordinate theme itself to the unit that immediately precedes it and that corresponds to the unit immediately preceding the main theme at the beginning of the exposition. Figure 33 illustrates the relationship between the local sonata form and the exposition of the overarching sonata form.

Throughout the local sonata form, the motto theme plays a form-articulating role at different hierarchical levels. Its return in mm. 105–122 in order to generate the effect of a thematic recapitulation is only the most obvious instance of this. In addition, the motto theme has a similar clarifying function for each of the other sections of the local sonata form, returning in mm. 1–10 before the exposition and in mm. 40–49 before the development. At a lower level, the return of motto material in mm. 19–24 helps to articulate the function of mm. 25–39 as a subordinate theme group within the exposition of the local sonata form.

The consequences of the subordinate theme group's simultaneous function as the recapitulation of the local sonata form reach as far as the recapitulation of the overarching sonata form (745ff). It too—and this is yet another argument in favor of a double-functional interpretation of mm. 105–172—is initiated by a return of the motto. Like the recapitulation of the motto in mm. 105–109, the one in m. 745 lacks the first few measures. Moreover, the recapitulation of the motto in the overarching sonata form is not followed by the recapitulation of the main theme, but by that of the subordinate theme. The motto and subordinate theme, which initially functioned as a recapitulation only in the dimension of the cycle, have ousted the exposition's main theme group from the beginning of the recapitulation in the dimension of the form.

Interpolation

Like Schoenberg's First, Zemlinsky's Second String Quartet contains three interpolated movements. The development of the overarching sonata form is separated from its recapitulation by a slow movement and a scherzo, and the recapitulation is separated from the coda by a finale. The formal organization of the

CHAPTER 8

EXPOSITION (beginning)

MOTTO THEME	MAIN THEME GROUP		LINK	TRANSITION		
	Main theme	Motto theme		Part 1	Part 2	Standing on the dominant
(f♯)	d					D: V
1–10	11–18	19–24		25–39		
				25–39		
				50–82	83–90	91–104
	d					D: V
Motto theme	Main theme	Transition	Link	Subordinate theme		
				Segment 1	Segment 2	Retransition
	EXPOSITON			DEVELOPMENT		

EXPOSITION (continued)

MOTTO THEME	SUBORDINATE THEME GROUP			CLOSING GROUP		
	a	B	a'	Conclusion	D	D
	D					
105–122	123–136	137–146	147–155	156–160	161–179	
D						CODA
	RECAPITULATION					

Figure 33: Zemlinsky, Second String Quartet: identification of the local sonata form with the exposition of the overarching sonata form

middle movements is unusually elusive. On the broadest scale, the slow movement is clearly a ternary form, with mm. 264–298 functioning as an exposition in D major (or at least one that constantly goes back to a D-major triad as a referential sonority), mm. °299–347 as a middle in the parallel minor, and mm. 348–360 as a much abridged recapitulation, again in D major. Within each of these large units, however, boundaries between smaller units are extremely fluid.

The analytical difficulties posed by the scherzo are of a different nature. Here, defining smaller units is easier and grouping adjacent units into larger ones relatively straightforward: units clearly belong together because they make use of the same themes, because of key relationships, or because they build up to a climax together. The scherzo can thus be divided into six large formal units: mm. 361–450, 451–517, 518–597, 598–631, 632–682, and 683–744.

Determining the function of each of these formal units, or identifying how exactly they join together to form a meaningful musical whole, is far less self-evident. All who have commented on the movement have considered the texture of mm. 632–682 to contrast starkly with that of the surrounding measures. Consequently, they have interpreted mm. 361–744 as a ternary pattern, with mm. 361–631 as the scherzo, mm. 632–682 as the trio, and mm. 683–744 as the recapitulation of the scherzo [Stephan 1976, p. 130; Weber 1977, p. 99; and Loll 1990, p. 160].[8] Even leaving aside the disproportion of sections resulting from this interpretation—271, 51, and 62 measures respectively—it remains problematic that the alleged recapitulation of the scherzo is restricted to the second of the four formal units that constitute the original scherzo section.

A more plausible option is to consider all—or almost all—large formal units listed above as operating at the same hierarchical level. In this case, one might consider hearing them as some kind of rondo form, with mm. 361–450 and mm. 598–631 functioning as the rondo theme and its return, and mm. 451–517, 518–597, 632–682, and 683–744 as the different episodes (A – B – C – A' – D – B). The problematic unit in this interpretation is the return of the rondo theme (A') in mm. 598–631. Not only is it very brief in comparison to most of the other units—especially if it is to be the only return of the rondo theme—but it also occupies a rather unusual position. Another possibility is to consider the two shortest formal units, mm. 598–631 and 632–682, as belonging together. This seems not entirely illegitimate, since the same thematic material prominently presents in both units. Moreover, it would result in a far more likely ternary form with an A – B – C – A' – B' design (shown in figure 34), in which A and A', and B and B', 90 and 85 measures and 66 and 61 measures long respectively, even correspond proportionally.

EXPOSITION		MIDDLE	RECAPITULATION	
A	B	C	A'	B'
361–450	451–517	518–597	598–682	683–744

Figure 34: proposed interpretation of the form of the scherzo of the Second String Quartet

The formal organization of the finale is significantly more transparent than that of the interior movements. Stephan calls it a "free rondo form with developmental elements" ("freies Rondo mit Durchführungselementen") [Stephan 1976, p. 131], but it seems more accurate to describe the movement as a sonata form with rondo implications, as shown in figure 35. The movement consists of a brief introduction (mm. 824–826), an exposition comprising an F♯-major main theme group (mm. 827–887), a transition (mm. 888–911), and a subordinate theme group in A major (mm. 912–948), a development (mm. 949–1026), an abridged recapitulation (mm. 1027–1108), and a coda (mm. 1109–1136). The rondo implications result from one additional return of the main theme in the middle of the development (mm. 990–997).

Introduction (mm. 824–826)

Exposition (mm. 827–948)
    Main theme group (mm. 827–887)   **F♯ major**
    Transition (mm. 888–911)
    Subordinate theme group (mm. 912–948)   **A major**

Development (mm. 949–1026)
    Segment 1 (mm. 949–989)
    Segment 2 (mm. 990–997): main theme restatement   **E major**
    Segment 3 (mm. 998–1026)

Recapitulation (mm. 1027–1108)
    Main theme group (mm. 1027–1064)   **F♯ major**
    Subordinate theme group (mm. °1065–1108)

Coda (mm. 1109–1136)

Figure 35: Zemlinsky, Second String Quartet: formal organization of the finale

All three interpolated movements are to a certain extent integrated in the overarching sonata form. Their tonal relation to the overarching sonata form is clear. The D major of the slow movement is not just the parallel major of the ("operating") tonic of the overarching sonata form, but simultaneously harks back to the key of the subordinate theme; the original minor tonic returns in the middle section of the slow movement. The scherzo is in D minor, and the finale is in F♯ major, the parallel major of the piece's "official" tonic.

In addition, there are numerous thematic connections between the interpolated movements and the overarching sonata form. The opening of the slow movement is related to the overarching sonata form by means of a technique we have been able to observe several times before, presenting familiar material in a new guise. As examples 32a and b illustrate, the opening melody of the movement clearly contains two prominent motives (or the head motive and one of its variants) from the quartet's motto theme. As shown in example 32c, the opening of the scherzo relates to the overarching sonata form in a very similar way, its first theme being built out of another variant of the motto's head motive.

Example 32: Zemlinsky, Second String Quartet: (a) motto (beginning) (mm. 1–4); (b) slow movement, opening melody (beginning) (mm. 264–265); (c) scherzo, first theme (beginning) (mm. 364–365)

In the scherzo, this is the only thematic connection to the overarching sonata form, but in the slow movement, thematic integration is more extensive. Towards the end of its exposition, from m. 286 onwards, the head motive of the middle part of the subordinate theme group (originally in mm. 137–139) features prominently, and in mm. 290–291, the upper voice of the subordinate theme group's concluding phrase (mm. 156–160) reappears. The same material comes back near the end of the recapitulation: the head motive of the subordinate theme group's middle part in mm. 351–353, the upper voice of its concluding phrase in mm. 354–356. Further thematic integration takes place in the middle section of the slow movement. Here, the D-minor chord with added augmented fourth from the beginning of the exposition's main theme group (m. 11) is emphatically restated twice (mm. 313 and 319). Interestingly, the thematic integration in the slow movement parallels its tonal relationship to the overarching sonata form: thematic recollections from the D-major subordinate theme group reappear in the D-major exposition and recapitulation of the slow movement, while references to the D-minor main theme group occur in its D-minor middle section.

The interpolated finale (mm. 824–1136) is preceded by a transition that prepares for it thematically. When the main theme group of the overarching sonata form is recapitulated from m. 801 onwards, the formal unit in mm. 804–807, which links two restatements of the second part of the main theme, already contains the characteristic rhythm of the finale theme (♩ ♪♪). In m. 814 the actual transition to the finale starts, a transition in which the finale's main theme gradually acquires a more tangible form. In spite of this preparation, the finale greatly contrasts with its environment. Most of the thematic material it uses is entirely unrelated to the overarching sonata form. There is only one exception. In mm. 1109–1136, just before the beginning of the coda of the overarching sonata form, the thematic material from the closing group of the exposition returns (or, in the dimension of the cycle, the coda of the first movement: mm. 161–198). Here, it functions as the coda of the finale, thus integrating this interpolated movement in the overarching sonata form.

All of the above are instances of indirect integration, relating an interpolated movement to a movement in the cycle that is identified with a section of the overarching sonata form. Late in the form, there is also one example of direct integration. In the coda of the overarching sonata form, more specifically from m. 1167 onwards, thematic material from the exposition of the slow movement is extensively recapitulated, thus integrating the slow movement directly into the overarching sonata form.

Several lines in the history of two-dimensional sonata form converge in Zemlinsky's Second String Quartet. Unsurprisingly, it is closely related to the large-scale tonal instrumental forms Schoenberg wrote in the years before, not only by its layout as a two-dimensional sonata form in general, but also in more specific ways. Its very complex tonal language is reminiscent of *Pelleas und Melisande*, its overall design, comprising a first movement that is identified with part of the overarching sonata form followed by three interpolated movements, echoes Schoenberg's First String Quartet, and the prominent use of a motto (theme) is reminiscent of the First Chamber Symphony.

At the same time, it would be misleading to overemphasize the proximity of Zemlinsky's String Quartet to Schoenberg's two-dimensional sonata forms. Many of the similarities listed above are only superficial. In comparison to Schoenberg's First String Quartet, for instance, the identification of the first movement with units of the overarching sonata form is realized in a very different way. The position of the interpolated movements in the overarching sonata form is also different. In Schoenberg's Quartet, the scherzo is interpolated in the middle of the development, the slow movement in the middle of the recapitulation, and the finale between the recapitulation and the coda of the overarching sonata form. In Zemlinsky's Quartet, the finale is also interpolated between the recapitulation and the coda. Both interior movements, however, appearing here in inverse order, are treated as one large interpolated block that is inserted between the short development and the recapitulation, suspending the overarching sonata form for a much longer period of time.

Similarly, the treatment of the motto in Zemlinsky's Quartet differs from that in Schoenberg's Chamber Symphony. As was shown in the last chapter, the motto in the Chamber Symphony does not yield the kind of thematic treatment that is so characteristic of the motto in Zemlinsky's Second String Quartet. Whereas the motto in Schoenberg's Chamber Symphony primarily serves to mark the beginnings and ends of movements in the dimension of the cycle, the motto in Zemlinsky's Quartet is mainly used to articulate the internal organization of the local sonata form.

That said, the differences between Zemlinsky's Second String Quartet and Schoenberg's two-dimensional sonata forms are no more significant than those between any of Schoenberg's two-dimensional sonata forms; Schoenberg's two-dimensional sonata forms still appear to be the primary context for Zemlinsky's Second String Quartet. The latter clearly engages in a dialogue with Schoenberg's two-dimensional sonata forms, adopting some of their characteristics, rejecting others, and sometimes finding new solutions for the same problems Schoenberg confronted.

Yet one might wonder whether Zemlinsky's Second String Quartet is in dialogue only with Schoenberg's two-dimensional sonata forms. Does it not engage in a similar way with two-dimensional sonata forms from the Liszt–Strauss tradition? This is an important question, both for our assessment of Zemlinsky's Second String Quartet itself and for our view of the phenomenon of two-dimensional

CHAPTER 8

sonata form in general. If the context of the Quartet is limited to Schoenberg's early instrumental music, the latter's overwhelming historical importance tends to overshadow it. In this context, Zemlinsky's Quartet risks being regarded merely as a belated appendix to Schoenberg's output; the nine years that separate its completion from that of Schoenberg's final two-dimensional sonata form, the Chamber Symphony, are a very long period of time when measured against the speed with which new music was evolving in Schoenberg's hands at the time.

At least one important characteristic of Zemlinsky's Quartet is distinctly un-Schoenbergian, and thus points beyond the Schoenberg context: the manner in which its local sonata form is identified with the exposition of the overarching sonata form. In his two-dimensional sonata forms, Schoenberg systematically identifies the local sonata form with the overarching sonata form's exposition and the first segments of its development. This strategy allows for the postponement of the recapitulation of the local sonata form until after the exposition of the overarching sonata form, thus bypassing the difficulty of having to build a recapitulatory movement in the exposition.

To identify the local sonata form with the overarching sonata form's exposition and only its exposition is a strategy that had not been used since Liszt's B-minor Sonata. Like Liszt in his Sonata, Zemlinsky thus fully exploits the analogies between the sections of a sonata form and the segments of a sonata-form exposition: the main theme group of the overarching sonata form corresponds to the exposition of the local sonata form, the transition of the overarching sonata form to the local sonata form's development, the overarching sonata form's subordinate theme group to the recapitulation of the local sonata form, and the closing group in the overarching sonata form to the coda in the local sonata form.

At the same time, in comparison to Liszt, Zemlinsky increases the recapitulatory effect of the subordinate theme group. In Liszt's Sonata, the recapitulation of the local sonata form is essentially off-tonic and at least initially not thematically articulated. The recapitulatory effect of the overarching sonata form's subordinate theme group is mainly generated by the very developmental nature of the transition that precedes it, the strong sense of arrival at the beginning of the subordinate theme group, and the recurrence of thematic material from the main theme group later in the subordinate theme group. Zemlinsky does all this and more. By opting for a tonal relationship between tonic minor and tonic major for the main and subordinate theme groups in the overarching sonata form, he enables them to relate to each other as an exposition and a recapitulation in the local sonata form in a very unambiguous way. The return of the motto at the beginning of the subordinate theme immediately highlights its simultaneous recapitulatory function by means of an unmistakable thematic return.

Notes

[1] "Ich ... arbeite fest an einem – Streichquartett!!" [Zemlinsky 1995, p. 97]. "Es wird nur 1 Satz haben, d.h. 4 Teile in einem Satz u. geht angeblich in fis moll" [p. 99].

[2] For a discussion of the harmonic language of the Second String Quartet see Loll 1990, pp. 178–195. Keys can often be determined solely by the appearance (sometimes repeatedly) of their tonic triad or pitch collection at rhetorically highlighted positions in the form; throughout the piece, functional harmonic progressions are extremely rare.

[3] Antony Beaumont's biography of Zemlinsky includes a convenient chart that compares the formal overviews from three important analyses of the Second String Quartet by Rudolf Stephan, Werner Loll, and Horst Weber [Beaumont 2000, pp. 236–237].

[4] This sonority pervades the entire quartet. Beaumont surmises that the chord's origin is in Schoenberg's *Pelleas und Melisande*. Because of its association with the so-called fate motive there (in m. 75, for instance), he interprets it as a cipher for "fate" [Beaumont 1995, pp. 35–36].

[5] Both authors significantly disagree about the length of the first movement. In Weber's analysis, it lasts until m. 104, while in Loll's, it is more than two and a half times as long (until m. 264). Stephan does not mention a first movement.

[6] Apparently, Weber does not hear mm. 415–434 as part of the development.

[7] Obviously, the note values are longer in mm. 105–109, but this is compensated for by the tempo, which is faster than at the beginning.

[8] Loll complements this view with an alternative interpretation. He suggests the possibility of regarding Zemlinsky's String Quartet not only as a one-movement sonata form and a four-movement sonata cycle, but also as a nine-movement cycle [Loll 1990, p. 160]. In this suite-like sequence, mm. 361–450 do not belong to the scherzo, but constitute an independent variation movement. As a result, Loll's scherzo begins only in m. 451. The main advantage of this perspective is that mm. 683–744 can be heard as a recapitulation of the scherzo's opening section in mm. 451–517. It is hardly probable, however, that two consecutive movements would share both tempo and key, or that they would be linked by numerous returns of thematic material from the earlier movement in the later one.

Conclusion

The significance of two-dimensional sonata form

In the preceding seven chapters, I have discussed the nine two-dimensional sonata forms by Liszt, Strauss, Schoenberg, and Zemlinsky explicitly as a group of interrelated compositions. In spite of their obvious connections to the much broader field of sonata form in general, these two-dimensional sonata forms constitute a context of their own, creating a subfield for the interpretation of each individual one of them. To be sure, the same group of works could have been studied in a much larger context. One could set out to measure them against a normative model of sonata form, and legitimately conclude that many characteristics typical of two-dimensional sonata form—the singularities in the exposition and the development of the overarching sonata form, the presence of interpolated interior movements, the often drastic modifications to the recapitulation, or the presence of an interpolated finale—are highly deformational. Yet one might also ask whether it is useful to continue regarding a particular form as a deformation of a given norm if deformations are as numerous and far-reaching as they are in two-dimensional sonata forms. What does it mean, moreover, to say that a particular musical form is a deformation? The mere identification of a number of deformational features does not get us much further, and using the concept of deformation as an analytical alibi for anything in a musical form that resists easy explanation would surely be simplistic. Rather, the concept of deformation should be embedded in a consistent analytical argumentation. If a particular feature of a composition is legitimately identified as a deformation, it should be possible to demonstrate how that deformation contributes to the way that specific composition works.

For the compositions analyzed in Chapters 2 through 8, this is possible only if the referential framework of normative sonata form is replaced by that of two-dimensional sonata form. From the latter perspective, everything that appears deformational from the point of view of normative sonata form falls into place and turns out to contribute to the articulation of the two-dimensional sonata form. Only initially does a two-dimensional sonata form invite interpretation within the referential framework of one-dimensional sonata form. From the dimensional disconnection onwards, indications that point in the direction of the more specific referential framework of two-dimensional sonata form rapidly increase.

There is also a more fundamental difference between one-dimensional and two-dimensional sonata form. The relationship between formal scheme and formal idea in a two-dimensional sonata form differs considerably from that in a one-dimensional sonata form. The basis of the latter is a formal scheme (even if that scheme was not necessarily in place as an abstract given at the time of composition). Although this scheme can accommodate considerable flexibility especially at the lower hierarchical levels of the form, its broad outlines—exposition with modulation, development, recapitulation, and coda—remain readily recognizable in practically every one-dimensional sonata form. This formal scheme as such does not coincide with the formal idea of the composition (for instance, a *per aspera ad astra* narrative trajectory). Rather, the formal scheme—which is, to a certain extent, invariable—serves as a vehicle for the realization of a formal idea. This formal idea, comparable to what Dahlhaus has called "the underlying idea" ("die zugrunde liegende Idee") in Beethoven [Dahlhaus 1987, pp. 183–191], is more abstract and can in principal be different in every composition.

In a two-dimensional sonata form, by contrast, the point of departure is not the formal scheme, but a formal idea, more specifically the idea of combining the sections of a sonata form with the movements of a sonata cycle at the same hierarchical level within a single-movement form. The specific shape this combination takes is by no means fixed. This is not to say that the formal scheme in a two-dimensional sonata form is not the vehicle of the formal idea; but, unlike a one-dimensional sonata form, it is the formal idea of a two-dimensional sonata form that is invariable, whereas the formal scheme can vary considerably.

Ever since Antonín Reicha described sonata form through the metaphor of drama, the traditional view of sonata form—obviously derived from a number of Beethoven's middle-period works—is that of a dynamic, goal- or even end-oriented form par excellence. Once set into motion, a sonata form heads unstoppably for its end. One of the tendencies thought to be characteristic of musical form later in the nineteenth century is the development of an epic type of sonata form. Three composers that are mentioned time and again in this context are Schubert, Bruckner, and Mahler. In each of these composers' sonata-form movements, the dynamic and goal-oriented nature of the form is undermined, either by an unusual—or at least un-Beethovenian—size, syntax, or melodic character of the themes or theme groups (Schubert), a bloc-like juxtaposition of large formal units (Bruckner), or the frequency of apparently non-functional episodes (Mahler).

Although this account is an almost caricature-like simplification of matters— not least because the epic type of sonata form has its origins in Beethoven too, as Adorno already recognized [Adorno 1960, p. 213]—it might at first seem that two-dimensional sonata form also participates in this tendency. When a movement of the sonata cycle is interpolated in the overarching sonata form, it temporarily suspends the continuation of that form. Therefore, this too might be interpreted as a fundamental difference between a two-dimensional and a (normative) one-dimensional sonata form. Yet the effect the movements of a sonata cycle have on the way the overarching sonata form functions in a two-dimensional sonata form is far less univocal than it initially seems. It depends on at least three factors: the kind of movement (a first movement, an interior movement, or a finale), its position (in the exposition, development, recapitulation, or coda), and its relationship to the overarching sonata form (identification or interpolation). In first movements that are identified with the initial formal units of the overarching sonata form, any effect that might interfere too strongly with the latter's functionality is deliberately avoided. This explains why in most two-dimensional sonata forms, the recapitulation of the local sonata form remains underexposed in order to avoid neutralizing the impact of the recapitulation of the overarching sonata form.

There are more diverse possibilities when it comes to interior movements. An interior movement does not significantly influence the overarching sonata form when it is identified with one of the latter's development segments. When it is identified with part of the exposition, however, it may threaten the continuation of the overarching sonata form. If the end of the exposition coincides with the end of the slow movement, this may lead to an apparent stagnation of the form at the end of the exposition. This is very much the case in *Ein Heldenleben*, while a similar situation at the end of the exposition of *Tasso* is avoided by the unexpected change in texture at the beginning of the second subordinate theme. Interior movements that are interpolated in the developmental space have a similar effect, and always suspend the continuation of the form. In spite of the often remarkable amount of thematic integration—direct or indirect, retrospective or prospective—they essentially remain foreign to the overarching sonata form. The strongest and most complex effect on the functionality of the overarching sonata form is exerted by movements of the sonata cycle that are located after the onset of the recapitulation. In the rare case in which an interior movement is located after the beginning of the recapitulation, it behaves differently from interior movements that are located elsewhere in the overarching sonata form. An interior movement in this position increases the end-oriented character of the overarching sonata form. This is what happens in Schoenberg's First String Quartet. Here, the interpolation of the slow movement in the middle of the recapitulation reduces the closural effect of the recapitulation and shifts the apex of the form to the coda. As was demonstrated in Chapter 6, this shift is emphasized by the large-scale tonal organization of the composition.

Interpolating a finale between the recapitulation and the coda leads to a similar result. The presence of such an unexpected amount of new élan after the beginning of the recapitulation clearly jeopardizes the latter's privileged position in the overarching sonata form, while at the same time increasing the emphasis on the coda. The identification of the finale with the recapitulation or coda equally increases the goal- or end-oriented nature of the overarching sonata form. If the finale is identified with the recapitulation, the latter's weight is increased by its double-functionality, in that it becomes an essential formal unit in the dimension of the cycle as well as in that of the form. If it is identified with the coda, the finale creates an even more end-oriented sonata form. As a double-functional formal unit, the coda becomes an essential rather than an optional section of the composition.

The history of two-dimensional sonata form does not end with the last two-dimensional sonata form discussed in the present study. Even within the limited geographical scope of Germany and Austria, composers continued to write two-dimensional sonata forms after Zemlinsky's Second String Quartet. Two examples from what might be called the periphery of Schoenberg's Viennese circle are Franz Schreker's Chamber Symphony of 1917 and Franz Schmidt's Fourth Symphony of 1932–33. Although by no means modeled on Schoenberg's Chamber Symphony, Schreker's eponymous composition does adopt the former's two-dimensionality as a generic convention. It consists of an introduction and a sonata form, into which the interior movements of a sonata cycle are interpolated. More specifically, the (relatively brief) development of the overarching sonata form is preceded by a slow movement and followed by a scherzo. Surprisingly, the slow movement reappears in its entirety between the recapitulation and the coda of the overarching sonata form. In Schmidt's Fourth Symphony, the first movement of the sonata cycle is identified with the exposition and development of the overarching sonata form (the development simultaneously functioning as a recapitulation). The slow movement and scherzo are interpolated between the development and recapitulation. The possibility of hearing the latter as simultaneously fulfilling the role of a finale entirely depends on the principle of cyclic completion.

In spite of the existence of successful two-dimensional sonata forms later in the twentieth century, the form's historical position changes after Schoenberg's Chamber Symphony. In Schoenberg's oeuvre, all instrumental works from *Verklärte Nacht* to the First Chamber Symphony are single-movement compositions in two-dimensional sonata form (or, in the case of *Verklärte Nacht*, a form related to two-dimensional sonata form). The same is true for his unfinished works from 1897 onwards. The transition to and the beginning of his atonal period, by contrast, are marked by a number of multi-movement instrumental compositions. Each of these—the Second String Quartet Op. 10, the Three Piano Pieces Op. 11, and the Five Orchestral Pieces Op. 16—constitutes a one-dimensional sonata cycle, or at least invites comparison with it [see Vande Moortele 2006a, pp. 62–70]. Two-dimensional sonata form in Schoenberg's oeuvre is, in other words, very closely tied to what Dahlhaus has called "musical modernism" ('die musikalische Moderne"): the period between the deaths of Wagner and Liszt and Schoenberg's first atonal compositions [Dahlhaus 1980, p. 277]. After the move to atonality, two-dimensional sonata form plays no role at all in Schoenberg's music. In a later stage of their development—from the 1920s onwards—composers of the Viennese School admittedly show a renewed interest in combining multi-movement elements in a single-movement form. Significantly, however, none of these works (including such diverse compositions as the second act of *Wozzeck*, the first scene from *Moses und Aron*, Schoenberg's Piano Concerto Op. 42 and String Trio Op. 45) really amounts to a two-dimensional sonata form as it is defined here.

From a broader perspective too, two-dimensional sonata form is very much a phenomenon of the musical modernism from around the turn of the twentieth century. After the advent of atonality, two-dimensional sonata forms were written only by composers who decided not to follow Schoenberg's move to atonality and continued to compose in an idiom typical of *die musikalische Moderne*. This is not to say that atonal music automatically outdated previous idioms and the forms associated with them; after Schoenberg's move to atonality, the part of two-dimensional sonata form in music history is not played. It remained a viable format (alongside more traditional multi-movement layouts) in younger symphonic traditions outside Central Europe until deep into the twentieth century; examples include Jean Sibelius' Seventh Symphony (1924) in Finland and Samuel Barber's First Symphony (1936) in the United States. Still, and even though Schoenberg and his followers initially occupied a very marginal position in their countries, it seems fair to say that after 1906 two-dimensional sonata form changed roles in Austria and Germany, from now on no longer figuring in the vanguard of music history.

Between roughly 1850 and 1910, however, two-dimensional sonata form was the locus par excellence of formal innovation in instrumental music. In the Austro-German world in the second half of the nineteenth century, formal experiments involving the combination of elements from sonata form and sonata cycle in a single-movement composition were the exclusive domain of composers of the *Neudeutsche Schule* and their adherents. This is, of course, hardly surprising. One of the debates between progressive and conservative composers—or rather between overtly and less overtly progressive ones—in the latter half of the nineteenth century centered on the discussion about the viability of traditional patterns of formal organization (the other debate being that over program versus absolute music). It is an oft-repeated fact that Liszt and his partisans held the opinion that traditional patterns of formal organization were worn out. Rather than disposing entirely of these forms, however, they attempted to revitalize them by treating them in innovative ways (an enterprise in which experiments such as the ones described in the previous chapters were a favorite tool). As has become clear in this study, two-dimensional sonata form played a similar role in the early instrumental music of Schoenberg. In this sense, he is clearly the heir to the *Neudeutsche Schule*. It is hardly a coincidence that Schoenberg started experimenting with two-dimensional sonata forms only when he ceased to be an exclusive champion of Brahms.

So strong a continuity between the New German and the Viennese Schools is at odds with the traditional view of Schoenberg's relationship with the different Austro-German compositional traditions in the nineteenth century. Traditionally, the Viennese School is regarded as a synthesis of two of the principal lines in nineteenth-century music history: the Beethoven–Brahms tradition on the one hand and the New German School (mainly Wagner himself) on the other. In his treatment of thematic-motivic development and form, Schoenberg, in particular, is often considered the direct heir of Beethoven and Brahms. In terms of pitch organization, he is believed to have continued Wagner's expansion of tonality that would eventually lead to atonality.

In the light of our findings this view must be revised. The Beethoven–Brahms tradition is, of course, of crucial importance for Schoenberg. But its influence on the formal organization of large-scale instrumental works predating the move towards atonality is not exclusive. In these compositions, the influence of the New German School is not restricted to pitch organization: their large-scale formal organization is also much indebted to post-Wagnerian progressive music— Strauss in particular—and this to a far greater extent than was hitherto believed. Schoenberg's instrumental music after *Pelleas und Melisande* thus paints a complex picture. Although Schoenberg moves away from the New German School in terms of aesthetics, choice of genre, and even thematic-motivic technique, he continues to use one of Liszt's and Straus's preferred patterns of large-scale organization.

▨ ☐ ▨

That two-dimensional sonata form played a role in music history mainly between roughly 1850 and 1910 is no coincidence. Two-dimensional sonata form is an answer—and here we come back to the initial hypothesis formulated in the introduction—to two central preoccupations of large-scale instrumental form in the post-Beethovenian nineteenth century. One is the search for a solution to the recapitulation problem in a sonata form, for a way of avoiding too close an analogy between the recapitulation and the exposition without neglecting one of the form's most fundamental requirements. The other is a strong tendency towards cyclic integration in multi-movement compositions, emphasizing that the separate movements in the multi-movement plan belong together intrinsically, rather than that they form a more or less random collection. Both preoccupations converge in two-dimensional sonata form. By combining a sonata form and a sonata cycle at the same hierarchical level in a single-movement composition, composers attempt both to achieve the highest possible degree of cyclic integration and to solve the recapitulation problem.

On the one hand, two-dimensional sonata form is the high point of the tendency towards cyclic integration, by far exceeding all previous attempts in that direction. Numerous other multi-movement compositions contain thematic relationships between different movements, display a through-composed multi-movement design, or suggest an overarching pattern of formal organization; some of them even combine all of these features. Yet in no previous type of cyclic multi-movement composition were the movements of the sonata cycle bound together so strongly as in a two-dimensional sonata form, where the separate movements are integrated into a fully-fledged overarching sonata form. On the other hand, two-dimensional sonata form is an attempt to solve—or at least mitigate—the recapitulation problem of sonata form. If in a two-dimensional sonata form the recapitulation of the overarching sonata form is identified with the finale of the sonata cycle, this adds to its weight as a formal unit. It not only acquires a double necessity—in the cycle as well as in the form—but also an increased independence from the exposition. If, by contrast, the finale is identified mainly with the coda, or is interpolated between the recapitulation and the coda, the apex of the form shifts from the recapitulation to the finale or the coda.

Concerns with the recapitulation problem run as a common thread through the history of two-dimensional sonata form from Liszt to Zemlinsky. It is hardly an exaggeration to say that almost every new two-dimensional sonata form comes with a new solution for it. In the B-minor Sonata, Liszt identified the finale with the recapitulation and the coda of the overarching sonata form. In *Tasso*, the finale is not identified with the entire recapitulation, but only with part of the recapitulation and all of the coda. In *Die Ideale*, each of the three themes from the exposition returns in a transformed shape. Strauss experimented with other strategies. In *Don Juan*, he incorporated the new theme from the development in his recapitulation to give it the character of a finale; in *Ein Heldenleben*, an initially orthodox and almost overly affirmative recapitulation soon gives way to citations from other compositions that override every analogy to the exposition. Schoenberg in his two-dimensional sonata forms detaches the finale from the recapitulation. In *Pelleas und Melisande* it is identified with the coda, in the First String Quartet it is interpolated between the recapitulation and the coda, and in the Chamber Symphony it is identified with the final segment of the recapitulation and the coda. Zemlinsky, finally, interpolates the finale between the recapitulation and the coda. His solution is at first sight similar to the one Schoenberg uses in his First String Quartet. Yet the finale in Zemlinsky's Quartet lacks the summative function that is so conspicuously present in Schoenberg's Quartet.

Although an answer to both crucial problems of nineteenth-century sonata form and sonata cycle, the combination of the movements of a sonata cycle with the sections of a sonata form at the same hierarchical level in a single-movement composition is itself deeply problematic. It engenders a very strong tension between both dimensions, which becomes particularly palpable when a movement of the sonata cycle is identified with one or several units of the overarching sonata form, or when a movement of the cycle is interpolated in the form. Although composers relentlessly attempted to solve this tension, it never entirely disappeared: the complete integration of both dimensions in a two-dimensional sonata form failed.

One does not have to agree with Adorno's idea of the mediation of music and society to see that the failure of two-dimensional sonata form to integrate sonata form and sonata cycle is in line with an Adornian image of post-1800 music history. After Beethoven—more exactly after Beethoven's middle period—the composition of large-scale and monumental musical forms grows increasingly problematic. Two-dimensional sonata form does more, however, than express the impossibility of the unbroken large form after Beethoven. It also highlights a tendency in Germanic art music in the second half of the nineteenth and early twentieth centuries to address problems of large-scale form in an explicit way. The greatest two-dimensional sonata forms by Liszt, Strauss, Schoenberg, and Zemlinsky tackle these problems head-on, but fail. Two-dimensional sonata form's failure—one is tempted to say: its heroic failure—to integrate sonata form and sonata cycle is, however, not a shortcoming; it is the hallmark of its historical position.

Appendix: Measure-Number Tables

Tasso
(Eulenburg)

A	27
B	52
C	99
D	131
E	145
F	216
G	309
H	382
I	417
J	447
L	496
M	529

Die Ideale
(Eulenburg)

A	°26	T	474
B	43	U	502
C	65	V	525
D	85	W	540
E	109	X	558
F	129	Y	586
G	158	Z	618
H	192	Tz	638
I	222	Aa	658
K	287	Bb	680
L	319	Cc	698
M	341	Dd	710
N	365	Ee	732
O	381	Ff	773
P	394	Gg	807
Q	407	Hh	827
R	425	Ii	849
S	453		

Don Juan
(Aibl Verlag/ Dover)

A	23
B	40
C	50
D	71
E	101
F	129
G	156
H	169
I	185
K	197
L	232
M	252
N	296
O	331
P	343
Q	365
R	379
S	386
T	402
U	421
V	447
W	474
X	490
Y	510
Z	521
Aa	543
Bb	556
Cc	569
Dd	596

Appendix

Ein Heldenleben
(Aibl Verlag/Dover)

1	13	**30**	260	**59**	510	**88**	729
2	21	**31**	274	**60**	514	**89**	737
3	29	**32**	288	**61**	518	**90**	745
4	37	**33**	296	**62**	522	**91**	753
5	45	**34**	302	**63**	530	**92**	762
6	52	**35**	309	**64**	538	**93**	774
7	62	**36**	317	**65**	546	**94**	788
8	68	**37**	323	**66**	554	**95**	796
9	76	**38**	328	**67**	560	**96**	804
10	84	**39**	336	**68**	566	**97**	811
11	90	**40**	345	**69**	574	**98**	819
12	98	**41**	354	**70**	580	**99**	828
13	110	**42**	369	**71**	584	**100**	834
14	124	**43**	378	**72**	590	**101**	846
15	129	**44**	392	**73**	598	**102**	858
16	145	**45**	402	**74**	607	**103**	866
17	153	**46**	410	**75**	614	**104**	871
18	161	**47**	416	**76**	625	**105**	878
19	169	**48**	423	**77**	631	**106**	883
20	175	**49**	430	**78**	639	**107**	890
21	182	**50**	443	**79**	653	**108**	897
22	190	**51**	449	**80**	659	**109**	909
23	200	**52**	457	**81**	666		
24	210	**53**	461	**82**	674		
25	215	**54**	469	**83**	682		
26	223	**55**	475	**84**	692		
27	234	**56**	488	**85**	705		
28	239	**57**	494	**86**	717		
29	255	**58**	506	**87**	723		

Pelleas und Melisande
(Universal Edition/Dover)

1	12	43	390
2	20	44	402
3	28	45	410
4	39	46	421
5	44	47	435
6	55	48	445
7	64	49	451
8	75	50	461
9	89	51	469
10	97	52	475
11	107	53	482
12	117	54	491
13	130	55	505
14	137	56	515
15	148	57	523
16	161	58	531
17	179	59	541
18	184	60	549
19	196	61	559
20	202	62	566
21	208	63	579
22	214	64	583
23	223	65	589
24	232	66	601
25	244	67	615
26	248	68	626
27	255	69	635
28	264		
29	268		
30	278		
31	287		
32	294		
33	302		
34	312		
35	322		
36	329		
37	346		
38	355		
39	365		
40	372		
41	377		
42	383		

Schoenberg, First String Quartet
(Verlag Dreililien)

A	97	H	784
B	200	I	872
C	301	K	952
D	366	L	1031
E	399	M	1122
F	532	N	1181
G	673	O	1270

Zemlinsky, Second String Quartet
(Universal Edition)

1	11	43	341	85	700	127	1060
2	16	44	348	86	709	128	1070
3	23	45	354	87	717	129	1081
4	30	46	361	88	723	130	1091
5	39	47	368	89	732	131	1099
6	48	48	382	90	740	132	1109
7	54	49	392	91	751	133	1122
8	62	50	400	92	757	134	1137
9	69	51	407	93	766	135	1147
10	75	52	414	94	777	136	1159
11	83	53	422	95	786	137	1167
12	91	54	429	96	795	138	1177
13	99	55	441	97	801	139	1185
14	105	56	451	98	808	140	1192
15	112	57	461	99	814	141	1202
16	123	58	468	100	820	142	1209
17	137	59	474	101	827		
18	143	60	483	102	833		
19	156	61	489	103	839		
20	161	62	497	104	849		
21	168	63	504	105	857		
22	180	64	510	106	867		
23	188	65	518	107	875		
24	199	66	527	108	881		
25	205	67	535	109	888		
26	212	68	542	110	902		
27	219	69	549	111	912		
28	229	70	556	112	922		
29	236	71	566	113	932		
30	246	72	574	114	940		
31	253	73	585	115	949		
32	264	74	592	116	959		
33	269	75	599	117	968		
34	276	76	611	118	977		
35	284	77	620	119	986		
36	290	78	632	120	994		
37	300	79	644	121	1001		
38	307	80	654	122	1013		
39	314	81	667	123	1025		
40	321	82	675	124	1034		
41	329	83	683	125	1043		
42	335	84	692	126	1052		

BIBLIOGRAPHY

ACKERMANN, Peter (1992), "Schönbergs 'Pelleas und Melisande' und die Tradition der symphonischen Dichtung," *Archiv für Musikwissenschaft*, 49, pp. 146–156.

ADORNO, Theodor Wiesengrund (1960), *Mahler: Eine musikalische Physiognomik*, in *Die musikalischen Monographien*, (*Theodor W. Adorno: Gesammelte Schriften*, 13, ed. Gretel ADORNO and Rolf TIEDEMANN), Frankfurt am Main: Suhrkamp, 2nd edition, 1977, pp. 149–319.

ALTENBURG, Detlef (1994), "Franz Liszt and the Legacy of the Classical Era," *19th Century Music*, 18, pp. 46–63.

— (1998), "Symphonische Dichtung," in *Die Musik in Geschichte und Gegenwart*, ed. Ludwig FINSCHER, *Sachteil*, 9, Kassel: Bärenreiter, col. 153–168.

BAILEY, Walter B. (1984), *Programmatic Elements in the Works of Schoenberg*, (*Studies in Musicology*, ed. George BUELOW, 74), Ann Arbor: UMI Research Press.

BEAUMONT, Antony (1995), "Schicksalsakkord und Lebensmotiv," in *Alexander Zemlinsky: Ästhetik, Stil und Umfeld*, (*Wiener Schriften zur Stilkunde und Aufführungspraxis*, Sonderband 1, ed. Hartmut KRONES), Vienna – Cologne – Weimar: Boehlau, pp. 27–43.

— (2000), *Zemlinsky*, London: Faber.

BENSON, Mark (1993), "Schoenberg's Private Program for the String Quartet in D Minor, Op. 7," *Journal of Musicology*, 3, pp. 374–395.

BERG, Alban (1918), "A. Schönberg, Kammersymphonie, op. 9: Kurze thematische Analyse," in *Alban Berg: Analysen musikalischer Werke von Arnold Schönberg*, (*Alban Berg: Sämtliche Werke*, ed. Rudolf STEPHAN and Regina BUSCH, *III. Abteilung: Musikalische Schriften und Dichtungen*, Band 1), Vienna: Universal Edition, 1994, pp. 119–130.

— (1920), "A. Schönberg, *Pelleas und Melisande*, op. 5: Kurze thematische Analyse," in *Alban Berg: Analysen musikalischer Werke von Arnold Schönberg*, (*Alban Berg: Sämtliche Werke*, ed. Rudolf STEPHAN and Regina BUSCH, *III. Abteilung: Musikalische Schriften und Dichtungen*, Band 1), Vienna: Universal Edition, 1994, pp. 83–96.

— (1994), "A. Schönberg, *Pelleas und Melisande*, op. 5: Thematische Analyse," in *Alban Berg: Analysen musikalischer Werke von Arnold Schönberg*, (*Alban Berg: Sämtliche Werke*, ed. Rudolf STEPHAN and Regina BUSCH, *III. Abteilung: Musikalische Schriften und Dichtungen*, Band 1), Vienna: Universal Edition, pp. 97–118.

BERGER, Christian (1997), "Die Musik der Zukunft: Liszts Symphonische Dichtung *Die Ideale*," in *Liszt und die Weimarer Klassik*, (*Weimarer Liszt-Studien*, ed. Detlef ALTENBURG, 1), Laaber: Laaber Verlag, pp. 101–114.

BIRKIN, Kenneth (2002), "'Ich dirigiere mit Vergnügen...': Liszt's Influence on Richard Strauss – Strauss Conducts Franz Liszt," *Studia musicologica academiae scientiarum hungaricae*, 43, pp. 73–92.

BOESTFLEISCH, Rainer (1990), *Arnold Schönbergs frühe Kammermusik: Studien unter besonderer Berücksichtigung der ersten beiden Streichquartette*, (*Europäische Hochschulschriften*, XXXVI/54), Frankfurt am Main: Peter Lang.

BONDS, Mark Evan (1991), *Wordless Rhetoric: Musical Form and the Metaphor of the Oration*, (*Studies in the History of Music*, ed. Lewis LOCKWOOD and Christoph WOLFF, 4), Cambridge (MA) – London: Harvard University Press.

BRINKMANN, Reinhold (1977), "Die gepreßte Sinfonie: Zum geschichtlichen Gehalt von Schönbergs Opus 9," in *Gustav Mahler: Sinfonie und Wirklichkeit*, (*Studien zur Wertungsforschung*, ed. Otto KOLLERITSCH, 9), Graz: Universal Edition – Institut für Wertungsforschung, 1977, pp. 133–156.

BROSCHE, Günter (1977), "Richard Strauss – Roland Tenschert: Briefwechsel 1943–1948," *Richard Strauss Blätter*, 10, pp. 1–10.

BRUHN, Siglind (2002), "*Pelleas und Melisande* Op. 5," in *Arnold Schönberg: Interpretationen seiner Werke*, 2 volumes, ed. Gerold W. GRUBER, Laaber: Laaber Verlag, vol. 1, pp. 36–60.

CAVANAGH, Lynn M. (1996), *Tonal Multiplicity in Schoenberg's First String Quartet*, Ph.D. diss., University of British Columbia.

CAPLIN, William E. (1998), *Classical Form: A Theory of Formal Functions for the Instrumental Music of Haydn, Mozart, and Beethoven*, New York: Oxford University Press.

CHERLIN, Michael (1994), "[Review of] Walter Frisch. *The Early Works of Arnold Schoenberg: 1893-1908*," *19th Century Music*, 18, pp. 174–185.

— (2007), *Schoenberg's Musical Imagination*, New York: Cambridge University Press.

DAHLHAUS, Carl (1970), *Analyse und Werturteil*, (*Musikpädagogik: Forschung und Lehre*, ed. Sigrid ABEL-STRUTH, 8), Mainz: Schott [English translation: *Analysis and Value Judgment*, trans. Siegmund LEVARIE, New York: Pendragon Press, 1983].

— (1974), "Schönberg und die Programmusik," in *Schönberg und andere: Gesammelte Aufsätze zur Neuen Musik*, Mainz: Schott, 1978, pp. 125–133 [English translation: "Schoenberg and programme music," in *Schoenberg and the New Music*, trans. Derrick PUFFETT and Alfred CLAYTON, Cambridge – New York: Cambridge University Press, 1987, pp. 94–104].

— (1976), "Liszts Bergsymphonie und die Idee der Symphonischen Dichtung," in *Jahrbuch des Staatlichen Instituts für Musikforschung Preußischer Kulturbesitz 1975*, ed. Dagmar Droysen, Berlin: De Gruyter, pp. 96–130.

— (1979), "Liszts Faust-Symphonie und die Krise der symphonischen Form," in *Über Symphonien: Beiträge zu einer musikalischen Gattung*, ed. Christoph-Helmut MAHLING, Tutzing: Schneider, pp. 129–139.

— (1980), *Die Musik des 19. Jahrhunderts*, (*Neues Handbuch der Musikwissenschaft*, ed. Carl DAHLHAUS, 6), Wiesbaden – Laaber: Laaber Verlag [English translation: *Nineteenth-Century Music*, trans. J. Bradford ROBINSON, Berkeley – Los Angeles: University of California Press, 1989].

— (1981), "Liszts Idee des Symphonischen," in *Klassische und romantische Musikästhetik*, Laaber: Laaber Verlag, 1988, pp. 401–412.

— (1987), *Ludwig van Beethoven und seine Zeit*, (*Große Komponisten und ihre Zeit*), Laaber: Laaber Verlag, 1987 [English translation: *Ludwig van Beethoven: Approaches to his Music*, trans. Mary WHITTALL, Oxford: Oxford University Press, 1991].

— (1988), "Liszt, Schönberg und die große Form: Das Prinzip der Mehrsätzigkeit in der Einsätzigkeit," *Die Musikforschung*, 41, pp. 202–213.

DALE, Catherine (2000), *Schoenberg's Chamber Symphonies: The Crystallization and Rediscovery of a Style*, Aldershot: Ashgate.

DANNREUTHER, Edward (1905), *The Romantic Period*, (*The Oxford History of Music*, 6), Oxford: Oxford University Press.

DARCY, Warren (1997), "Bruckner's Sonata Deformations," in *Bruckner Studies*, ed. Timothy L. JACKSON and Paul HAWKSHAW, Cambridge: Cambridge University Press, pp. 256–277.

DÖMLING, Wolfgang (1985), *Franz Liszt und seine Zeit*, (*Große Komponisten und ihre Zeit*), Laaber: Laaber Verlag, 1985.

FINSCHER, Ludwig (1998), "Zyklus," in *Die Musik in Geschichte und Gegenwart*, ed. Ludwig FINSCHER, *Sachteil*, 9, Kassel: Bärenreiter, col. 2528–2537.

FLOROS, Constantin (1980), "Die Faust-Symphonie von Franz Liszt: Eine semantische Analyse," in *Franz Liszt*, (*Musik-Konzepte*, ed. Heinz-Klaus METZGER and Rainer RIEHN, 12), Munich: Edition Text+Kritik, pp. 42–87.

FRISCH, Walter M. (1984), *Brahms and the Principle of Developing Variation*, (*California Studies in 19th Century Music*, ed. Joseph KERMAN), Berkeley – Los Angeles: University of California Press.

— (1993), *The Early Works of Arnold Schoenberg: 1893-1908*, Berkeley – Los Angeles: University of California Press.

— (2003), *Brahms: The Four Symphonies*, (*Yale Music Masterworks Series*), New Haven – London: Yale University Press.

GERLACH, Reinhard (1966), *"Don Juan" und "Rosenkavalier": Studien zu Idee und Gestalt einer tonalen Evolution im Werke Richard Strauss'*, (*Publikationen der Schweizerischen musikforschenden Gesellschaft*, II/13), Bern: Haupt.

GREY, Thomas (1988), "Wagner, the Overture, and the Aesthetics of Musical Form," *19th Century Music*, 33, pp. 3–22.

HAIMO, Ethan (2006), *Schoenberg's Transformation of Musical Language*, New York: Cambridge University Press.

HAMILTON, Kenneth (1996), *Liszt: Sonata in B Minor*, (*Cambridge Music Handbooks*, ed. Julian RUSHTON), Cambridge: Cambridge University Press.

— (1997), "Liszt," in *The Nineteenth-Century Symphony*, ed. D. Kern HOLOMAN, (*Studies in Musical Genres and Repertories*, ed. R. Larry TODD), New York: Schirmer, pp. 142–162.

HANSEN, Mathias (1993), *Arnold Schönberg: Ein Konzept der Moderne*, Kassel: Bärenreiter.

HATTESEN, Heinrich Helge (1990), *Emanzipation durch Aneignung: Untersuchungen zu den frühen Streichquartetten Arnold Schönbergs*, (*Kieler Schriften zur Musikwissenschaft*, ed. Friedhelm KRUMMACHER and Heinrich W. SCHWAB, 33), Kassel: Bärenreiter.

HEPOKOSKI, James (1992a), "Fiery-Pulsed Libertine or Domestic Hero? Strauss's *Don Juan* Reinvestigated," in *Richard Strauss: New Perspectives on the Composer and his Work*, ed. Bryan GILLIAM, Durham NC: Durham University Press, pp. 135–175.

— (1992b), "Structure and Program in *Macbeth*: A Proposed Reading of Strauss's First Symphonic Poem," in *Richard Strauss and his World*, ed. Bryan GILLIAM, Princeton: Princeton University Press, pp. 67–89.

— (1993), *Sibelius: Symphony No. 5*, (*Cambridge Music Handbooks*, ed. Julian RUSHTON), Cambridge: Cambridge University Press.

— (1997), "Elgar," in *The Nineteenth-Century Symphony*, ed. D. Kern HOLOMAN, (*Studies in Musical Genres and Repertories*, ed. R. Larry TODD), New York: Schirmer, pp. 327–344.

— (2001), "Beethoven Reception: The Symphonic Tradition," in *The Cambridge History of Nineteenth-Century Music*, ed. Jim SAMSON, Cambridge: Cambridge University Press, pp. 424–459.

— (2002), "Back and Forth from *Egmont*: Beethoven, Mozart, and the Nonresolving Recapitulation," *19th Century Music*, 25, pp. 127–154.

— (2006), "Framing *Till Eulenspiegel*," *19th Century Music*, 30, pp. 4–43.

— (2009), "Sonata Theory and Dialogic Form," in William CAPLIN, James HEPOKOSKI, and James WEBSTER, *Musical Form, Forms, and Formenlehre: Three Methodological Reflections*, ed. Pieter BERGÉ, Leuven: Leuven University Press, pp. 71–89.

HEPOKOSKI James, and Warren DARCY (2006), *Sonata Theory: Norms, Types, and Deformations in the Late Eighteenth-Century Sonata*, New York – Oxford: Oxford University Press.

HORTON, Julian (2005), "Bruckner's Symphonies and Sonata Deformation Theory," *Journal of the Society for Musicology in Ireland*, 1, pp. 5–17.

HUMAL, Mart (1999), "Structural Variants of Sentence in Main Themes in Beethoven's Sonata Form," in *A Composition as a Problem II*, ed. Mart HUMAL, Tallinn: Estonian Academy of Music, pp. 34–48.

JACKSON, Timothy L. (1997), "The Finale of Bruckner's Seventh Symphony and the Tragic Reversed Sonata Form," in *Bruckner Studies*, ed. Timothy L. JACKSON and Paul HAWKSHAW, Cambridge: Cambridge University Press, pp. 140–208.

— (1999), *Tchaikovsky. Symphony No. 6 (Pathétique)*, (*Cambridge Music Handbooks*, ed. Julian RUSHTON), Cambridge: Cambridge University Press.

KAPLAN, Richard (1984), "Sonata Form in the Orchestral Works of Liszt: The Revolutionary Reconsidered," *19th Century Music*, 8, pp. 142–152.

KENNEDY, Michael (1984), *Strauss's Tone Poems*, London: BBC.

KEYM, Stefan (1998), "Originalität oder Epigonentum? Zur motivisch-thematischen Struktur der 'b-Moll-Sonate' von Julius Reubke im Vergleich mit Liszts 'h-Moll-Sonate'," *Die Musikforschung*, 51, pp. 34–46.

KIRBY, Frank E. (1995), "The Germanic Symphony of the Nineteenth Century: Genre, Form, Instrumentation, Expression," *Journal of Musicological Research*, 14, pp. 193–221.

KOCH, Heinrich Christoph (1793), *Versuch einer Anleitung zur Composition*, vol. 3, Leipzig: Böhme, reprint Hildesheim: Olms, 1969.

KOHLER Ralf-Alexander, and Markus BÖGGEMAN (2002), "I. Streichquartett op. 7," in *Arnold Schönberg: Interpretationen seiner Werke*, 2 volumes, ed. Gerold W. GRUBER, Laaber: Laaber Verlag, vol. 1, pp. 73–94.

KOKKINIS Nikos, and Ralf KWASNY (1999), *Arnold Schönberg. Pelleas und Melisande (Nach dem Drama von Maurice Maeterlinck). Symphonische Dichtung für Orchester Opus 5. Kritischer Bericht – Skizzen – Entstehungs- und Werkgeschichte – Dokumente (Arnold Schönberg: Sämtliche Werke*, ed. Rudolf STEPHAN etc., IV.B.10), Mainz – Vienna: Schott – Universal Edition.

KLEIN, Michael (2005), *Intertextuality in Western Art Music*, Bloomington – Indianapolis: Indiana University Press.

KROSS, Siegfried (1990), "Das 'Zweite Zeitalter der Symphonie' – Ideologie und Realität," in *Probleme der symphonischen Tradition im 19. Jahrhundert*, ed. Siegfried KROSS and Marie Luise MAINTZ, Tutzing: Schneider, pp. 11–36.

LA MARA (1894), *Letters of Franz Liszt*, transl. Constance BACHE, vol. 2, London: Charles Scribner Sons.

LOLL, Werner (1990), *Zwischen Tradition und Avantgarde: Die Kammermusik Alexander Zemlinskys*, (*Kieler Schriften zur Musikwissenschaft*, ed. Friedhelm KRUMMACHER and Heinrich W. SCHWAB, 34), Kassel: Bärenreiter.

LONGYEAR, Rey M. (1973), "Liszt's B Minor Sonata: Precedents for a Structural Analysis," *The Music Review*, 34, pp. 198–209.

MAHNKOPF, Claus-Steffen (1994), *Gestalt und Stil: Arnold Schönbergs Erste Kammersymphonie und ihr Umfeld*, (*Bärenreiter Hochschulschriften*), Kassel: Bärenreiter.

MARX, Adolf Bernhard (1857), *Die Lehre von der musikalischen Komposition*, 4 volumes, vol. 3, Leipzig: Breitkopf und Härtel, 1845/3rd ed. 1857.

MEYER, Leonard B. (1967), *Music, the Arts, and Ideas: Patterns and Predictions in Twentieth-Century Culture*, Chicago – London: The University of Chicago Press.

NEWLIN, Dika (1980), *Schoenberg Remembered: Diaries and Recollections, 1938–1976*, New York: Pendragon Press.

NEWMAN, William S. (1969), *The Sonata since Beethoven*, Chapel Hill: The University of North Carolina Press.

PFANNKUCH, Wilhelm (1963), "Zu Thematik und Form in Schönbergs Streichsextett," in *Festschrift Friedrich Blume: Zum 70. Geburtstag*, ed. Anna Amalie ABERT and Wilhelm PFANNKUCH, Kassel: Bärenreiter, pp. 258–271.

PUFFETT, Derrick (1995), "'Music that Echoes within One' for a Lifetime: Berg's Reception of Schoenberg's 'Pelleas und Melisande'," *Music and Letters*, 76, pp. 209–264.

RETI, Rudolph (1951), *The Thematic Process in Music*, New York: MacMillan.

RIEMANN, Hugo (1905), *Grundriß der Kompositionslehre (musikalische Formenlehre)*, 2 volumes, vol. 1: *Algemeine Formenlehre*, Berlin: Hesse, reprint 1922 [originally published as *Katechismus der Kompositionslehre* in 1889].

SAFFLE, Michael (2002), "Orchestral Music," in *The Liszt Companion*, ed. Ben ARNOLD, Westport, CT: Greenwood Press, pp. 235–279.

SCHÄFERS, Matthias (1998), "Zur Formkonzeption von Arnold Schönbergs 'Pelleas und Melisande' op. 5," in *Musik als Text: Bericht über den Internationalen Kongreß der Gesellschaft für Musikforschung, Freiburg im Breisgau 1993*, 2 volumes, ed. Hermann DANUSER and Tobias PLEBUCH, vol. 2: *Freie Referate*, Kassel: Bärenreiter, pp. 388–391.

— (2001), "'…daß dasjenige, das den Anstoß zur Entwicklung gegeben hat, auch das erste ist, das uns wieder abstößt…': Arnold Schönberg und Richard Strauss," in *Autorschaft als historische Konstruktion: Arnold Schönberg – Vorgänger, Zeitgenossen, Nachfolger und Interpreten*, ed. Andreas MEYER and Ullrich SCHEIDELER, Stuttgart – Weimar: Metzler, 2001, pp. 117–157.

SCHIBLI, Sigfried (1984), "Ein Stück praktisch gewordener Ideologie: Zum Problem der komplexen einsätzigen Form in Frühwerken Arnold Schönbergs," *Archiv für Musikwissenschaft*, 41, 1984, pp. 274–294.

SCHMALFELDT, Janet (1995), "Form as the Process of Becoming: The Beethoven-Hegelian Tradition and the 'Tempest' Sonata," *Beethoven Forum*, 4, pp. 37–71.

SCHMIDT, Christian Martin (1978), "Formprobleme in Schönbergs frühen Instrumentalwerken," in *Bericht über den 1. Kongreß der Internationalen Schönberg-Gesellschaft*, (*Publikationen der Internationalen Schönberg-Gesellschaft*, 1, ed. Rudolf STEPHAN), Vienna: Lafite, pp. 180–186.

— (1986a), *Arnold Schönberg. Streichquartette I. Kritischer Bericht – Skizzen – Fragmente* (*Arnold Schönberg: Sämtliche Werke*, ed. Rudolf STEPHAN et al., VI.B.20), Mainz – Vienna: Schott – Universal Edition.

— (1986b), "Schönbergs 'very definite – but private' Programm zum Streichquartett Opus 7," in *Bericht über den 2. Kongreß der Internationalen Schönberg-Gesellschaft*, (*Publikationen der Internationalen Schönberg-Gesellschaft*, 2, ed. Rudolf STEPHAN and Sigrid WIESMANN), Vienna: Lafite, pp. 230–234.

— (1990), "Die 'Aufhebung' der Symphonie Beethovens in Liszts symphonischer Dichtung," in *Probleme der symphonischen Tradition im 19. Jahrhundert*, ed. Siegfried KROSS and Marie Luise MAINTZ, Tutzing: Schneider, pp. 523–535.

SCHMITZ, Arnold (1923), *Beethovens "Zwei Prinzipe,"* Berlin – Bonn: Dümmler.

SCHMITZ, Eugen (1904), "Liszts H-Moll-Sonate: Eine hermeneutische Studie," *Allgemeine Musik-Zeitung*, 31, pp. 451–453 and 470–471.

SCHOENBERG, Arnold (1907), "Streichquartett op. 7 von Arnold Schönberg," in *Schönberg, Berg, Webern: Die Streichquartette der Wiener Schule*, ed. Ursula von RAUCHHAUPT, Munich: Ellerman, 1971, pp. 11–13.

— (1949a), "Analyse der Kammersymphonie," in *Stil und Gedanke: Aufsätze zur Musik* (*Gesammelte Schriften* 1, ed. Ivan VOJTĚCH), Frankfurt am Main: Fischer, 1976, pp. 440–445.

— (1949b), "Analyse von 'Pelleas und Melisande'," in *Stil und Gedanke: Aufsätze zur Musik* (*Gesammelte Schriften* 1, ed. Ivan VOJTĚCH), Frankfurt am Main: Fischer, 1976, pp. 437–439.

— (1949c), "My Evolution," in *Style and Idea: Selected Writings of Arnold Schoenberg*, ed. Leonard STEIN, New York: St. Martin's, 1975, pp. 79–92.

— (1949d), "Notes on the Four String Quartets," in *Schönberg, Berg, Webern: Die Streichquartette der Wiener Schule*, ed. Ursula von RAUCHHAUPT, Munich: Ellerman, 1971, pp. 36–66.

— (1954), *Structural Functions of Harmony*, ed. Leonard STEIN, New York – London: Norton (rev. edition 1969).

— (1958), *Ausgewählte Briefe*, ed. Erwin STEIN, Mainz: Schott.

— (1967), *Fundamentals of Musical Composition*, ed. Gerald STRANG and Leonard STEIN, London: Faber & Faber.

SCHWEIZER, Klaus (1970), *Die Sonatensatzform im Schaffen Alban Bergs*, (*Freiburger Schriften zur Musikwissenschaft*, ed. Hans Heinrich EGGEBRECHT, 1), Stuttgart: Musikwissenschaftliche Verlagsgesellschaft.

SEIDEL, Wilhelm (1986), "Schnell – Langsam – Schnell: Zur klassischen Theorie des instrumentalen Zyklus," *Musiktheorie*, 1, pp. 205–216.

STEINITZER, Max (1911), *Richard Strauss*, Berlin – Leipzig: Schuster und Loeffler.

STEPHAN, Rudolf (1976), "Über Zemlinskys Streichquartette," in *Alexander Zemlinsky: Tradition im Umkreis der Wiener Schule*, (*Studien zur Wertungsforschung*, ed. Otto KOLLERITSCH, 7), Graz: Universal Edition – Institut für Wertungsforschung, pp. 120–136.

STEPHAN, Rudolf and Regina BUSCH (1994), "Zur Textgestalt," in *Alban Berg: Analysen musikalischer Werke von Arnold Schönberg)*, (*Alban Berg: Sämtliche Werke*, ed. Rudolf STEPHAN and Regina BUSCH, *III. Abteilung: Musikalische Schriften und Dichtungen, Band 1)*, Vienna: Universal Edition, 1994, pp. xxix–xxxii.

STRANG, Gerald (1967), "Editor's Preface," in Arnold SCHOENBERG, *Fundamentals of Musical Composition*, ed. Gerald STRANG and Leonard STEIN, London: Faber & Faber, pp. xiii–xv.

STRAUSS, Richard (1949), *Betrachtungen und Erinnerungen*, ed. Willi SCHUH, Zürich: Atlantis.

STRAUSS, Gabriele (1996), *Lieber Collega! Richard Strauss im Briefwechsel mit zeitgenössischen Komponisten und Dirigenten*, vol. 1, (*Veröffentlichungen der Richard-Strauss-Gesellschaft*, ed. Franz TRENNER, 14), Berlin: Henschel.

SWIFT, Richard (1977), "I/XII/99: Tonal Relations in Schoenberg's *Verklärte Nacht*," *19th Century Music*, 1, pp. 3–14.

TALBOT, Michael (2001), *The Finale in Western Instrumental Music*, (*Oxford Monographs on Music)*, New York – Oxford: Oxford University Press.

TARUSKIN, Richard (2005), *The Nineteenth Century*, (*The Oxford History of Western Music*, 3), New York – Oxford: Oxford University Press.

TENSCHERT, Roland (1944), *Dreimal sieben Variationen über das Thema Richard Strauss*, Vienna: Frick.

THIEME, Ulrich (1979), *Studien zum Jugendwerk Arnold Schönbergs: Einflüsse und Wandlungen*, (*Kölner Beiträge zur Musikforschung*, ed. Heinrich HÜSCHEN, 107), Regensburg: Bosse.

TORKEWITZ, Dieter (1995), "Liszts *Tasso*," in *Torquato Tasso in Deutschland: Seine Wirkung in Literatur, Kunst und Musik seit der Mitte des 18. Jahrhunderts*, ed. Achim AURNHAMMER, (*Quellen und Forschungen zur Literatur- und Kulturgeschichte der germanischen Völkern*, ed. Ernst OSTERKAMP and Werner RÖCKE, 3), Berlin – New York: de Gruyter, pp. 321–347.

VANDE MOORTELE, Steven (2005), 'Die Funktion des Mottos in der zweidimensionalen Sonatenform bei Schönberg und Zemlinsky', in *"form follows function" – zwischen Musik, Form und Funktion: Beiträge zum 18. internationalen studentischen Symposium des DVSM (Dachverband der Studierenden der Musikwissenschaft) in Hamburg 2003*, ed. Till KNIPPER, Martin KRANZ, Thomas KÜHNRICH & Carsten NEUBAUER, Hamburg: Von Bockel, pp. 331–341.

— (2006a), "'Absolut nicht symphonisch'? Schönbergs Fünf Orchesterstücke und die Gattungskonventionen der Symphonie," *Musik und Ästhetik*, 36, pp. 57–70.

— (2006b), "Form, Program, and Deformation in Liszt's *Hamlet*," *Dutch Journal of Music Theory*, 11, pp. 71–82.

— (2007), "Form as Context: Zemlinsky's Second String Quartet and the Tradition of Two-Dimensional Sonata Form," in *Zemlinsky Studies*, ed. Michael FRITH, London: Middlesex University Press, pp. 99–111.

— (2008), "Beyond Sonata Deformation: Liszt's Symphonic Poem *Tasso* and the Concept of Two-Dimensional Sonata Form," *Current Musicology*, 86, pp. 41–62.

— (2009), "The First Movement of Beethoven's *Tempest* Sonata and the Tradition of Twentieth-Century '*Formenlehre*'," in *Beethoven's* Tempest *Sonata: Perspectives of Analysis and Performance*, (*Analysis in Context: Leuven Studies in Musicology*, 2), ed. Pieter BERGÉ, co-ed. Jeroen D'HOE and William CAPLIN, Leuven: Peeters, pp. 293-314.

WALKER, Allan, Maria ECKHARDT, and Rena CHARNIN-MUELLER (2001), 'Liszt, Franz', in *The New Grove Dictionary of Music and Musicians, Second Edition*, ed. Stanley SADIE and John TYRRELL, 14, London: MacMillan, pp. 755–877.

WALTER, Michael (2000), *Richard Strauss und seine Zeit*, (*Große Komponisten und ihre Zeit*), Laaber: Laaber Verlag.

WEBER, Horst (1977), *Alexander Zemlinsky*, (*Österreichische Komponisten des 20. Jahrhunderts*, 23), Vienna: Lafite.

WEBERN, Anton (1912), "Schönbergs Musik," in *Arnold Schönberg*, Munich: Piper, pp. 22–48.

WEBSTER, James (1992), "The Form of the Finale of Beethoven's Ninth Symphony," *Beethoven Forum*, 1, pp. 25–62.

WELLESZ, Egon (1921), *Arnold Schönberg*, Leipzig: Tal.

WERBECK, Walter (1996), *Die Tondichtungen von Richard Strauss*, (*Dokumente und Studien zu Richard Strauss,* ed. Stephan KOHLER, 2), Tutzing: Schneider.

WILKE, Rainer (1980), *Brahms, Reger, Schönberg: Streichquartette. Motivisch-thematische Prozesse und Gestalt*, (*Schriftenreihe zur Musik*, 18), Hamburg: Wagner.

ZEMLINSKY, Alexander (1934), "Jugenderinnerungen," in *Arnold Schönberg zum 60. Geburtstag*, Vienna: Universal Edition, pp. 33–35.

— (1995), *Briefwechsel mit Arnold Schönberg, Anton Webern, Alban Berg und Franz Schreker*, ed. Horst WEBER, (*Briefwechsel der Wiener Schule*, ed. Thomas ERTELT, 1), Darmstadt: Wissenschaftliche Buchgesellschaft.

Index of Names and Works

A
Ackermann, Peter 124
Adorno, Theodor W. 54, 196, 202
Altenburg, Detlef 60
Arditti Quartet 157

B
Bailey, Walter 102, 123, 156
Barber, Samuel
   Symphony no. 1 199
Beaumont, Antony 193
Beethoven, Ludwig van 2, 6, 31, 54, 131, 156, 196, 200, 202
   Große Fuge Op. 133 57
   Leonore overture no. 3 Op. 72b 79
   Piano Sonata in C major Op. 2 no. 3 133
   Piano Sonata in C major Op. 53 (*Waldstein*) 79
   Piano Sonata in D minor Op. 31 no. 2 (*Tempest*) 58, 212, 214
   Symphony no. 9 in D minor Op. 125 7, 33
Benson, Mark 128
Berg, Alban 104–9, 113–8, 124f, 160f, 174, 178
Berlioz, Hector
   Benvenuto Cellini Op. 23 (overture) 44
   King Lear Op. 4 43
   Le Corsaire Op. 21 44
Berwald, Franz
   String Quartet in E♭ major 57
Birkin, Kenneth 81
Boestfleisch, Rainer 156
Böggeman, Markus 156
Bonds, Mark Evan 3, 9

Brahms, Johannes 6, 101, 131, 155, 200
   Symphony no. 3 in F major Op. 90 29
   Violin Sonata no. 3 in D minor Op. 108 174, 178
Brendel, Franz 78
Brinkmann, Reinhold 159
Brosche, Günter 99
Bruckner, Anton 9, 101, 196
   Symphony no. 1 in C minor 60
   Symphony no. 8 in C minor 29
Bülow, Hans von 82, 99
Busch, Regina 124

C
Caplin, William E. 8, 11, 13ff, 31f, 79, 99, 156
Cavanagh, Lynn C. 132, 156
Cherlin, Michael 6, 27f, 124, 148, 156f
Chopin, Frédéric
   G-minor Piano Trio Op. 8 79
   Piano Sonata in C minor Op. 4 79

D
Dahlhaus, Carl 2, 9, 25, 28ff, 33, 37, 42, 45, 51, 58, 60f, 63, 108, 123, 156f, 196, 199
Dale, Catherine 123, 177
Dannreuther, Edward 62
Darcy, Warren 3f, 8f, 31, 47, 83f, 120, 156, 178
Dehmel, Richard 102
Dömling, Wolfgang 49f, 58
Draeseke, Felix 59
Dvořák, Antonín 7

F

Floros, Constantin 62, 78
Franck, César 7
Frisch, Walter 6, 27, 35, 41, 57, 60, 102, 110, 123ff, 131, 133, 138, 156f, 162ff, 167, 172, 174, 177f

G

Gerlach, Reinhard 99
Grey, Thomas 78

H

Haimo, Ethan 6, 105f, 115, 124, 156, 161, 167, 177
Hamilton, Kenneth 9, 58, 63f, 156
Hansen, Mathias 28
Hattesen, Heinrich Helge 29, 157
Haydn, Joseph 2, 31
Hepokoski, James 2–5, 8f, 31, 47, 54, 64f, 79, 82–7, 91f, 120, 156, 178
Horton, Julian 3
Humal, Mart 99

J

Jackson, Timothy 9, 29, 178

K

Kaplan, Richard 62, 65, 78
Kennedy, Michael 99
Keym, Stefan 78
Kirby, Frank E. 60f
Koch, Heinrich Christoph 9
Kohler, Ralf-Alexander 156
Kokkinis, Nikos 103, 123f
Kross, Siegfried 60
Kwasny, Ralf 103, 123f

L

Lasalle Quartet 157
Liszt, Franz 1, 5–9, 20f, 23ff, 27–30, 35–79, 81f, 87, 98f, 101, 103, 122f, 127, 154, 156, 175, 181, 191f, 195, 199–202
Ad nos, ad salutarem undam 35
Après une lecture de Dante 35
Ce qu'on entend sur la montagne 62f
Die Ideale 5, 59, 62f, 71–78, 82, 87f, 98, 122, 154, 175, 201
Eine Faust-Symphonie 9, 62, 79
Festklänge 60, 62
Hamlet 60, 62, 65, 79, 214
Hungaria 62
Les préludes 62f, 78, 79
Mazeppa 62
Orpheus 60, 62, 78
Piano Concerto in A major 35
Piano Sonata in B minor 1, 5f, 20, 23ff, 27, 29f, 35–60, 62, 65, 69, 73, 76, 78, 127, 156, 175, 192, 201
Prometheus 60, 62, 78, 79
Tasso: Lamento e trionfo 5, 59f, 62–71, 78f, 82, 98, 118, 197, 201
Loll, Werner 179, 183, 187, 193
Longyear, Rey 51

M

Maeterlinck, Maurice 103f, 106, 108, 127, 211
Mahler, Gustav 101, 196, 207f
Mahnkopf, Claus-Steffen 156f, 174f, 177
Marx, Adolf Bernhard 3, 16–19, 31f, 52, 156
Mendelssohn-Bartholdy, Felix 54
Meyer, Leonard B. 19
Moscheles, Ignaz 7
Mozart, Wolfgang Amadé 2, 31
    Piano Sonata in D major K311 173

N
Newlin, Dika 127, 128
Newman, William 1, 20–5, 28, 30f, 35, 44, 50f, 59

P
Pfannkuch, Wilhelm 102, 123
Prazak Quartet 157
Puffett, Derrick 107f, 124

R
Ratz, Erwin 8
Redlich, Carl 123
Reicha, Antonín 196
Réti, Rudolph 31
Reubke, Julius 59, 78
Riemann, Hugo 16ff, 32

S
Saffle, Michael 62
Saint-Saëns, Camille 7
Schäfers, Matthias 117, 123f
Schibli, Sigfried 28
Schmalfeldt, Janet 33, 58
Schmidt, Christian Martin 72, 109, 124, 128, 156
Schmidt, Franz
  Symphony no. 4 in C major 198
Schmitz, Arnold 156
Schmitz, Eugen 35
Schoenberg, Arnold 1, 5f, 8, 11, 13f, 24-31, 59, 78, 99, 101–200
  Chamber Symphony in E major Op. 9 1, 5, 59, 123, 127f, 156, 159–80, 183, 191–2, 198, 202
  Five Orchestral Pieces Op. 16 31, 199
  Gurrelieder 123
  Hans im Glück 102
  Moses und Aron 199
  Pelleas und Melisande 5, 101–25, 127, 132, 151, 154, 156, 159, 160f, 176f, 179, 190, 193, 200, 202
  Piano Concerto Op. 42 199
  String Quartet in D major 102
  String Quartet no. 1 in D minor Op. 7 1, 5, 24f, 29f, 122, 127–57, 159, 167, 176, 179, 183, 191, 197, 202
  String Quartet no. 2 in F♯ minor Op. 10 179
  String Trio Op. 45 199
  Toter Winkel 102
  Verklärte Nacht Op. 4 101f, 123, 159, 198, 213
Schreker, Franz
  Chamber Symphony 198
Schubert, Franz 196
  Piano Sonata in B♭ major D960 133
  Wanderer Fantasy 7, 37, 56f
Schumann, Robert 54, 60
  Manfred overture Op. 115 44
  String Quartet in A minor Op. 41 no. 1 58
  Symphony no. 3 in E♭ major Op. 97 (Rhenish) 60
  Symphony no. 4 in D minor Op. 120 7, 29, 35ff, 56f, 198
  Szenen aus Goethes Faust WoO 3 (overture) 44
Schweizer, Klaus 124
Seidel, Wilhelm 32
Sibelius, Jean
  Symphony no. 7 in C major Op. 105 199
Skrjabin, Alexander 7
Smetana, Bedřich 7
Stein, Erwin 156

Steinitzer, Max 99
Stein, Leonard 128
Stephan, Rudolf 124, 179, 187f, 193, 215
Strang, Gerald 11, 13
Strauss, Richard 1, 5f, 8, 59, 78, 81–99, 101f, 110, 123f, 154, 175, 191, 195, 200ff
  Aus Italien Op. 16 81
  Don Juan Op. 20 5, 81–93, 98f, 109f, 118, 122, 154, 175, 201
  Ein Heldenleben Op. 40 5, 81f, 93-99, 121, 197, 201
  Guntram Op. 25 97
  Macbeth Op. 23 92
  Taillefer Op. 52 103
  Till Eulenspiegels lustige Streiche Op. 28 102, 210
Swift, Richard 123

T
Talbot, Michael 55, 123, 154
Taruskin, Richard 61
Tchaikovsky, Ilyitch 7, 9, 29, 210
  Symphony no. 6 in B minor Op. 74 9, 29
Tenschert, Roland 81, 208
Thieme, Ulrich 101f

V
Viole, Rudolf 59

W
Wagner, Richard 43, 78, 81, 101, 199, 200, 209, 215
  Lohengrin 81
  Rienzi (overture) 43
  Tannhäuser 78, 81
Walker, Alan 59, 78
Weber, Horst 183, 187, 193
Webern, Anton 24f, 32, 103, 124
Webster, James 31, 33
Wellesz, Egon 123
Werbeck, Walter 81, 88, 93, 99
Wolf, Hugo 101
Wolzogen, Ernst von 103

Z
Zemlinsky, Alexander 103, 127
  String Quartet no. 2 in F♯ minor 5f, 179–93, 198f, 202

www.ingramcontent.com/pod-product-compliance
Lightning Source LLC
Chambersburg PA
CBHW071204240426
43668CB00032B/2073